D. M. Kerly

An Historical Sketch of the Equitable Jurisdiction of the Court of Chancery

Being the Yorke Prize Essay of the University of Cambridge for 1889

D. M. Kerly

An Historical Sketch of the Equitable Jurisdiction of the Court of Chancery
Being the Yorke Prize Essay of the University of Cambridge for 1889

ISBN/EAN: 9783337013899

Printed in Europe, USA, Canada, Australia, Japan

Cover: Foto ©Suzi / pixelio.de

More available books at **www.hansebooks.com**

AN HISTORICAL SKETCH

OF THE

EQUITABLE JURISDICTION OF THE COURT OF CHANCERY.

London: C. J. CLAY AND SONS,
CAMBRIDGE UNIVERSITY PRESS WAREHOUSE,
AND
STEVENS AND SONS, LIMITED,
119 AND 120, CHANCERY LANE,
LAW PUBLISHERS AND BOOKSELLERS.

Cambridge: DEIGHTON, BELL AND CO.
Leipzig: F. A. BROCKHAUS.
New York: MACMILLAN AND CO.

AN HISTORICAL SKETCH

OF THE

EQUITABLE JURISDICTION OF THE

COURT OF CHANCERY.

BEING THE YORKE PRIZE ESSAY OF THE UNIVERSITY OF
CAMBRIDGE FOR 1889.

BY

D. M. KERLY, M.A., LL.B.,

FELLOW OF ST JOHN'S COLLEGE, CAMBRIDGE;
OF THE INNER TEMPLE, BARRISTER-AT-LAW.

CAMBRIDGE:
AT THE UNIVERSITY PRESS
1890

[*All Rights reserved.*]

PREFACE.

WHILE so many books have been published upon every branch of the text of English Law, it is strange that so little attention should have been paid to its history. Reeves' History is still the only account of the progress and development of the common law as a whole, and no similar history of the great rival system of equity has ever appeared. Much has been written, indeed, upon the origin of the extraordinary jurisdiction of the Chancellors, and upon the genesis of particular branches of equity, as, for instance, trusts. The learned work of Spence, and the admirable introduction to the Close Rolls by Sir Duffus Hardy are accepted authorities on the origin of English equity, and quite recently new light has been thrown upon the subject by a number of essays in the *Law Quarterly Review*, and by Mr Pike's introductions to the Year Books of 12, 13, and 13, 14 Edward III. in the Rolls series. The second part of the first volume of Spence contains, besides the account of the rise and establishment of the equitable jurisdiction of the Court of Chancery already referred to, a description of equity at, and before the end of the reign of Charles I., a large part of which, however, is based upon inferences drawn from decisions of Lord Nottingham and other Chancellors who belong to the period following the Rebellion. These scattered fragments are, so far as I am aware, the only history of equity we have.

The following essay does not pretend, in any way, to fill the gap, or to rival the elaborate history of the common law mentioned above. Its aim, as indeed its size sufficiently suggests, is far less ambitious. An attempt has been made to sketch the rise, development and progress of the Court of

Chancery as a Court of Equity, and to give a summary account of the introduction and development of some of the leading principles which the court adopted, and of the procedure by which they were embodied in practice. Obviously, so large a subject could be treated within the limits of the essay in outline only.

I have derived much assistance from Spence and from the introductions and essays referred to above, and, as regards the history of the court, and of the Chancellors who presided over it, from Parkes' *History of the Court of Chancery* and Lord Campbell's *Lives of the Chancellors*, and for the materials of the 12th chapter, on the growth of modern equity, I have drawn largely upon the stores collected in White and Tudor's *Leading Cases*. My indebtedness to these and the other works and authorities of which I have made use is fully acknowledged in the notes.

I have added, in the notes to the 12th chapter, some references, (printed in heavy type) to recent cases in which the principles summarised in the text have been discussed and illustrated, in the hope that, with their assistance, the account of the leading cases and of the doctrines established by them given in that chapter may be useful as a first introduction to a study of modern equity. The majority of the recent cases are taken from Brett's *Leading Cases in Modern Equity*, where the facts of, and extracts from the judgments in the cases are set out, and I am indebted to Mr Brett and his publishers for permission kindly accorded to me, to make use of his valuable collection.

I have to thank my friend Mr A. Wood Renton for his kindness in reading the proof sheets of the essay.

D. M. KERLY.

1, GARDEN COURT,
TEMPLE.
July, 1890.

CONTENTS.

CHAPTER I.

	PAGE
Introduction	1
The Judicial System of Mediæval England, and the relation of the King, the Council and Parliament to it	7
The King's Courts	8
Procedure by writ	9
Writs *consimili casu*	10
Equity and the action on the case	11
Judicial power of the King	13
Judicial power of the Council	17
Judicial power of the Parliament	19
Subsequent history of these powers	21

CHAPTER II.

The Chancellor	23

CHAPTER III.

The Establishment of the Chancellor's jurisdiction	26
References to him under Edward I.	27
References to him under Edward II.	28
References to him under Edward III.	30
The Court of Chancery fixed at Westminster	31

CHAPTER IV.

Petitions of the Commons against the Chancellor's jurisdiction, and Statutes relating to it	37
Petitions under Richard II.	38
Statute as to costs in Chancery	39

	PAGE
Petitions under Henry IV.	41
The Statute against reversing judgments	42
Petition against the subpœna	43
Examination of the Defendant in Chancery	44
Later petitions against the Chancery	45

CHAPTER V.

The Chancery from the reign of Richard II. to the reign of Elizabeth, and the Bills in the Calendars 47

SEC. 1. *Procedure and Pleading.*

Contents of the Calendars	48
Common Law in Chancery	49
Constitution of the Court	57
The Bill	61
Examples of bills	62
The Writ	66
Answer and reply	67
The mode of taking evidence	68
The decree	69

SEC. 2. *The relief sought.*

A. Where the common law remedy could not be obtained	71
B. Where the common law process was used oppressively or fraudulently	72
C. Forgery and duress	73
D. Where no remedy was contemplated by the common law	76
Discovery	77
Uses and trusts	79
Contracts	87
Specific Performance	88
Injunction	89
Equity under Henry VIII.	92

CHAPTER VI.

From Wolsey to the Commonwealth. The Chancellors	94
Wolsey, the last of Ecclesiastical Chancellors	94
Sir T. More	96
Lawyers as Chancellors	97
Lord Ellesmere	99
Influence of precedent and of Roman Law in early equity	100
Lord Bacon's Speech on taking his seat as Chancellor	103
His orders	104
Lord Coventry	105

CHAPTER VII.

	PAGE
The struggle for pre-eminence	107
Injunctions	107
Law and equity under Elizabeth	108
The contest over injunctions	109
The Earl of Oxford's case	111
Threat of a præmunire	113
The reports to the King	114
The King's decree	115
Development of equity consequent upon this victory	116

CHAPTER VIII.

From Wolsey to the Commonwealth. Procedure and Practice	118
The bill, and process to compél appearance	119
The answer	120
Examination of witnesses	121
Dilatoriness of the procedure	122
The hearing and the decree	123
Motions and references	124
Suits *in forma pauperis*	126
Officers of the Court	127

CHAPTER IX.

From Wolsey to the Commonwealth. The matters dealt with by the Court, and the relief given	129
Uses and Trusts	130
The Statute of Uses	133
The Statute of Wills	134
Trusts after the Statute of Uses	135
Administration	139
Wills	141
Charities	142
Separate Estate	142
Mortgages	143
Fraud and Accident	145
Suretyship	146
Specific Performance	147
Accounts	148
Injunction	149
Discovery	151
Criminal Jurisdiction	153

CHAPTER X.

	PAGE
The attempted reforms under the Commonwealth	154
Abuses of the Chancery	155
Whitelock's Orders	156
Proceedings in Parliament	157
The Chancery Amendment Bill	159
Cromwell's Ordinances	161
Failure of the reformers	163

CHAPTER XI.

The Court of Chancery from the Restoration to the retirement of Lord Eldon	164
Clarendon's Orders	164
Development of real property law	165
Development of equity	166
Appeals to the House of Lords	167
The Chancellors of the 17th and 18th centuries	169
Lord Nottingham	169
The Statute of Frauds	171
Attacks on the Chancery in Parliament	172
Somers' Act	173
Lord Macclesfield	174
Lord Hardwicke	175
Lord Thurlow	179
Improvement of the Law	181
Lord Eldon	182

CHAPTER XII.

Growth of modern equity 184

SEC. 1. *The general characteristics of the leading cases.*

The leading cases	186
Scarcity of reports	187
Arguments in the leading cases	188
Influence of Roman Law upon equity	189

SEC. 2. *The doctrines of the leading cases.*

1. Trusts, voluntary settlements, trustees' receipts, executory trusts, precatory trusts, the trustee, investment of trust money, remuneration of the trustee 192
Conversion 202
Joint ownership 205

	PAGE
Assignment of choses in action	206
Powers, illusory appointments, fraud on a power	207

2. Administration, payment of debts out of real estate, the interpretation of wills 210
Legacies, satisfaction of debts, ademption of legacies by advancements, substitution of legacies, ademption of specific legacies . 213
    Marshalling 215
    Election 217
    Restraints on marriage 218

3. Married Women's property, equity to a settlement, the wife's reversion, mortgage of the wife's estate 220

4. Infants 225

5. Mortgages, redemption and foreclosure, tacking, consolidation . 227
    Vendor's lien 233
    Equitable mortgages 234
    Notice 234

6. Fraud, standing by 237
    Catching bargains 240
    Undue influence 242

7. Mistake, (1) in expression, parol evidence, rectification of wills, construction of releases, (2) in matter of substance, unilateral mistake 243
    Compromise 249

8. Penalties 250

9. Sureties 251

10. Specific performance, part performance, time not of the essence of the contract, specific performance a discretionary relief, agreements between husband and wife 253

11. Injunction 258
    Equitable waste 259

12. Discovery 260
    Purchase for valuable consideration without notice . . . 261

CHAPTER XIII.

Reform in chancery .	264
The demand for reform	264
Uncertainty of the law	266
Costliness of equity	267
The six clerks	267
Evidence in chancery	268
The pleadings	269
Delay in chancery	270

CONTENTS.

	PAGE
Appointment of additional judges in equity	272
The master's offices	273
Lord Eldon's commission	274
The Orders of 1828 and 1831	275
The Chancery Regulation Act, 1833	275
Reforms in the law, and in the common law courts	276
Sir George Turner's Act and Lord Cottenham's orders	277
Summary procedure in equity	279
Last reforms of the Masters' offices	280
The Chancery Commission of 1850	281
Its reports on jurisdiction and evidence	281
Extension of summary procedure	283
Abolition of the Masters	283
New rules as to pleading and parties	284
Summons at chambers	284
Issues of law abolished	285
Further changes in the mode of taking evidence	285
The Consolidated Orders of 1860	287
The Common Law Procedure Acts	288
The Auxiliary jurisdiction in equity superseded	288
The proposals of 1860 to give further equity powers to the common law courts	289
Substantive reforms in equity	290
Fusion of equity and common law	292
The Judicature Acts	293

TABLE OF ABBREVIATIONS.

Abbreviations.	References. Chiefly to Reports.
Ap. Ca.	Law Reports. Appeal Cases
Atk.	Atkyns
B. and P.	Bosanquet and Puller
B., Bea.	Beavan
Beames	Orders in Chancery
Bing.	Bingham
Bro. Ab.	Abridgement
Brooke	,,
Bro. C. C.	Brown's Chancery Cases
Bulst.	Bulstrode
Burr.	Burrows
C. D.	Law Reports, Chancery Division
Cal.	Calendars of the Proceedings in Chancery
Camp.	Campbell's Lives of the Chancellors
Cas. in Chy.	Cases in Chancery (Ed. 1735)
Chy. Cas.	,, ,,
1, 2, 3, Ch. Cas.	,, ,,
Cas. Talbot	Cases in Equity in the time of Talbot
Cas. Temp. Finch.	Reports tempore Finch
Ch. Cas.	Choice Cases in Chancery (Ed. 1672)
Ch. Rep.	Reports in Chancery (Ed. 1736)
Ch.	Law Reports, Chancery Appeals
Cl. Roll.	Close Rolls
Cl. and F.	Clark and Finelly
Co.	Coke's Reports
Co. Inst.	Coke's Institutes
Cox	(Ed. 1816)
Cr. and Ph.	Craig and Phillips
Cro. Car.	Croke's reports of the reign of Car. I.
Cro. Jac.	,, ,, ,, ,, James I.
D. F. and Jo.	De Gex, Fisher and Jones
D. G. J. and S.	De Gex, Jones and Smith
D. G. and J.	De Gex and Jones
Dick.	Dickens (Ed. 1803)
Digby	Digby's History of Real Property (3rd Ed.)
Dow	Dow's Reports, House of Lords
Dr. and W.	Drury and Warren
Drew.	Drewry

TABLE OF ABBREVIATIONS.

Abbreviations.	References. Chiefly to Reports.
Eq. Ca. Ab.	Equity Cases Abridged
Free.	Freeman
Giff.	Giffard
Gilb.	Gilbert's Reports
H. L. C.	House of Lords Cases
Ha.	Hare
Inst.	Coke's Institutes
J. and W.	Jacob and Walker
Jac.	Jacob
K. and J.	Kay and Johnson
L. J. Ch.—Q. B.	Law Journal Chancery—Queen's Bench
L. R. Eq.	Law Reports Equity
L. R. H. L.	Law Reports, House of Lords
Law Quar. Rev.	Law Quarterly Review
Lev.	Levinz
M. and Cr.	Mylne and Craig
Madd.	Maddock
Mer.	Merivale
Mod.	Modern Reports
Monro	Acta Cancellariæ
P. W.	Peere Williams (Ed. 1826)
Parkes	History of Chancery
Prec. Chy.	Precedents in Chancery
Q. B. D.	Law Reports, Queen's Bench Division
Rep.	Coke's Reports
Rep. in Chy.	Reports in Chancery (Ed. 1736)
Rolle	Rolle's Abridgements
Rot. Parl.	Parliamentary Rolls
Russ.	Russel
Salk.	Salkeld
Sch. and Lef.	Schoales and Lefroy
Seton	Seton on Decrees (4th Ed.)
Show. P. C.	Shower's Parliamentary Cases
Sim.	Simon
Smith, L. C.	Smith's Leading Cases (9th Ed.)
Spence	Spence's Equitable Jurisdiction
Swan.	Swanston
T. R.	Term Reports
Term Rep.	,, ,,
Toth.	Tothill (Ed. 1649)
Ves.	Vesey (Junior)
Ves. Snr.	Vesey Senior (Ed. 1818)
Vern.	Vernon (Ed. 1828)
Vin. Ab.	Viner's Abridgement
W. and T.	White and Tudor's Leading Cases (6th Ed.)
Warren	Law Studies (3rd Ed.)
Y. and C. Ex.	Younge and Collier's Exchequer in Equity

INTRODUCTION.

THE Court of Chancery merged by the Judicature Acts with the Courts with which it had so long been contrasted administered a system of rules and principles which were very unlike those administered by the Chancellor in the early days of his judicial dignity, if indeed the Chancellor in those early days can be said to have administered any system of rules or principles at all. Writers on the later Equity had no difficulty in showing that the decisions of Lord Eldon's successors were as closely reasoned, and as well grounded on precedent as any given in a Court of Common Law, and that the ruling of the Chancellor, the Vice-Chancellors, or the Master of the Rolls could be anticipated with as much confidence as that of a judge. The difficulty they found was rather to discover on what general principle those laws which were Equity could be distinguished from those which were Common Law, and to explain in any rational manner why it should be necessary in some cases to go to one side of Westminster Hall, in some to the other, and in some to both, to obtain redress which was promised by the laws of the land. Technical equity had come, in fact, to have no special connection with equity in the sense of justice, that is, the common or average idea of what ought to be. Blackstone[1], writing in the middle of the 18th century, in terms which would have been more accurately applied to a later period, shows that modern 'Equity' makes no claim to moderate in any given case the rigour of the Common Law, for there are many hard cases in which it offers no relief; that in

---

[1] *Commentaries*, Vol. III. p. 430.

the administration of it no special regard is paid to the spirit as opposed to the letter of the law, for all Courts use the same rules of interpretation; that its scope cannot be summed up under the heads of fraud, accident and trust, for, while questions coming under each of these are determinable in the ordinary Courts, a Court of Equity deals also with questions coming under none of them; and that, as already said, judges in Equity pay a due respect to precedents and to the customs of the Court. In fact, he says[1], "the system of our Courts of Equity is a laboured connected system, governed by established rules, and bound down by precedents, from which they do not depart, although the reason of some of them may perhaps be liable to objection." And Mr Justice Story[2], later on, defined Equity jurisprudence as "that portion of remedial justice which is exclusively administered by a Court of Equity as contradistinguished from that portion of remedial justice which is exclusively administered by a Court of Common Law."

It will appear in the course of this essay that, with the exception of the very small boundary marked out by Statute, which itself was often infringed, the equitable jurisdiction of the Chancellor was at first, and for many centuries remained, untrammelled by definite rule. The decrees of the Court of Equity down to, at least, the reign of Elizabeth were, in Blackstone's words[3], "rather in the nature of awards, formed on the sudden *pro re nata*, with more probity of intention than knowledge of the subject, founded on no settled principles as being never designed, and therefore never used for precedents," though they were indeed influenced and moulded by the current notions of morality, in the formation of which the great stores of an older system played an important part, and from time to time, but in an irregular and occasional manner, as the scanty references to Chancery in the Year Books show, affected by a repugnance to interfere with what were taken to be fundamental principles of Common Law. This was the Equity whose standards Selden indignantly compared to the length of the Chancellor's foot.

[1] *Commentaries*, Vol. III. p. 432.
[2] Story's *Equity Jurisprudence*, c. 1, § 25.
[3] Vol. III. p. 433.

Sir Henry Maine has suggested that the earliest laws originated in the "themistes" or decrees of an arbitrary and uncontrolled judge being found to contain, in the long run, a number of constant principles. The same case arising again and again with slightly varying circumstances is found to call for the same decision, and so a rule is formulated and laid down prospectively. In just the same way, in a particular class of cases, our modern English Law, erecting the jury as the judge of what is average or reasonable care or conduct, gradually obtains from repeated verdicts a rule to fit the more marked cases, and what was a 'question of fact' becomes a 'question of law[1].' I shall endeavour to show that the development of our system of Equity, its growth from the rudimentary stage, in which the personal conscience of the judge, the arbitrium of a single *bonus vir*, assisted by the principles and rules of morality, and occasionally the vague traditional course of the Court, decided each individual case, to that in which such legislation *ex post facto* almost entirely ceased to occur, was carried out by an analogous process.

Right and legal remedy are expressly declared by a maxim of our law to be correlative terms, and a modern jurist in defining rights deals only with such as may be enforced or defended in the Courts of the State, but these notions, it must be borne in mind, are essentially modern, and are based upon the near coincidence in a developed State of the areas covered by positive law and by positive morality, and upon the permanent presence of a legislature ready and willing to grant to the Courts new or altered powers wherever the sense of the community declares that a particular case is unprovided for, or wrongly treated, by the law. The state of things in England, in the thirteenth century, was entirely different; that there was 'no remedy at the Common Law,' was only too apparent in many a hard case, not only where the Common Law did not contemplate a remedy, but where it did and its machinery failed to provide one.

The legislature indeed was not altogether inactive, and from time to time elaborate codes dealing both with procedure

[1] *The Common Law*, Holmes Lecture, III. p. 123.

and with substantive law, were enacted by it; for instance, the Statute of Marlebridge[1], and the Statute of Westminster the first[2] were enacted, for "the Reformation of Statutes and Laws, whereby the Peace and Tranquillity of the People may be preserved, and wherein convenient remedy by the King and his Lieges ought to be applied," as the preamble of the former Statute states. Still it was both difficult to reach and hard to move, and, in most cases even of admitted hardship, a mediæval statesman would undoubtedly have declared, as the Judges and the Chancellor himself on many occasions did, that it were better a single individual should suffer than that the law and constitution of the land should be changed. Under these circumstances sources of redress other than the ordinary courts of law were looked to. The King himself, his Council, and, after its erection, Parliament, could be petitioned for aid, and from the gradual devolution of the judicial prerogatives of these upon the Chancellor arose his extraordinary jurisdiction.

The following pages commence with a summary account of judicial powers of the different Courts of the Kingdom, and of the King, the Council and Parliament in the 13th and 14th centuries, and of the peculiarities in the Chancellor's position which led to the gradual transference from the King, the Council and Parliament to him of applications for redress, where it was difficult or impossible to obtain it 'at common law.'

The process was so far complete by the end of the reign of Edward III. that the Chancery was established as a regular Court, already administering most of what was afterwards called its common law jurisdiction, (when a distinction as yet not definitely drawn, was made, extending to both procedure and principle,) and administering also equitable relief. The gradual advance to this stage is traced by the aid of the records of orders and indorsements made upon petitions addressed to the other powers transferring them to the Chancellor's care.

The new jurisdiction was not set up without considerable opposition. The House of Commons throughout the 15th century made repeated attacks upon it and the methods of

[1] 52 Hen. III. c. 1.   [2] 3 Edward I.

its administration, and, though these were unsuccessful, they led to the passing of several important statutes, and they throw so much light on the Court of Chancery, and upon the popular feeling in regard to it, that I have thought it not out of place to give a short account of them.

From the 17th year of Richard II. the bills and proceedings in Chancery were recorded and preserved, and, in the 5th chapter, an attempt is made to construct from the collection of those published by the Record Commissioners a sketch both of the relief granted by the Court and of the manner in which it was administered. A strict adherence to chronological sequence would have been equally difficult and unprofitable in this, as in the later portions of the book, and I have therefore adopted the plan of dividing the five centuries of the existence of the Court of Chancery into four periods: from Richard II. to Elizabeth, from Elizabeth to the Commonwealth, from the Restoration to the retirement of Lord Eldon, and from that event to the Judicature Acts.

I have attempted in each of the first three periods to describe and illustrate the procedure and the leading doctrines of the Court as a Court of Equity, and in the second and third, to sketch, in general outline, the alterations from time to time of the spirit in which these doctrines were worked out, and the share taken by the great Chancellors in moulding and developing their jurisdiction. The private lives of the Chancellors, their political achievements, and the important part they took in the growth and consolidation of the constitution of England have nothing to do with the subject of this essay, but the history of Equity is bound up with the alterations which many of them introduced into its principles and practice, and large areas of its jurisdiction are identified with such names as those of Ellesmere, Nottingham, Hardwicke, and Eldon. It is therefore so far only as they left their individual marks upon the jurisdiction that any reference is made to the Chancellors who presided in the Court.

The 10th chapter is wholly taken up with an account of the attempted, but unsuccessful reforms of Equity and its administration under the Commonwealth, and the 13th with the far-reaching reformation actually effected during the present century.

Incidental questions, such as the relation of the Common Law side of Chancery to the Equity side, the weight of precedents in early times, and the influence of Roman Law upon our own Equity, have been discussed at points in the narrative where they became of special prominence, and, in accordance with the general plan of making chronological order subordinate to convenience, in discussing them, I have often taken both a backward and a forward glance at the history of the matters involved. Thus when the final settlement of the right of Chancery to grant injunctions to sterilise judgments at law is reached in the reign of James I., I have referred to the earlier grants of such injunctions and to far later opinions as to the expediency of allowing them.

Propositions of fact, in a work dealing with legal history, which are unsupported by authority are entirely out of place. They are intruders which are entitled to no respect. And if in the following pages illustration and detail appear to be sometimes unnecessarily profuse, I must plead in excuse my anxiety to offer the means of verification for the opinions and statements put forward.

CHAPTER I.

The Judicial System of Mediæval England and the Relation of the King, the Council and Parliament to it.

THE records of Mediæval England which remain to us bear witness, not only to the extreme litigiousness of all classes of Englishmen of the time, but also to the great variety and number of courts to which, in one cause or another, recourse could be had[1]. The Norman Kings in introducing the High, or King's Courts, had not abrogated the jurisdiction of the local and personal courts which existed in every district. The Lord had his manorial courts and claimed to exercise judicial functions through his Council as the King himself did[2], and the Sheriffs and the Aldermen of the towns held pleas; the tenants in ancient demesne claimed that no writs ran against them to answer in the King's Courts, and every official of a court, lay or ecclesiastical, which exercised a particular jurisdiction claimed to answer in that court, and in that court only, for all matters, whether otherwise falling within its particular jurisdiction or not.

The Courts of Law.

The most important Courts, by far, in the 13th century, and especially towards its close, were the King's Courts. Henry II. had reorganised the Curia Regis, reducing the number of its judges from 18 to 5, and directing them "quod illi quinque audirent omnes clamores regni et rectum facerent; et quod a Curia Regis non recederent, sed ibi ad audiendum clamores

---

[1] See *The Coming of the Friars and other essays*, Jessop; and Introductions to the Year Books of Edward III., Pike. Blackstone, Vol. III. ch. IV.

[2] See 15 R. 2. c. 12 (enacting that no one should be made to answer for his *freehold* before the council of a lord).

hominum remanerent; ita ut, si aliqua questio inter eos veniret quæ per eos ad finem duci non posset; auditui regi præsentaretur, et sicut ei, et sapientioribus regni placeret, terminaretur[1]." This was probably the origin of the King's Bench as a distinct tribunal. The 11th article of Magna Carta separated Common Pleas from other suits in the King's Court, and thence arose the Court of Common Pleas, which became a fixed Court sooner than the other Courts, although it was not immediately fixed by this article at Westminster, as is sometimes supposed, for it is found in Session at York so late as the reign of Edward III. At the beginning of the reign of Henry III. we find also the Exchequer as a distinct division, but, until the end of that reign, the judges of the two Benches and the Exchequer remained interchangeable, the Chief Justiciar being the recognised head of all. The office of the Justiciar lost its importance after the fall of Hubert de Burgh, the Chancellor, who had no connection with any of the Courts, succeeding to the position of judicial preeminence, and the three Courts became quite distinct, and soon began to develope diversities of procedure.

Besides these Courts, and as auxiliary to them, were the itinerant justices who went circuit and held assizes of *nisi prius*, by virtue of special commissions, which, though at first entrusted to persons other than the judges of the three Courts, for instance to Serjeants-at-law, and on one or two occasions to the Chancellor, were ultimately almost invariably entrusted to them alone.

The presence and jurisdiction of these Courts of the King tended constantly to diminish the importance of the local courts already mentioned, and gradually to restrict their functions to the determination of matters of small importance[2]. Thus it became a principle that, except as to land in ancient demesne, a claim touching a freehold must be made in the Common Pleas[3], or might, as of course, be removed there, and

[1] Introduction to the Close Rolls. Hardy, p. xxv, quoting Benedic Abbas 206.

[2] 6 Edward I., c. 8 (no suit for less than 40s. in the King's Courts).

[3] In spite of the provision of Magna Carta (c. 24) that the writ of *precipe* should not issue concerning any tenement whereby a freeman might lose his court. See *History of Real Property*, Digby, p. 71.

the right of hearing appeals on pleas of false judgments given in the courts of the King's tenants was reserved to the King's Bench.

The King's Courts had originally been established by the King's authority, and their jurisdiction in cases between subject and subject was in every case based upon the King's Writ. "Non potest quis sine brevi agere" Fleta wrote[1] in the reign of Edward I., and the same rule had been laid down in the preceding reign by Bracton. The writ had originally no connection whatever with the relief sought[2], it had been a general direction to do right to the plaintiff, or as the case might be, but, long before the time now referred to, this had been changed. A particular writ had come to be the only appropriate commencement of an action for a particular redress, and all writs to commence actions were now issued from the Chancery, an office over which the Chancellor presided. It appears that even after the writ obtained by the plaintiff had come to be connected with the remedy sought for, until about the time of Glanvil, a writ to suit each case was framed and issued, but the Provisions of Oxford (1258) expressly forbade the Chancellor to frame new writs without the consent of the King and his Council. It followed that there were certain writs, each applicable to a particular state of circumstances and leading to a particular judgment, which could be purchased by an intending plaintiff. These writs were described as writs "de cursu," and additions to their number were made from time to time by direction of the King, of his Council or of Parliament.

<small>*Procedure by Writ.*</small>

The early statutes contain a number of new forms of writs. Thus the statute of Westminster II., after enacting that lands given to a man and the heirs of his body shall not be alienable by the tenant-in-tail, proceeds thus, "and forasmuch as in a new case new remedy must be provided, this manner of writ shall be granted to the party that will purchase it: Præcipe A quod juste, etc., reddat E manerium de F cum suis pertinentiis quod C dedit tali viro et tali mulieri et heredibus de ipsis viro et muliere exeuntibus."

---

[1] *Fleta*, 2, c. 13 (written circ. 15 Edward I.).

[2] *History of Procedure*, Bigelow, ch. 4.

The inadequacy of the common form writs to meet every case was, to some extent, remedied by the 24th Chapter of the Statute of Westminster II., which, after providing for one or two particular cases to meet which no writ existed, provides further that "whensoever from henceforth it shall fortune in Chancery that in one case a writ is found, and in like case falling under like law is found none, the clerks of the Chancery shall agree in making a writ or shall adjourn the Plaintiffs until the next Parliament, and the cases shall be written in which they cannot agree, and be referred until the next Parliament; and, by consent of the men learned in the Law a writ shall be made, that it may not happen, that the King's Court should fail in ministering justice unto Complainants." In his commentary on this statute Coke asserts that it is merely declaratory of the Common Law, and Mr Bigelow has shown that, as already said, in earlier times the framing of writs had certainly not been restricted to merely copying precedents[1]. The power of extending the jurisdiction of the King's Courts to new cases, and of adapting it to the growing needs and changing circumstances of the community by the construction of new writs, revived or created by the statute, was not however so taken advantage of as to remove the constraints placed upon that jurisdiction by the connection between writs and forms of action. It appears that it was the custom for a plaintiff to state his grievance to the Chancellor or his clerks and for them to find or frame him an appropriate writ, for Fleta[2] tells us that there were associated with the Chancellor "clerici honesti et circumspecti, domino Regi jurati, qui in legibus et constitutionibus Anglicanis notitiam habeant pleniorem; quorum officium sit supplicationes et querelas conquerentium audire et examinare, et eis super qualitatibus injuriarum ostensarum debitum remedium exhibere per brevia Regis," but this cannot be taken to mean that a writ was designed to fit every case. The words of the statute give no power to make a completely new departure; writs are to be framed to fit cases similar to, but not identical with, cases falling within existing

Writs 'consimili casu.'

[1] *History of Procedure*, ch. 4.
[2] *Fleta*, 2, 13, § 1. From § 14 it appears that parties sometimes brought their own draft writs to be sealed.

writs, and the examples given in the statute itself are cases of extension of remedies against a successor in title of the raiser of a nuisance, and for the successor in title of a person who had been disseised of his common. Moreover the form of the writ was debated upon before, and its sufficiency determined by the judges, not by its framers, and they were, as English judges have always been, devoted adherents to precedent. In the course of centuries, by taking certain writs as starting points, and accumulating successive variations upon them, the judges added great areas to our Common Law, and many of its most famous branches, assumpsit and trover and conversion for instance, were developed in this way, but the expansion of the Common Law was the work of the 15th and subsequent centuries, when, under the stress of eager rivalry with the growing equitable jurisdiction of the Chancery, the judges strove, not only by admitting and developing actions upon the case, but also by the use of fictitious actions, following the example of the Roman Prætor, to supply the deficiencies of their system.

It is often alleged that by a liberal construction of this statute, the need for the Chancellor's extraordinary jurisdiction would have been avoided. Austin with characteristic vigour of language says that "Equity arose from the sulkiness or obstinacy of the Common Law Courts, which refused to suit themselves to the changes which took place in the opinions and circumstances of society[1]." Blackstone writes to the same effect: this "provision, (with a little accuracy in the clerks of the Chancery, and a little liberality in the judges, by extending rather than narrowing the remedial effects of the Writ) might have effectually answered all the purposes of a Court of Equity, except that of obtaining discovery by the oath of the Defendant[2]," and the idea is not confined to modern writers, for a judge of the reign of Edward VI. said that "the subpœna would not be so often used as it is, if we paid heed to actions upon the case" (such as the one before the Court) "and maintained the jurisdiction of this Court and other Courts." The suggestion is however

Whether equity could have been developed through actions on the case.

[1] *Jurisprudence*, p. 635.
[2] *Commentaries*, Vol. III. p. 51 (citing the passage following from Y. B., 21 Edward IV. 23).

an unfounded one. It assumes that the equitable jurisdiction wholly arose from the insufficiency of the Common Law, while in fact that insufficiency accounts for but a very small part of the work which fell to the early Chancellors, if the character of that work can be judged from the applications made to their successors in the 15th century, which are the earliest of which we have any continuous record. The Chancellor's power at first was far more often called in to remedy or prevent a breakdown or miscarriage of the ordinary system than to supply omissions which it contemplated or recognised. The suggestion assumes also that the Common Law Courts were intended to supply a remedy in aid of every right the law allowed, but this is also contrary to the fact, as will be shown later on. It implies moreover that the statute rightly or liberally interpreted would have allowed every relief subsequently given in Chancery to have been given in the Common Law Courts; now if it was open to the judges to offer relief to every legitimate claimant in their courts, it is somewhat extraordinary they should have declined to do so, for so eager were the judges of the Exchequer and the King's Bench to attract business, and its concomitant emoluments, to their own Courts, that at an early date it was necessary to forbid the Exchequer holding Common Pleas, and in face of this prohibition, by the well known fictitious allegation of 'quominus,' that Court finally evaded the restriction, and the King's Bench followed suit with the fictitious 'Bill of Middlesex.' It is not however true that without wholly revolutionising their procedure, as well as extending their jurisdiction, the Courts could have offered the kinds of relief that Equity ultimately gave. The varied and flexible decrees, indeed, applicable to suits between numerous parties, and involving intricate and inter-dependant questions, decrees which were not delivered in every case as finally determining the suit and settling the rights of the parties, as were the simple judgments for plaintiff or defendant at Common Law, were of far later date than that of the origin of the equitable jurisdiction, but it seems clear that by no conceivable process of development of the Common Law on the lines of this statute could they have been obtained.

Blackstone himself excepts discovery, and if he could have foreseen the development of Equity in the half century following the publication of his Commentaries, he would no doubt have enlarged the exception. The experiment has, in fact, been tried, and tried under most favourable conditions by judges to whom the legislature had denied the equitable powers they themselves were anxious to possess, in some of the American States[1], and it resulted in failure, and in the grant by the legislature of an extraordinary jurisdiction based upon that of the English Chancery.

The Courts of the King and the subordinate local and franchise Courts were not regarded as offering a remedy for every civil wrong. Their work had down to the time of Edward I. been largely supplemented by the Ecclesiastical Courts, which had claimed to decide all cases where the faith of the party was pledged and broken, as well as cases of marriage and testament, but as the power of the lay lawyers increased, and the jealousy of the Church, which afterwards became so marked a feature of English social life, grew stronger, the former class of cases was withdrawn from the cognizance of these Courts by successive statutes. But the jurisdiction of the Common Law Courts was also supplemented by the judicial powers of the King, or his delegates, who afterwards became the Privy Council, sitting for him, and his Council of nobles and great officers, which afterwards developed into Parliament.

Judicial powers outside the courts of law.

The Norman Kings were not only the 'fountains of justice,' as our modern constitutional phrase puts it, but were its actual administrators, and probably the absolute power of issuing decrees on disputes between their subjects was the last part of their prerogative which would have been called in question. Complaint indeed was made of the issue of writs of execution without trial being had, and this Magna Carta forbids, but the right of the King to both try and determine was not disputed or curtailed till long after this

The King.

---

[1] Pennsylvania and Massachusetts, see "Administration of Equity through Common Law Forms." Sydney G. Fisher, 1 *Law Quarterly Review*, p. 455, and "Chancery in Massachusetts," Edwin H. Woodruff, *ibid.* 5, p. 370.

period¹, though he gradually ceased to exercise it, and Richard II. was advised not to interfere "in his proper person in any matter touching the law or party," but to leave it to his Council "to do what belonged to law and his honour and estate²."

The ordinance of Henry II. already quoted created or adopted a higher tribunal than the King's Court then made a permanent body², for it directed a reference in cases of disagreement between the judges, and in cases of difficulty, to the King and the wiser men of the kingdom, that is to the King in Council with a body which, during the 13th and 14th centuries, consisted of the Chancellor, the Treasurer and the Judges and other great officers and dignitaries who were summoned to assist the King as his permanent advisers. The earlier kings sat continually in person in this body, John, for instance, sat in his house day after day for judicial business, but as the more absorbing interests of continental wars and domestic politics came to occupy the attention of the later Plantagenets they gradually ceased to do so, and 'Coram Rege' became a mere formal expression in the Council, as in the King's Bench.

The King, who bound himself by his coronation oath 'to administer 'æquam et rectam justitiam' to all, not only heard appeals from his Courts but interfered continually in their working, and generally for reasons which are sufficiently suggested by the phrase repeatedly occurring in the Year Books, 'the Plaintiff purchased a writ,' and by the well-known Chapter of Magna Carta.

The following case, which is stated at length in Mr Pike's Introduction to the Year Book 12 and 13 Ed. III.⁴, will illustrate the nature and extent of this interference. It began in the ninth year of Edward III.

John de Boddenho brought an assize of Novel Disseisin against *John de Derby* in respect of a Chapel at Bedford. The Defendant alleged that he held it 'ex collatione Domini Regis,' and produced a writ under the

Boddenho's case.

---

¹ (Statutes were passed under Edward I. and Edward III. to restrain the King's irregular interferences with the Common Law.)
² *Proceedings of the Privy Council*,
Vol. I. p. 84.
³ Introduction to the Close Rolls, Hardy, p. xxv.
⁴ p. xcv.

Privy Seal addressed to the judges, forbidding them to proceed without consulting the King, whereupon the judges adjourned to speak with the King. Afterwards the Plaintiff produced another writ close, purporting to have been granted on a petition 'coram nobis et concilio nostro in Parliamento nostro,' which directed the judges to proceed to take the assize. On the day named for the assize the Defendant produced a third writ close, which asserted the King's title again and directed the judges to give no judgment against the Defendant. A fresh jury was then impannelled, and the matter was again adjourned.

When it came on again the Defendant had another writ setting up a new case, that the Plaintiff had renounced his title, and directing the judges to investigate the alleged renunciation, and to take care no harm happened to the rights of the King or to the Defendant, but this time the Plaintiff had his writ in reply ready, given as before on petition in Parliament, and directing the Court to proceed, and the assize at last was taken. It found that the Chapel was in the collation of the Mayor and Burgesses, not of the King, and that the Plaintiff was seised and had never renounced. This was by no means the end of the case, but the records contradict each other as to what happened next, and the last entry states that there was a writ of error to the King's Bench.

This is perhaps a flagrant instance of interference with the ordinary course of justice, and no doubt the allegation of a claim on behalf of the King is a peculiarity, but many similar cases occur in the records[1]. They are the more striking that they occur in direct breach of the enactments that "There shall no writ from henceforth that toucheth the Common Law go forth under the Petty Seal[2]," and that "it is accorded and established that it shall not be commanded by the Great Seal nor the Little Seal to disturb or delay common right (commune droit), and that, though such commandments do come, the justices shall not leave to do right in any point[3]."

---

[1] See, for instance, Introduction to Y. B., 12 and 13 Edward III., Pike, p. xciii.

[2] 28 Edward I. c. 6.

[3] 2 Edward III. c. 8.

Applications for redress or assistance then were made to the King, not only by way of appeal from decisions of the Courts, but also where matters were pending before the judges, and they were also made, as appears from the Rolls of Parliament, the published proceedings of the Privy Council, and the Close Rolls, in many cases without any reference to the Courts at all. They were made by Petition addressed either to him alone, or to him in Council or in Parliament. Petitions made to the King alone and answered by him occurred long after the reign of Richard II. The following Petition was addressed to Henry IV. "A n$\overline{re}$ ts excellent t ts redoute S^r, n$\overline{re}$ Seigno^r le Roy," the King's tenants of Feltham pray that he will forbid the Officers of the Bishop of London to disturb their right of common, which they enjoy under a grant of Edward III. "p^r Dieu t en oever de Charitie,...consideraunt ts g^{a}cious Seigno^r $\bar{q}$ les ditz suppliantz sont si poveres q'ils ne p^r.ount endurer lez costages p^r avoir remedye p la comune ley." The indorsed order is that right be done, and a writ granted to the Petitioners[1].

The Petition is interesting, although it belongs to a much later epoch than that we are now considering, because it shows the survival to a time when the authority of the Courts was even more firmly established, and when the Chancellor's Equity was an important institution, of the power of redress inherent in the King, and also because of its resemblance in form to the Petitions presented in the Chancery. So late as the reign of Elizabeth petitions of this class were presented to the Queen, and were referred by her to the Chancellor[2].

The Council, says Mr Hardy[3], "had an absolute jurisdiction over all the proceedings in the Courts below;"
The Council. ..."if any litigant felt himself aggrieved, he applied for redress to the Council, in the same manner as he would have applied to the King before the latter committed his prerogative of distributing justice and equity to his council." Application was made to it[4], "where from the heinousness of

---

[1] *Proceedings of the Privy Council*, Vol. II. p. 110.

[2] There are several instances in Munro's *Acta Cancellariæ*.

[3] Introduction to the Close Rolls,

p. xxvi, and see Stubbs' *Constitutional History*, Vol. II. p. 273.

[4] *Equitable Jurisdiction*, Spence, Vol. I. p. 330.

the offence, or the rank or power of the party, or any other cause, there was likely to be an impediment to a fair trial, or to the attainment of appropriate redress in the ordinary tribunals. So also when by force and violence,"—and, it may be added, fraud or local prejudice,—"justice was prevented taking its ordinary course. The Council on such application either took the case into their own hands, or gave specific directions in regard to it according to the circumstances of the case. Where a party was suffering imprisonment by the process of an inferior Court the double remedy of a *Subpœna* against the pursuing party, and a writ of *Habeas Corpus cum causa* was sometimes given. The Council had the power of issuing writs into all special jurisdictions or Franchises, as Wales and Ireland, which, with their other extraordinary powers, gave them surpassing capabilities beyond those of any other Court except the Court of Chancery" (after its establishment).

The Council here referred to, was a body of permanent salaried officials, the most important of whom was the Chancellor, who presided in it and directed its business. It met daily, and had from time to time associated with it the lords and great ecclesiastical dignitaries specially summoned to attend its meeting, and it then sat as the "Great Council," which was distinct from Parliament, but which blended with Parliament when sitting. The Great Council ultimately, when, under Edward III., the constitution of Parliament became fixed, merged into it, and the permanent Council became distinct and separate, during the Session of Parliament as at other times, and received the title of the 'Privy Council.'

The description of the work of the Council given above is fully borne out by the ordinance made for its governance in 13 Richard II.[1] This provides that the Council shall meet at 8 or 9 o'clock a.m. at the latest, and shall take the King's business first; that it shall send matters touching the Common law to the judges, matters touching the office of the Chancellor into Chancery, and those touching the office of the Treasurer into the Exchequer; that all matters which cannot

[1] *Proceedings of the Privy Council*, Vol. I. p. 18.

be disposed of without the special grace of the King shall be sent to him to have his advice and will declared concerning them, and that all other matters sent to the Council for their advice, and others of great charge shall be determined by those of the Council who are present, and the officers; and then follows a direction that "all other bills of the people of small importance be examined and disposed of before the Keeper of the Privy Seal and others of the Council who should be present at the time." This last provision, which recalls some general orders of reference of petitions to the Chancellor of earlier date which will be mentioned later on, is supposed to have founded the Court of Requests, a minor Court of Equity which was practically abolished by a decree of the Queen's Bench under Elizabeth[1].

The following case of 1 Edward II., which is reported in the Abbreviatio Placitorum[2], will serve to illustrate the manner and occasion of applications to the Council under that King.

The tenants of the King's Manor of Carbeston, which was a manor of 'ancient demesne,' petitioned the Council for relief against the Abbot of Welbeck who had inclosed certain arable land and woods, and the Council, having read the petition, agreed that the petitioners should go before the King's Bench, and that there justice should be done, and they sent the petition to the judges, who gave the parties a day for hearing. The Abbot pleaded that the land was his, but he also objected that he ought not to answer without the King's writ. To this objection the tenants replied that, their manor being of ancient demesne, no writ ran within it except the "little writ close of the King," and that they could have no remedy except by petition. Judgment was given that the facts should be found by a Jury, and the petitioners were told to obtain a writ against the Abbot if they thought it would be any assistance to them. What finally happened does not appear. The ground of the application to the Council here was the lack of remedy in the ordinary course at the Common Law.

---

[1] Spence, Vol. I. p. 351, Coke, *Inst.* v. 97.   [2] p. 302, R. 2.

The King and the Council were not the only authorities which might be applied to for assistance: the Great Council of the Realm sat from time to time under the earlier Kings, and under Edward I. and his son and grandson it developed into Parliament, and exercised the right of hearing petitions and granting relief upon them, and, as its power increased, it manifested much jealousy of the exercise of a similar power by the Council and by the Chancellor.   *Parliament.*

In the Parliament of Lincoln in 1315 it was ordered[1] that the Chancellor, the Treasurer and the Judges should lay before Parliament cases pending before them in their places which they could not decide without its aid, that what ought to be done in regard to them might be done by it. And a Statute of 14 Edward III.[2], reciting that "divers mischiefs have happened, for that in divers courts, as well in the Chancery, as in the King's Bench, the Common Bench and in the Exchequer, before Justices assigned, and other justices deputed to hear and determine, the judgments have been delayed sometime by difficulty, and sometime by divers opinions of the judges and sometimes for some other cause," enacted that in every Parliament triers of petitions should be appointed with power, on complaint being made to them of such delays, to call for the proceedings in the delayed causes, and to discover from the justices what was the reason of the delays, and either (with the advice of the Chancellor, the Treasurer and others of the King's Council) to give judgment themselves, or, if the matter were of great difficulty, to bring it before Parliament.

The case of Boddenho at the beginning of the reign of Edward III. has already been cited to show how the King, or his Council in his name, interfered in the course of justice, and the same case shows Parliament interfering to redress the balance. The following case of about the same date, is an instance of a dispute between the judges and Parliament upon a point of law.

[3] Geoffrey Staunton sued John Staunton and his wife

---

[1] *Rot. Parl.* I. p. 350 (*a*).
[2] Statute 1, c. 5.
[3] Introduction to Year Book, 13 and 14 Edward III., Pike, p. xxxvii. The record of the proceedings in Parliament is in *Rot. Parl.* III. p. 122.

Amy in formedon in the Common Pleas. The Defendant Amy vouched her husband and co-defendant to warranty, and assigned a fine by which one T, who had an estate in the tenements claimed by her husband's gift, conveyed to her and her husband. The Plaintiff averred that T had no estate in the tenements. Thereupon Amy denied the admissibility of this averment, but offered to answer over if it were held admissible. The Plaintiff then presented a petition to the King in Council in Parliament alleging that the offer to answer over was inserted by the clerks by misprision. Parliament agreed that the Plaintiff's averment was admissible, and that Amy could make no further answer as the parties had abode judgment absolutely, and two writs were sent to the judges directing them to proceed to judgment, and a third one requiring them to do so or to show cause why they delayed. Thereupon there was a new argument in Court, in the course of which Stonore C. J. said that the decision of Parliament was bad law, and no judgment was given.

The Plaintiff presented another petition to Parliament, and the Clerk of Parliament was sent to tell the judges to go on, or to bring the record into Parliament for judgment there. They did the latter, and Parliament gave judgment for the Plaintiff. Error was next sued in the King's Bench, and both parties, in turn, petitioned Parliament, and ultimately a writ was sent to the King's Bench to proceed 'ad finalem discussionem negotii,' and, the defendants abandoning their case, the Plaintiff applied for, and obtained execution.

From this sketch of the judicial powers of the King, Council and Parliament, it will be seen that the Common Law Courts were not at any time sufficient for the needs of the country, and that the existence of civil rights which they were incompetent to protect was, even in the infancy of the present Courts, fully recognised. These judicial powers were the roots from which the Chancellor's equitable jurisdiction grew, for the petitions craving their aid were continually referred to the Chancellor for him to consider and answer, until the reference became so much a matter of course that parties indorsed their petitions over of their own motion, and the Chancellor's power to grant relief in the nature of that granted by the King's Council and Parliament became so firmly established that petitions were addressed, in the first instance, directly to him.

The custom of granting relief in matters of private right by Parliament and the Council continued long after the reign of Edward III. when the practice of direct application to the Chancellor became common. A petition to the King of the reign of Henry IV. has already been quoted, and numerous similar petitions are to be found in the Parliament Rolls and the proceedings of the Privy Council under Richard II. and his successors.

Subsequent history of the judicial powers of the Council and of Parliament.

The Statute 4 Henry IV. c. 23, which complains "that after judgment given in the Courts of our Lord the King the parties be made to come upon grievous pain, sometimes before the King himself, sometimes before the King's Council, and sometimes in Parliament, to answer there anew," and enacts that, after judgment, the "Parties and their heirs shall be thereof in Peace" until the judgment be undone by attaint or error, shows clearly that the old powers were then still in full force and exercise. In 1460 the Lords of Parliament actually tried, and decided on the right of the Duke of York to the Crown, the Chancellor pronouncing the judgment, and they resolved[1] that "every persone high and lowe suing to this high court of Parlement of right must be herd, and his desire and petition understaud," but a century before this, the rule had been adopted that Parliament ought to relieve only those who could find no remedy elsewhere[2].

The interference of the Council in cases touching freedom of the person, and rights of property, was the subject of continual attack from the time of Edward III. onward, as being a breach of the Great Charter, and many statutes were passed to restrain it[3]. Had these Statutes been observed, the Courts of Equity would never have arisen. Later on, when the attack

---

[1] 1 Camp. 366, *Rot. Parl.* v. 375 (a).

[2] See Lord Chancellor Scrope's Address to a parliament of 2 Richard II., *Rot. Parl.* III. p. 55, and the order on a petition, 13 Richard II., *Rot. Parl.* III. p. 259.

[3] 5 Edward III., c. 9; 25 Edward III., c. 18; 28 Edward III., c. 3; 37 Edward III., c. 18; Taswell Langmead, p. 178, et seq.

was made directly upon the Chancellor's growing jurisdiction, the King and his advisers were more cautious, and the petitions of the Commons for abolition of the jurisdiction were not allowed to become statutes. The power of the King or his Council to issue 'privilegia,' or to displace the legal rights of the subject in particular cases, was definitely lost in the struggles of the 17th century, but it had long before become obsolete, although James I. claimed to possess it as well as other dead branches of the prerogative. The Private Bill in Parliament is at the present day, a direct descendant of the old Petition and Answer.

CHAPTER II.

THE CHANCELLOR.

BEFORE dealing in detail with the reference of petitions to the Chancellor, which led to the conferment upon him of an extraordinary jurisdiction analogous to that of the King, Council and Parliament, it will be convenient to consider shortly the position of the Chancellor in and before the reign of Edward III. His office as the King's Secretary, Chaplain of his Chapel, and Keeper of his Seal was a very ancient office. Coke declares that it had existed from extreme antiquity[1], and it certainly existed before the Conquest. By reason of his position as custodian of the Great Seal he was the head of the office in which the King's Charters were inrolled, and whence the original writs were issued, in the manner already described. All the petitions to Parliament and the Council passed through this office, and the records concerning them were there inrolled, and, where relief was granted upon them, as for instance that the judges should proceed with an action, it was usually carried into effect by a writ close out of the Chancery[2]. From the time Becket held the office it became of importance and dignity next after that of the Justiciar only. William Fitz Stephen, one of Becket's Clerks, describes the Chancellor[3] as sealing all the King's ordinances and being present, even though unsummoned, at all his councils. Nothing was done without the Chancellor's consent and advice either in the Curia or in the Exchequer. It does not appear that he regularly

---

[1] 4 *Inst.* 78.
[2] *Rot. Parl.* II. p. 123 et passim, Introduction to Year Book, 13 and 14 Edward III., p. xliii.
[3] *Constitutional History*, Stubbs, I. p. 647.

held any Court of his own before the reign of Edward II., and the antiquity assigned by Coke and Blackstone to his Common Law jurisdiction is far too great. Fleta, writing in the reign of Edward I., merely refers to his control over the issue of writs, and says nothing of his holding any Court. He does say, however, that recognizances and contracts were inrolled in the Chancery, and judicial writs issued to the Sheriffs to enforce them out of the Chancery, just as by the judges themselves. If the recognizance were newly enrolled, when the creditor came to complain of the non-observance of the agreement, immediate execution issued, but if it were not, the debtor was summoned on a certain day to show cause why execution should not be had, and if he appeared and said nothing in point, or failed to appear, the writ to the Sheriff issued. "Ex hac quidem constitutione," adds the writer[1], "oriuntur brevia judicialia in cancellaria sicut coram ipsis justiciariis." The Statute of Merchants 13 Edward I. which created the Statute Staple, expressly reserved the power of the Chancellor and Justices to take recognizances in form by law, usage and manner provided. Perhaps in these inquiries may be found the first beginning of the Chancellor's separate jurisdiction. It is clear that by the date now considered the Chancellor was looked upon as a judicial personage[2]. Becket, Chancellor under Henry II., was panegyrised as "qui regni leges cancellat iniquas, et mandata pii principis æqua facit," and Neville, Chancellor under Henry III., is referred to as "singulis sua jura, præcipue pauperibus, juste reddens et indilite." He was too, as we have seen, the President of the Council, which was greatly occupied with judicial work, and since the fall of Hubert de Burgh and the abolition of the Justiciarship, he was in fact 'head of the law' in the kingdom[3]. So important had his office become that, from the reign of Henry III. onwards, continual demands were made that he should be elected by

[1] *Fleta*, 2, 13.
[2] Campbell, Vol. I. Early Chapters. Spence, Vol. I. p. 334.
[3] (See letter to Lord Chancellor Langton from Milicent de Mohaunt, thanking him for his assistance in a suit, and asking for further aid, No. 1755, Royal Letters, cited in Horwood's Introduction to Year Book, 30 and 31 Edward I., p. lxxxi.)

the Council or Parliament, or with their assent. He had indeed already become, what Bacon's Selden calls him, 'the kingdom's darling.' The Statute 28 Edward I. c. 5 expressly associates the Chancellor with the Judges and directs him and them to follow the King, "so that he may have at all times near him some sages in law which be able duly to order all such matters as shall come into the Court at all times when need shall require."

It is not then surprising that when the King or the Council appointed a delegate or commission to hear and decide petitions, the Chancellor should have been almost invariably chosen, with or without assistants, marked out as he was for such duties, not only by his connection with the administration of the law, with the King's grants and mandates under seal, and with the presentation and recording of the petitions, but also by his position as a great cleric, and, in most cases, the head of the chief Ecclesiastical Court in the kingdom, for such he usually was, since by reason of that position he could lay special claim to a knowledge of what 'conscience,' 'right,' 'justice,' 'honesty' or 'law and reason,'—the terms employed in the references to him—demanded.

CHAPTER III.

THE ESTABLISHMENT OF THE CHANCELLOR'S JURISDICTION.

The reign of Edward I.

THE earliest general reference of petitions to the Chancellor is found in an ordinance of 8 Edward I.[1] After complaining of the multitude of petitions presented to the King, most of which could be dealt with by the Chancellor or Judges, that ordinance provides that all petitions that touch the Seal shall go first to the Chancellor, and those that touch the Exchequer to the Exchequer, and those that touch the justices or the law of the land to the justices, and those that touch the Jurie to the justices of the Jurie. And if the matters are so great, or so much of grace, that the Chancellor and the others cannot do what is asked without the King, then they shall take them to the King to know his will, and that no petition come before the King and his Council except by the hands of the said Chancellor and the other chief ministers; so that the King and his Council may be able, without the embarrassment of other business, to attend to the important business of his kingdom and his foreign lands. This, it is clear, conferred no special jurisdiction on the Chancellor, who is mentioned as one, and along with others, of the chief ministers, while matters of grace are distinctly reserved to be dealt with by the King himself. The matters touching the seal, I presume, refer to the formalities required to authenticate the King's grants and mandates, and the issue of original writs, and perhaps also the revocation of improper grants, which would show, if that be so, that what was afterwards the

[1] Introduction to Close Rolls, Hardy, p. xxviii. Stubbs, *Const. Hist.* II. p. 263.

Common Law Jurisdiction of the Chancellor was already in operation or was now first created. The matters touching the justices or the law of the land have obviously reference to ordinary administration of justice, and to delays and irregularities therein which the judges could of themselves correct.

There is another ordinance[1] of 21 Edward I. which is to the same effect and shows that the earlier one was either temporary only, or that it had not been observed.

Lord Campbell[2] gives a list of nearly a dozen decrees of the Council in the reign of Edward I. upon petitions referring them to the Chancellor. One is a petition for the King's Letters Patent of protection, and the answer to the supplicant is "veniat ad cancellariam, ut fiat ei quod graciose fieri poterit," another is for the appointment of a *custos* for a convent, and it is ordered that the Chancellor shall appoint one, a third is answered "cancellar: vocat justic: provideat eis remedium, et aliis in hoc casu perpetuo duratur," evidently directing the Chancellor with the help of the judges to frame an original writ for a new case, to become 'de cursu.' Several of the other decrees, however, direct a hearing in the Chancery, and that justice shall be done. This is the case of a complaint of ejectment from a right of pasture, and of a dispute as to the jurisdiction of the Archbishop of Canterbury, which, for all that appears, might have been tried in the ordinary Courts.

Lord Campbell[3] also mentions a writ under the Privy Seal directed to the Chancellor and Master of the Rolls enclosing a petition and requiring them to give such remedy as to them should appear to be consonant to honesty.

These cases were as yet, however, only sent to the Chancellor as a convenient referee, and he had no exclusive jurisdiction in respect of them. Thus in the case last mentioned he is associated with the Master of the Rolls, and in a case of 33 Edward I. the matter in question is committed to him and the Treasurer, and they are directed to consult with the Judges. In that case the Plaintiff complained that the Defendant, the Queen, to whom certain lands had been conveyed by a fine, had

---

[1] Stubbs, *loc. cit.*
[2] Vol. I. p. 186.
[3] *Ibid.*, citing from "The Judicial Authority of the M. R."

seized others not conveyed, and so he petitioned the King, and the King by his writ sent him before the Judges. The Judges however could not proceed because of errors in an inquisition, which it appears had been taken, and in the pleadings, and therefore the King sent the writ to the Treasurer of England and the Chancellor that they, after consultation with the judges, might proceed to judgment. This, added the order, was not to be taken as a precedent[1]. The record describes the proceedings as upon a 'monstre de droit,' which was the proper form of action to recover property held by the King, and was afterwards appropriated to the Common Law side of Chancery or the Exchequer, but it does not appear that the King was interested in this case.

In the course of the next reign the Chancellor began to sit regularly for judicial business, as appears from the entry already referred to on the Rolls of the Parliament of Lincoln in 1315[2] where, after reciting the appointment of triers of petitions, it is added, that it was ordered that the Chancellor, the Treasurer and the Judges of both Benches should bring before Parliament cases pending before them 'in their places' which they could not decide without its help.

The reign of Edward II.

There is a record too of 13 Edward II.[3] which shows that cases were regularly heard in the Chancery by the Chancellor, and that it was the custom then, as in later times, not to try matters of fact in that Court. It appears that in this case the pleading and procedure exactly resembled that of the ordinary Common Law Courts. The nature of the claim is not stated, but it was probably based upon a recognizance or other acknowledgment inrolled in the court, for the report is as follows: "Henry de Ernestfest, after inspecting the said acquittance, pleaded 'non est factum suum' and this he was prepared to verify ('et hoc optulit verificare &c.'). And, as this kind of cause, according to the custom of England, cannot be determined in the Chancery, the Chancellor adjourned the parties to the King's Bench ('in curia Regis coram ipso Rege

---

[1] *Abbreviatio Placitorum*, 256, R. 46.
[2] *Rot. Par.* I. p. 350 (a), cited in Campbell.
[3] *Abbreviatio Placitorum*, p. 336, Rot. I.

ad faciend & recipiend qd jur' fu'it & raconis &c.'). The jury found that the acquittance was not the deed of the said Henry, and therefore, concludes the record, 'let Ricardus Messinge be taken' &c. The Rolls of Parliament show that a very great variety of business was at this time referred to the Chancellor, especially cases in which the Crown was concerned, for these had come to be regarded as specially appropriable to him. Thus, to a petition[1] complaining of the seizure of a ship for the then expected war, by the King's officers, it was answered 'videtur consilio quod execucio hujus peticionis spectat ad officium cancellarii. Ideo tradatur cancellario." In the same year, 19 Edward II., there is a petition addressed to the Chancellor directly, begging his attention to an earlier petition which had been referred to him by Parliament and praying that he would, by writ, direct the judge to bring the record and proceedings in an action of the suitor's before himself[2].

In the Parliament of 1320[3] a petition alleging ejectment and personal outrage, for which, though the petitioner had sued out twelve writs, she had obtained no relief, was sent for hearing to justices to be assigned in Chancery, on account of the poverty of the petitioner, and a petition complaining of forcible ejectment was similarly dealt with on account of the enormity of the wrong.

Sir Duffus Hardy collected from the Rolls a large number of answers endorsed on petitions of this reign, referring them to the Chancery, and from them it clearly appears that judicial enquiries were regularly made there[4]. Several of the petitions are concerned with claims affecting the King's rights, which, as already said, were now specially appropriated for the Chancellor's determination, and which formed the chief part of his common law jurisdiction, but many deal with matters of grace only, and in some it is expressly stated there is no remedy at the Common Law. There are several allusions in the answers

[1] *Rot. Parl.* i. p. 433 (b), 19 Edward II. (cited in Campbell i. p. 209).
[2] *Rot. Parl.* i. p. 437 (a). No. 25. (There are a large number of references to Chancery, with or without directions as to the method of suing there, in this year.)
[3] *Rot. Parl.* i. p. 372, No. 11.
[4] Campbell, Vol. i. p. 206.

to the custom of the Chancery as the rule by which the decision was to be guided, and sometimes 'law and reason' or 'reason' were to supply the determining principles, but generally the matter was committed to the Chancellor to do what 'ought to be done,' or 'what justice demands,' or without any specific direction at all. In two cases he was directed to summon counsel: where the Prior of the Church of the Trinity at Canterbury complained of an infringement of his right to the goods of his under-tenants convicted of felony, the answer was 'Monstre sa chartre en Chancellerie et le Chanc: apele a lui conseil s'avise ceoq soit meus a fere de cest besoigne;' and where the Archbishop of York complained of a prohibition to his court, it was 'Veigne en Chancellerie et mestre sa chartre; et le Chancellier apele a lui conseile, face ceo qe face a faire,' and in another case, that of a petition for the recovery of a moiety of a manor, he was told to call to his assistance some of the Council and the Serjeants at Law, and to do what of law and reason ought to be done.

The answers tell us moreover that the custom of calling a respondent to show cause, which had prevailed in the previous reign in regard to recognizances, was sometimes adopted in considering remitted petitions, but the more general course, as yet, appears to have been to issue a commission to find the facts by inquisition returnable into the Chancery, a plan always adopted in the case of escheats and forfeitures.

During the reign of Edward III. the Chancery as a Court for hearing causes became fully established, and was fixed, where it remained for so many centuries, at Westminster in the Hall rebuilt by the King and William of Wykeham[1]. The record of the delivery of the Great Seal to Lord Chancellor Sadyngton says he received it "in the King's Great Hall at Westminster in the place where the Chancellor usually sits among the Clerks of the Chancery to exercise his office[2]." Coke[3] says that the Court had become stationary before this reign " in a certayne place, to the great benefit and ease of

The reign of Edward III.

[1] *History of the Coif*, Pulling, p. 78. Camp. I. p. 214, Stubbs, *Const. Hist.* II. p. 267.
[2] *Rot. Cl.* 19 Edward III., p. 2. Camp. I. p. 246.
[3] 2 *Inst.*, p. 552.

the subject," but in this he is incorrect, for, as we have seen, Edward I. expressly required the Chancellor to accompany him in those extraordinary peregrinations which he, as his predecessors, made continually through the kingdom, and both in his reign and the next there are entries of the purchase of pack-horses to carry the Chancery Rolls[1]. The Commons petitioned the King in the year 1364 to make the King's Bench stationary at Westminster or York 'where the Common Bench remains,' and though the King refused to bind himself, the Court did in fact sit regularly at Westminster from his reign onwards.

In the 22nd year of his reign Edward published his famous writ to the Sheriff of London[2], reciting that he was much occupied with matters concerning the State, and his own business, and directing that all matters proper to be brought before him, whether relating to the Common Law, or to the special grace of the King, should be brought, the matters touching the Common Law before the Lord Chancellor (the Archbishop of Canterbury elect) to be disposed of by him, and the other matters touching the grant of the King's grace before the Chancellor, or the keeper of the Privy Seal, and that they or one of them should transmit to the King the petitions which they could not dispose of without consulting him, together with their or his opinion thereon, so that on reading it and without it being necessary to make any further suit to the King, he might indicate his will in the matter to the Chancellor or keeper of the Privy Seal, and that thenceforth no other business of the kind should be brought before the King himself.

This writ is sometimes referred to as if it were a kind of statutory warrant for the existence of the Chancellor's extraordinary jurisdiction, but if this were so it could hardly have escaped the attention of the earlier writers. Coke does not mention it, nor do Bacon and his fellows in their report to King James I.[3], and in the numerous petitions and complaints

[1] Camp. I. p. 270.
[2] Printed in Camp. I. p. 248, and Stubbs, *Const. Hist.* p. 269. (Many of the copies of the early statutes and ordinances on the records are addressed to particular sheriffs.)
[3] *Post*, ch. VII.

of the Commons against the Chancellor's interference with the Common Law, no reference is made to it. It was probably a merely temporary measure due to the King's engrossment in the French War, and in the siege and capture of Calais, and long afterwards, petitions were made to the King and were sometimes heard and answered by him in person, while the jurisdiction of the Council probably attained its most vigorous operation under Edward's successor, Richard II. Lord Campbell suggests that the Common Law business of which the writ speaks was the issue of original writs, but this was the Chancellor's regular office, and applications would normally only be brought to the King in case of his refusal, it seems more probable therefore that it is to requests for interferences with the ordinary course of the Common Law, such as those in Boddenho's and the other cases cited above, that allusion is made.

The records however show[1] that about this time reference to the Chancellor in cases of difficulty in, or of the absence of the ordinary remedy at Common Law had become the usual course. Sir Duffus Hardy suggests that the Council, who still accompanied the King, being deprived of the Chancellor's assistance after he began to remain regularly at Westminster, were compelled to refer petitions to him to a greater extent than before, and hence the indorsement 'adeat in Canc:' or 'sequatur in Canc:' on petitions addressed to the Council become very common towards the end of the reign. The judges themselves occasionally sought the Chancellor's assistance as appears from the following interesting case[2]. It was an action for a debt of 200 marks, or pounds (the reports differ), due on a bond conditioned for the payment of 100. The Defendant pleaded payment and acceptance of 100, but did not aver payment on the day. The Plaintiff replied that he took the 100 on account only. The first hearing ended (apparently) in judgment for the Plaintiff, but the case came on again, and the judges then said they would speak to the

[1] Introduction to the Close Rolls, Hardy, p. xxviii.
[2] Year Book, 46 Edward III. Mich.

23, and 47 Edward III. Mich. 14, cited in Jenkyns' *Six Centuries of Reports*, but these are misstated.

Chancellor, and on the next day, by the advice of the Chancellor and all the Judges, they gave judgment for the Plaintiff, the Defendants to be in mercy, and, as to the 100 paid, the Plaintiff to get nothing. The Chancellor did not until long after develope any special equity alleviative of the hardships of the Common Law, and he is here seen advising that a penalty be enforced, without any suggestion of relieving the debtor.

The following decrees on petitions to Parliament complaining of judgments at law may be added as further evidence of the establishment of the delegated jurisdiction in Chancery. They are cited by Lord Campbell[1]. "Let this Petition be referred to the Chancery, and let the Chancellor cause to be summoned before him the Counsel of Madame (the Petitioner, who was seeking relief against a judgment in the Common Pleas,) to appear in Chancery on a certain day, and also the King's serjeants and some of the justices, and, if nothing be shown or said which may reasonably disturb the judgment, or if the Counsel of Madame do not choose to appear, then let a writ issue to the justices where the plea was depending before judgment to proceed according to the law and the usages of the land."

"Let this Petition be referred to the Chancery, and there let evidence, which the said Geoffrey says he hath to manifest the loss of the aforesaid commodities, be received, and that justice was not done him in his suit for recovery of losses in these parts, and therefore let speedy remedy be ordained him according to the law used in such cases."

Still more conclusive evidence of the thorough establishment of the Chancery as a Court is afforded by the proceedings in relation to a Petition to the King and Council, of the Clerks in Chancery by which they claimed, and obtained, with the consent of Parliament, the privilege of being sued only in their own Court[2].

The jurisdiction of the Chancellor in respect of claims by the King in this reign was further developed by the Statute

---

[1] Vol. I. p. 271, *et seq., Rot. Parl.* II. p. 206; (21 and 22 Edward III.) and p. 437 (temp. Edward III.).

[2] Camp. *loc. cit. Rot. Parl.* II. p. 154.

36 Edw. III. (13) which provides that if an escheator seize lands, and the escheat be challenged, the escheator shall send the inquest into Chancery, and a writ shall be delivered him to show the cause of the seizing in the Chancery, and the Challenger may there traverse[1] the office or otherwise show his right, and from thence the matter shall be sent into the King's Bench for final discussion.

The references and applications to the Chancellors were not however confined to cases of the King's claim, nor does it appear that any distinction was drawn between such cases and others in regard to procedure, as yet, or indeed for long after. But this point will be considered later on.

The following is an example of the petitions directed to the Chancellor himself in this reign. It will be noticed that it asks generally for 'a remedy,' and that in support of a common law right, as it alleges. Its form closely resembles, on the one hand, the petitions of the time to Parliament and to the Council, and, on the other, the earlier bills of the next reign which are printed in the Chancery Calendars. It commences thus[2]: "Au Chanceller n're seign' le Roi monstre William…," and it alleges that the Petitioner, a parson, claims certain tithes, which the Dean of Wymborne claims also in respect of a free chapel of the King. The petitioner had commenced a suit in the Ecclesiastical Court, but a prohibition had issued out of Chancery to stay it because of the assertion of the King's claim, "p'quey le dit William prie a v're g*ciouse seign'ie q'vous pleise ordiner remedie q'sa dite esglise ne soit disherite encontre co'e droit." The indorsement states that the Petitioner, in person, and the Dean, by his attorney, appeared in the Chancery at Westminster, and a day was given them "ad faciend' & recipiend' de contentis in ista petic'o'e quod cur' d'ni Regis considerav'it." A comparison of this case with that of Boddenho, stated above, which occurred earlier in the reign, where a similar defence involving the King's right was raised, shows

---

[1] "Et illoeques soit oie sanz delay de *traverser loffice* ou autrement mon*strer son droit*, et dilloeques mande *devant le Roi* affaire finale discussion, sanz attendre autre mandement."

[2] It is quoted in the Introduction to the Close Rolls, Hardy, p. **xxix**, 38 Edward III.

here a prohibition issuing from the Chancery and an application to the Chancellor to remove it, in place of the corresponding orders of the King and petitions to Parliament in the earlier case, and, although the new ways have not yet superseded, and for long after did not supersede, the old, their existence marks the birth of the Chancellor's jurisdiction.

Towards the end of the reign a Statute[1] was passed, dealing, as was the custom with our early statutes, with many different matters,—Purveyance, the Jurisdiction of Mayor of the Staple, and the stipends of priests,—which contains the provision "that if any man feel himself aggrieved contrary to any of the articles above written or other contained in divers statutes, and will come into the Chancery, or any for him, and thereof make his complaint, he shall presently there have remedy by force of the said articles and statutes without elsewhere pursuing to have remedy." This, as the writ to the Sheriff discussed above, has been regarded by some as a special authority for the Chancellor's jurisdiction, but it seems more probable that Coke's explanation[2], that the statute refers only to remedy by obtaining a writ to commence an action in the ordinary Common Law Courts, is correct. The concluding words point in this direction and were probably inserted to prevent the King's purveyors, against whom the Statute was chiefly directed, from objecting to the jurisdiction of the ordinary Courts. A similar direction had been given by Edward II. in answer to a complaint from the Commons of unlawful arrests[3]; "ceux qi sont pris par tele accisement veignent en Chancellerie et averout dreyt," and another is found in the statute 15 Richard II. Cap. 12.

I have now traced the Chancellor's Court down to its full establishment as a Court holding regular sittings, in which the Chancellor heard, very often by remittance from Parliament or the Council, and sometimes at least by original application, 'matters of grace' to which the ordinary procedure was for some reason or other not applicable, or was not applied. These cases were heard on a direct complaint setting out the

---

[1] 36 Edward III., c. 9. (A later chapter from this statute, touching escheats, has already been cited.)
[2] 4 *Inst.* 82.
[3] *Rot. Parl.* I. 430. 19 Edward II.

facts upon which it was based without any technicality, and without the writ which in the Common Law Courts was at once the commencement of the action[1], and the foundation of the judge's jurisdiction to try it. Besides these matters the Court had other business to deal with, the *scire facias* upon recognizances and to annul the King's Charters wrongly granted, petitions of right and traverses of office, and actions by and against the officers of the Court. These latter were dealt with, in most cases, according to the ordinary common law procedure[2], as in later times when the division between the Common Law and Equity sides of Chancery became established they always were, but so far as we have gone, and for long afterwards, as the bills preserved in the Tower show, the procedure by bill was often applied to them also.

[1] Spence, Vol. I. p. 338.
[2] *Post*, p. 53. Spence, Vol. I. p. 337. See also the case of *Mareshal v.* *Bemburgh*, Y. B. 12 and 13 Edward III., Pike, p. 96.

CHAPTER IV.

PETITIONS OF THE COMMONS AGAINST THE CHANCELLOR'S JURISDICTION, AND STATUTES RELATING TO IT.

FROM the beginning of the reign of Richard II. and for more than a century afterwards continual complaints were made in Parliament of the interference of the Chancellor in matters cognisable in the Common Law Courts, and their terms throw much light on the growing importance of the Chancery Court, and show how it was steadily usurping the place formerly occupied by the Council,—which, as we have seen, had met with a precisely similar attack in the reigns of the Edwards,—and by Parliament itself in the redress of private wrongs. The fact that these complaints all came from the Commons suggests that they may have been prompted rather by the professional jealousy of the Common Law lawyers, who, though often forbidden to sit, were found in the Lower House in large numbers, than by any real abuse of the Chancellor's powers.

In 1 Richard II. the Commons petitioned that no Writ issuing out of the Chancery, Letter of the Privy Seal or secret be directed to any one to cause him to come before the Council of the King, or any other, to answer for his frank tenement or things appurtenant thereto, as hath been heretofore ordained, but "that the Common Law of the land be maintained to have its due course."[1] The reply promised that none should be so made to answer finally, provided that, at the suit of a party, where the King and his Council should be credibly

---

[1] Quoted in the *History of the Court of Chancery*, Parkes, p. 39. *Rot. Parl.* III. p. 44.

informed as to maintenances, oppressions and other outrages, in places where the Common Law was not able to have its due course, the Council might send for the alleged offender to find surety to answer for his misprision and for good behaviour.

From this petition and reply it is plain that the two characteristic features of the Chancery proceedings, the summons to appear and answer without any original writ directed to the Sheriff, that is essentially the 'subpœna,' and the examination of the party complained of, a thing not allowed in civil or criminal proceedings at the Common Law, were already in regular use by the Council, having been borrowed perhaps by the Chancellors and other Canonists who sat in it from the procedure of the Courts Christian where both had long been established.

It has been suggested[1] that until a much later time the Chancellor enforced in his Court nothing but the Common Law, and that what the Commons complained of was, not the supercession of an older system by a newer, of the *jus civile* by the *jus honorarium*, but the practice of the Common Law in a new Court. What relief the Chancellor gave and what matters his Court was occupied with, can only be discovered from the bills which have been preserved and the meagre references in the Year Books, but the cases cited above and Commons' petitions themselves clearly show that it was something other than mere Common Law. Thus in 7 Richard II. the Commons prayed "that from henceforth there be directed out the Chancery no letter under the Privy Seal, for the disturbance of the possession of any subject of the King, without due process and answer of the party, *especially when* the party is ready to do what the law demands," and the King replied[2] "let those who feel themselves hurt individually show their grievance to the Chancellor, who will provide them a remedy." Again in 13 Richard II.[3], the Commons presented two petitions to the King, one asking that "neither the Chancellor nor any other person may make any ordinance

---

[1] "Early Eng. Equity:" Mr Justice Holmes, 1 *Law Quar. Rev.* p. 163.
[2] Introduction to the Close Rolls, Hardy, p. xxix. *Rot. Parl.* III. p. 162.
[3] Hardy, *loc. cit. Rot. Parl.* III. pp. 266, 267.

against the Common Law, or ancient custom of the realm, and the statutes already made or to be made in this present parliament, but that the Common Law may run impartially for all the people, and that no judgment given shall be annulled without due process of Law, and the other that "none of the King's lieges be made to come by writ of *Quibusdam certis de causis*, nor by any other such writ, to appear before the Chancellor or the King's Council to answer for any matter for which remedy might be obtained at Common Law, on penalty of a fine of £100 on the Chancellor and loss of office on the clerk who issued the writ." To each of these the King returned an evasive answer.

Four years later the Commons petitioned again[1]: "that, inasmuch as many liege subjects of the Kingdom, by untrue suggestions made as well to the Council of our Lord the King as in the Chancery of our Lord the King, are enjoined to appear before the said Council, or in the Chancery, upon a certain penalty, upon a certain day, by which the loyal subjects of the Kingdom are unjustly harassed and aggrieved, to the great damage of your said liege subjects, and to the utter destruction of their estate, without remedy in the meantime to be had for the damages and cost: That you please to ordain and establish in this present Parliament, that the Chancellor of England for the time being shall have full power to cause the parties complaining in such writs, under a certain penalty, to find sufficient pledge and surety to make satisfaction to the party Defendant in case the suggestion be not true. And that the said Chancellor shall have full power to assess and tax the costs and damages so coming to the party Defendant from the party Plaintiff, and shall cause execution for the false suggestion aforesaid," and then, lest this be taken to authorise the Chancellor to try actions touching freeholds, or triable at Common Law, a proviso was inserted in the petition that such actions be tried only before the Justices, as had been accustomed. The King replied, that he willed that the Chancellor for the time being should have power to ordain and award damages

Power to give the Defendant costs.

[1] Parkes, p. 41. *Rot. Parl.* III. p. 323.

according to his discretion, and the recorded petitions in Chancery show that this power was frequently exercised; security for costs being often given by the Plaintiff during Richard's reign, that is long before the Statute of 15 Henry VI. was passed to[1] more fully carry out the intention of the above petition. That Statute required the Plaintiff to give security for the costs before the issue of the Subpœna to summon the Defendant to answer. It had fallen into disuse before the reign of James I.

These attacks upon the Chancery did not prevent the House of Lords sending petitions to be dealt with there. Thus in 15 Richard II. two petitions to the King and the Lords of Parliament[2], one of which was a complaint by a convent of an interference with its exclusive right to bury the persons dying within a certain district, and the other a complaint that the Respondent refused to enforce a recognizance which the Complainant's debtor had entered into with him for her use, were both indorsed "Soit ceste peticion mandez en la Chancellerie, et le Chanceller par auctorite du Parlement face venir les parties devant luy en la dite Chancellerie, et illocquez la matire en ceste peticion compris diligeaument vicue et examine, et oiez les resons d'une parti et dautre, outre soit fait par auctorite de Parlement ce que droit et reson et bone fay et bone conscience demandent en le cas." In the same year an act was passed[3] which directed persons aggrieved by being called upon to answer before the Council of any lord, set up in imitation of the King's Council, to apply to the Chancellor. Probably this application was intended to refer to the Chancellor's ministerial duties only, as issuer of original writs, but whatever the intention of the statute, application was certainly made to him by bill in some cases, at least within the mischief of it[4].

In the second year of Henry IV. there is a petition couched in terms much more friendly to the Court of Chancery. It prays[5] "that, because great mischiefs happen in the Court of

[1] 4 *Inst.* p. 84, *post*, p. 66.
[2] *Rot. Parl.* III. p. 297. Introduction to the Close Rolls, Hardy, p. xxix.
[3] *Ante*, p. 35. 15 Rich. II. c. 12.
[4] *Freeman v. Pontrell*, 1 Cal. p. xlii.
[5] Campbell, Vol. I. p. 308. *Rot. Parl.* III. p. 474.

Chancery by the discussion of all pleas in matters traversed in the said Court, and by the Judges of the two benches being taken out of their Courts to assist in the discussion of such matters," traverses may be sent into the King's Bench or the Common Pleas to be discussed and determined according to law. The King answered that the Chancellor had already discretion to send them. Lord Campbell apparently looks upon this as the origin of the practice of sending issues into the King's Bench for trial, but that practice was far older than the statute and was recognised by the escheats statute[1] already referred to. In the earliest times of reference to the Chancery an inquisition was often directed to be taken by a commission appointed for the purpose and returned into the Chancery for discussion and judgment, a course similar to that adopted in the other Courts, which often had the facts found for them by the Sheriff and a jury[2].

Two years later an Act[3] was passed to suppress violent disseisins and seizures of chattels, which were stated to be of daily occurrence, and by which the injured parties were often so utterly despoiled that they had nothing left wherewith to "pursue their right." The remedy proposed is "that if the party grieved or other lawful man for him, will make affiance in his name, that the entry was made in such forcible manner, that the Chancellor of England for the time being shall have power by his discretion to grant a special assize in this case to the party grieved of whatsoever value the tenements be, without suing to the King." The penalty on the disseisor to be a year's imprisonment and double damages to the Plaintiff, and in the special assize there to be named one of the Justices of one Bench or the other, or the Chief Baron of the Exchequer if he be a man of law.

Power to grant a special assize in cases of outrage.

This statute points to the great vice of the administration of the Common Law all through the 13th, 14th, and 15th centuries, its failure to give redress where the injured party was poor, and unable to pay the

Absence of remedy for poor plaintiffs.

---

[1] 36 Edward III., and see the case cited, *ante*, p. (28), of 13 Edward II. *Abbreviatio Placitorum*, p. 336, R. 1.

[2] For instance see *Abbreviatio Placitorum*, p. 305, R. 72.

[3] 4 Henry IV. c. 8.

fees by which alone the original writs could be obtained, and for the reduction of which the Commons often petitioned with no better results than promises, which seem never to have been fulfilled, that special consideration should be given to applications by poor plaintiffs. The sufferer's inability to sue might well be produced, as the statute says, by the wrong itself, so that the very magnitude of the outrage secured its immunity from punishment, and perhaps in addition gave the injurer means to corrupt the jury of his neighbours or the local officials, sheriffs and others, in whose hands the execution of the Common Law process lay. The power given to the Chancellor by this statute to appoint a commission to try the charge on the bare complaint of the party, or the sworn complaint of his agent, recalls the directions on petitions referred from Parliament and the Council, of which examples have already been given, that an inquest be directed out of the Chancery to try the truth of the petition. It would seem however that the examination of the Defendant himself on oath, in the Chancery, or by a Commission elsewhere, had by this time generally superseded all other modes of investigating charges made before the Chancellor, for this was the procedure adopted in regard to the petitions preserved in the Tower.

The Parliament which sanctioned the exercise by the Chancellor of the special power just considered, in a later chapter of the same statute decreed[1] that, "whereas as well in pleas real as in pleas personal, after judgment given in the courts of our Lord the King, the parties be made to come upon grievous pain, sometimes before the King himself, sometimes before the King's Council and sometimes in Parliament to answer there anew, to the great impoverishing of the parties aforesaid and in subversion of the Common Law of the land," thenceforth, after judgment the parties and their heirs should be thereof in place until the judgment be reversed by 'attaint' or 'error.' This enactment formed one of the main weapons in the hands of the Common Law party in the great contest over the right of the Chancellor to

Judgments only to be reversed by attaint or error.

[1] 4 Henry IV. c. 23.

issue injunctions to stay proceedings upon judgments obtained at law, which came to a head under Coke and Ellesmere in 16 James I. Bacon and his fellows, who drew the report to the King upon which the dispute was decided, argued that the extraordinary jurisdiction of the Chancellor is not here intended to be restrained, for the Chancellor is not expressly mentioned, and moreover the statute was made upon one of two petitions from Parliament, of which the other, which never became law, expressly attacked that jurisdiction. An account of the report and of the whole discussion will be given at a later stage.

There seems little doubt that the statute was taken to bind the Chancellor, at the time and for long afterwards, for it appears to have been actually pleaded and allowed in the reign of Henry VI. in answer to a petition complaining of an unconscientious judgment[1].

The following petition of 3 Henry V.[2] shows that the frequent exercise of what may be called the Chancellor's original jurisdiction was then regarded as of recent date. It shows too that summons by subpœna for personal examination had already become the common course in his Court. The petition opens with a complaint of writs of Subpœna and Certiorari sued out of the Chancery and Exchequer for matters determinable at Common Law: "which never were granted or used before the time of the late King Richard when John Waltham heretofore Bishop of Salisbury, of his craft made, found, and commenced such innovations against the form of the Common Law of your realm," and, it continues: "whereas by reason that your justices of either Bench, when they ought to attend in their places to enter pleas and take inquests for the deliverance of your people, are occupied upon examinations upon such writs,"—to the loss of both King and people—"on which examinations there is great clamour and noise, by divers persons not aware of the law, without any record thereon entered in your said places, and upon which pleas they cannot determine but by the examination and oath

Petition against the Subpœna.

[1] *Beek v. Hesill*, 2 Cal. xii. (cir. 10. Hen. VI.) [2] Parkes, p. 48. *Rot. Parl.* iv. p. 84.

of the parties, according to the form of the civil law, and the law of the Holy Church in subversion of the Common Law,"— and Defendants are compelled to find sureties to keep the peace: therefore the Commons pray the King to ordain "that every person who shall sue such writs shall put all the cause and matter of his suit in the said writs, and that all such writs in the Courts out of which they shall issue, shall be inrolled in the said Courts and made patent and shall remain for the Defendants therein, without being returned in the said Courts,"—the Defendant in any case determinable at common law to recover £40 as a debt from the Plaintiff. The petition goes on to complain of 'writs called informations' issued out of the Exchequer, and to suggest that all writs contrary to the ordinance and the proceedings upon them shall be void. The King rejected the prayer.

It is difficult to understand why so great an aversion should exist to the examination of a defendant as this and subsequent petitions display, an aversion which seems to have made the procedure of the Star Chamber the chief ground of objection to its jurisdiction in the 17th century, and which still retains in our law, though now in reference to crimes and penalties only, the maxim 'nemo debet prodere seipsum.' Perhaps the accident of the procedure having been borrowed, either directly, or through the Council, from the Canon Law accounts for what is to modern notions so unreasonable an objection. Certainly the Church was at this time exceedingly unpopular in Parliament, which again and again advised Henry IV. to seize its property and apply it to founding new peerages, to charity, and to his own use. The Chancery was naturally identified with the Church, since, with few exceptions, of which the lawyers Parnying and Thorpe under Edward III. are the most important, the Chancellors were always Churchmen, and generally Archbishops and Cardinals, until the appointment of Sir Thomas More by Henry VIII. Perhaps the devotion of the Common Law lawyers to their own system, which rejected the testimony of the parties to any litigation, and their natural jealousy of its rising rival, at once prompted the objection and suggested its form.

Examination of the defendant.

The John Waltham referred to in the petition was Master of the Rolls in 5 Richard II. and afterwards became Keeper of the Seal. The invention of the Sub‑ pœna was not his, as the Commons supposed, nor did he first add the penalty to the writ 'Quibusdam causis,' as Lord Campbell suggests[1]. All the essential parts of the Subpœna are to be found in writs issued by the authority of Parliament and the Council during the reign of Edward III., and the use of the penal clause in statutes and orders of all descriptions was much older[2]. For instance[3], the Serjeants were, from the time of Edward II. appointed to aid the King with their advice, under a penalty. The earliest writ[4] in the Chancery Calendars directs Richard Stormesworth, the defendant, "for certain causes propounded before us (Richard II.) and our Council," to appear, in his proper person, "before us and our said Council in our Chancery on Tuesday next after the feast of St Martin the Bishop to answer to those things which shall then there be objected to thee on our part, and further to do and receive what our Court shall consider in this behalf;" and this, it continues, "under the peril (sub periculo) which may ensue, thou shalt in no wise omit, and have there this writ." Later on the penalty was generally a fixed sum, and the bills pray that a writ to answer 'under a great pain' may be directed to the defendant, but it does not appear that these penalties were ever enforced; the judges indeed denied the power of the Chancellor to fine, saying that he could imprison only, and the Exchequer refused to enforce a fine imposed in Chancery and estreated there[5].

Origin of the Subpœna.

It is unnecessary to dwell further upon the petitions of the Commons against the interference of the Chancellor, and his competition with the ordinary Courts. They continued during the reigns of Henry VI. and Edward IV., and they suggested various remedies for the evil complained of; for instance, in 1 Henry VI., that

Later petitions against the Chancery.

---

[1] Campbell, Vol. I. p. 296.
[2] Introduction to Close Rolls, Hardy, p. xxx. Note. Close Rolls. 37 Edward III., 1 *Law Quar. Review*, p. 162.
Note (2). 16 Richard II. c. 2.
[3] Pulling, *Order of the Coif*, p. 31.
[4] Cal. I. p. v. 18 Richard II.
[5] *Post*, p. 89.

no subpœna should be allowed until two judges had certified that the Plaintiff had no remedy at Common Law[1], and in 15 Henry VI. that an action should lie for bringing a man into Chancery for matters determinable at law[2], but nothing came of them, except a temporary provision in 9 Henry V. that the plea of a Common Law remedy should be a good answer to a bill[3], and the statute[4] requiring the Plaintiff in Chancery to give security for costs, which has already been referred to. The King even refused[5] to enact that if any man indorsed his bill or petition with the words "by the authority of Parliament let this bill or petition be sent to the Council of the King or to the Chancellor of England," without authority, he should be punished. Perhaps in this case, as Lord Campbell says, because he would not recognise the right of the Commons to interfere upon petitions presented, as, since the division of the Houses, all petitions in Parliament touching private redress had been presented, to the Lords[6].

---

[1] Parkes, p. 53. *Rot. Parl.* IV. p. 189.
[2] *Rot. Parl.* IV. p. 501.
[3] Parkes, p. 52. *Rot. Parl.* IV. p. 156.
[4] 15 Henry VI. (made on the petition of that year last cited).
[5] 8 Henry V. *Rot. Parl.* IV. p. 127.
[6] In *Rot. Parl.* VI. p. 144, is an order containing a direction that, if anything be done contrary to the order, the Chancellor may hear complaint of it by Bill as he accustomed to do on a writ of subpœna. The reference to this in Vin Ab. Chancery, is wrongly printed 14 Edward III., it should be Edward IV.

CHAPTER V.

THE CHANCERY FROM THE REIGN OF RICHARD II. TO THE REIGN OF ELIZABETH, AND THE BILLS IN THE CALENDARS.

SECTION 1. *Procedure and Pleading.*

FROM the 17th year of Richard II. materials for writing the history of the Court of Chancery become more abundant, for after that time the bills presented to the Chancellor, or specimens of them, were preserved, and a selection of those now remaining of dates earlier than the reign of Elizabeth has been printed in the first two volumes of the Proceedings in Chancery[1]. I shall now attempt to describe the procedure of the Court, the relief it gave, and the nature of the matters which came before it, by the aid of these materials. There are no data, so far as I am aware, for an account of the progress either of its procedure or of its jurisdiction during the period, except of the most summary kind, and it will be convenient therefore to treat the whole of the petitions[2] together, without attempting to divide them into chronological groups, merely marking incidentally such indications of development or alteration as they supply, and marking these with the caution, that, as the records under consideration represent a selection only, and not the whole of the business done, the conclusions drawn, and above all any negative conclusion, based

---

[1] These are referred to hereafter as "the Calendars" (Cal.).

[2] I use the terms bill and petition indifferently as the records of this time do, no distinction appears to be made in their use down to the reign of Elizabeth.

for instance on the first appearance of a particular form, must be taken as tentative only.

Contents of the calendars. The bills begin in the 17th year of Richard II., the year of the passing of the Statute to enable the Chancellor to give a successful Defendant costs. None have been found of the reign of Henry IV., and but few of that of his son, but after this they became numerous. The records consist of the bills and, after written answers were introduced, the answers and further pleadings, with, in some cases, the examinations of the Defendants and others, in some the decrees made, and occasionally copies of the writs issued. There are besides a few miscellaneous entries of documents connected with particular suits: thus there is a letter from the Earl of Derby to the Chancellor, enclosing a bill[1] addressed to the Chancellor by one of the Earl's tenants, and asking him to grant relief upon it "in case that the law will permit it;" and there are two similar letters missive[2] from Henry V., when in France in 1419, to his Chancellor accompanying bills which had been addressed, and actually presented to, and considered by, the King himself. The first of the King's letters directs the Chancellor that the "foresaide supplicacon wel understanden and considered by yow, ye doo calle before yow bothe parties speciffied in the same supplicacion, and thaire causes herd, that ye doo unto hem both right and equite, and in espial that ye see that the porer partye suffre no wrong, but that ye make suche an ende in this matiere y^t we be no more vexed hereafter with thaire complaints." The other letter is in similar terms, but contains a statement that the King had information, outside the bill, of the great maintenance of the defendants. Both the enclosed bills were of the ordinary kind, except that they were addressed to the King, instead of to the Chancellor, and the second is indorsed with a decree by the Council, although it was remitted to the Chancellor, for the issue of writs of subpœna, the penalty to be in the Chancellor's discretion, and the writs to be served by the Sheriff.

[1] 1 Cal. p. vii.   [2] 1 Cal. p. xvi.

Before discussing the procedure in Chancery of this period as it is displayed by the Calendars, it will be necessary to consider the relation of what were afterwards respectively known as the Common Law and the Equity sides of the Court. Reference has been repeatedly made in the preceding pages to the Common Law business of the Chancellor, but, so far, I have not attempted to distinguish it from the rest of his judicial work, for, as has already appeared, the two grew up side by side, and, for the most part, in the same manner.

The Common Law and the Equity sides of Chancery.

Coke, writing in the seventeenth century, of the Court of Chancery, as he knew it, says[1], "In the Court of Chancery are two Courts, one ordinary, 'corum domino rege in cancellaria,' wherein the Lord Chancellor or Lord Keeper of the Great Seal proceeds according to the right line of the law and statutes of the realm, 'secundum legem et consuetudinem Angliæ,' another extraordinary, according to the rule of equity, 'secundum æquum et bonum.'" "The ordinary Court holds pleas of *scire facias* for the repeal of the King's letters patent, of petitions, and *monstrans de droits*, traverses of offices, partitions in Chancery, of *scire facias* upon recognizances in this Court, writs of *audita querela* and *scire facias* in the nature of an *audita querela.*" "In these if the parties descend to issue, this Court cannot try it by jury, but the Lord Chancellor or Lord Keeper delivereth the record by his own proper hands into the King's Bench to be tried there, because for that purpose both Courts are accounted but one; and after trial had to be remanded into the Chancery, and there judgment to be given." To this list of matters belonging to the Common Law side Mr Spence[2] adds executions on statutes, and pleas of all personal actions by or against any officer of the Court, and he says, "the proceedings in all or most of these cases were by Common Law process, not by petition or bill; but the Chancellor never had authority to summon a jury....The Chancellor in the exercise of his ordinary or Common Law jurisdiction could not advert to matters of conscience." All the older authors agree in regarding the Common Law side of

[1] 4 Inst. 79.   [2] 1, p. 336.

Chancery as of greater antiquity than the other, and in representing its procedure as, from the first, analogous to that of the other Courts, and the very name *extraordinary jurisdiction* was framed to connote the variation of the equity side from the normal jurisdiction and procedure of that called ordinary. It has recently, however, been shown by Mr Pike[1] that in some cases, at least, in matters outside its 'ordinary jurisdiction' the Court of Chancery in early days adopted and allowed a procedure closely analogous to that of the Common Law Courts, and, on the other hand, the records show that the ordinary jurisdiction was often exercised through the extraordinary procedure. I shall now point out the characteristic differences of these procedures, and then attempt to estimate the extent to which either was in this period appropriated to one or the other division of the Chancellor's work.

The system of pleading at Common Law had already become scientific at the end of the reign of Edward I.[2] and during the two succeeding reigns it took the definite shape it retained down to the present century. An action commenced with a writ to the Sheriff to which the Defendant appeared. The Plaintiff then, by the mouth of his Counsel, till, under Edward III., written pleadings were introduced, put in his declaration, consisting of 'Counts' or succinct statements of the allegations on which he relied, framed in alternative forms, but so as in every case to follow the writ. The Defendant thereupon *pleaded*, stating his answer to each Count on one or more grounds, the Plaintiff *replied* to the Pleas, and then the Defendant *rejoined*, and so on. The declaration, pleas, reply, rejoinder, &c. being all generally described as *pleadings*. Either party instead of pleading to the last pleading of his adversary could *demur* to it, alleging some ground of insufficiency in law of the facts as stated to support the claim or defence, or alleging want of form, and the demurrer was tried and determined. Finally, when all disputed points of law and pleading which arose had been decided, if

Procedure at Common Law.

---

[1] "Common Law and Conscience in The Ancient Court of Chancery." 1 *Law Quar. Review*, p. 443.

[2] Introduction to Year Book. 30 and 31 Edward I. Horwood, p. xxvii.

the action had not itself been disposed of, one party concluded to the Country, that is, appealed to a jury upon the facts then left in issue, and the other party replied with a 'similiter,' and the cause stood for the hearing, after which judgment was given on the verdict of the jury.

In Chancery the procedure by bill and answer, as it appears in the records of this period, was in many respects different from this. The Plaintiff commenced with a *bill* in which he set out the facts of the case, as he alleged them, and asked for relief, and generally for a Subpœna to compel the appearance of the Defendant for examination. The Defendant put in his *answer*, in which he usually both demurred to the bill and pleaded matters in reply to it, and also denied the truth of its allegations and set out his own version of the story.

Procedure in Equity.

The Plaintiff then *replied* to the answer, in the same manner as the Defendant had replied to the bill, and the Defendant rejoined to the reply, and so on, one case in the records getting as far as a surrebutter. There are also instances of amended bills, and of a cross bill by a Defendant. In after times these further pleadings beyond the answer were dispensed with, amended bills and answers serving to bring out the points in issue, and pleas and demurrers were separated from the answers and employed and treated with the accuracy, and in the manner of the Common Law Courts. Thus Lord Bacon[1] distinguishes a plea, which he says imports matter foreign to the bill, from a demurrer, which does not. At some stage in the proceedings the Defendant was examined on oath in the Chancery, or elsewhere by a commission, on the matters alleged in the bill. Before the introduction of written answers, of which the first instance recorded is in 21 Henry VI.[2], there seems to have been no distinction between the examination and the answer. In later times it became the custom to add to the bill a series of interrogatives to which the Defendant made written answers whose truth he swore to, but during the present period the examination was always *vivâ voce*. When the pleadings were finished the parties produced witnesses who

[1] In his Orders. [2] *Arkenden v. Starkey.* 1 Cal. xxvi.

gave their evidence orally in the Chancery or to Commissioners, and tendered such documentary evidence as they had, and the judgment or decree was made.

From this sketch it will be seen that the main distinctions between the two systems at this time were the commencement by original writ,—implying a grant of jurisdiction from the King in the particular case,—and the trial of the issues of fact by the jury, in the one, and the personal summons, by subpœna, of the Defendant, and his examination on oath, in the other. There was a further distinction in some cases, in that at Common Law the judges pronounced judgment on their own authority, conferred by the writ, while in Chancery the Chancellor made his order by the advice, or with the consent of the Council, or of specified persons, or of the judges sitting with him.

Mr Pike has discovered and published a case of *Hals* v. *Hyncley*[1] heard in the Chancery in the seventh year of Henry V., which so far as is known is the earliest case which can be traced right through all its proceedings from bill to decree, and which, though concerned with matters in the 'extraordinary jurisdiction,' is inrolled among the County Placita records, which are generally taken to relate to the Common Law business only. The proceedings, except that they commence by bill and that the Defendant was brought into Court by subpœna, are throughout closely analogous to those adopted in the Common Pleas of the day, and they are closed by the Plaintiffs appealing to the jury: "et haec omnia petunt quod inquirantur per patriam," the Defendant joining issue with the 'similiter.' The issue so joined was neither tried by the Chancellor upon the examination of the Defendant and Witnesses, nor by being sent into the King's Bench, but by a special commission under the Great Seal to three judges to try the truth of the matter by a jury of the County, and to return the inquisitions into the Chancery. The Jurors found for the Plaintiffs, and, on the return, the Plaintiffs moved for judgment, which is recorded in these words, "super quo habita super premissis matura et

Common Law procedure in equity matters. Hals v. Hyncley.

[1] 1 *Law Quar. Review*, p. 445.

diligenti deliberatione cum Justiciariis et Servientibus dicti domini Regis ad Legem, ac aliis peritis de Consilio suo in Cancellaria prædicta existentibus, de eorum avisamento *consideratum est* quod predicti (the Plaintiffs) ad possessionem suam manerii et advocationis prædictorum cum pertinentiis, una cum exitibus de eodem manerio a predicto die Mercurii perceptis, restituantur."

From this Mr Pike infers that, down to the reign of Henry V., at least, no sharp line had been drawn between the Common Law and the Equity proceedings in Chancery. This inference is supported by a study of the records in the Calendars, and of the references from the Council and Parliament to the Chancellors cited above, which amply establishes the converse proposition to that suggested by this case, namely, that the procedure by bill, subpœna and examination was frequently applied to the matters enumerated above as belonging to the Common Law jurisdiction, and to others which must be classed with these. Thus there are references[1] under Edward I. of two petitions, one touching the grant of Letters Patent, and the other concealment of dower, the former directing the suppliant "veniat ad cancellariam, ut fiat ei quod graciose fieri poterit," the latter the Defendants "veniant coram Cancellario et respondeant Regi de concealamento, et ibi fiat remedium tam pro Rege quam pro Petente;" and amongst the references of the reign of Edward II. there are numerous petitions[2] dealing with the matters above mentioned, one or two of which (e.g. a petition touching the King's rights in a hospital, and another touching a ship) are expressly said to belong to the Chancellor's office, and a remedy is directed to be given upon them in Chancery, in some cases summarily, in some on the return of an inquisition issued thence to find the facts. Among the bills printed in the Calendars are several which relate to and complain of claims made on the King's behalf: for example, the second in the first volume which complains of failure to obtain redress by a *scire facias* obtained from the King by petition, and the petition of Lord

Equity procedure in Common Law matters.

[1] Campbell, Vol. I. p. 186.   [2] Campbell, Vol. I. p. 207.

De Grey[1] in the second volume, which complains of seizure of the Plaintiff's lands into the King's hands by the Lord-Lieutenant of Ireland, and prays that the Lord-Lieutenant may be ordered to return the "whole tenor of all manner of records and evidences, and the cause of the seizure abovesaid, with all offices and inquisitions which are in the said Chancery of Ireland" into the Chancery of England, and to these may be added the frequent applications, which in after time would have been for 'supplicavits' to compel the Defendants to find surety of the peace. There is nothing whatever in the form of the bills in these cases, or in the recorded proceedings upon them, to suggest that they were dealt with in any manner different from that adopted in regard to the other bills in the collection.

On the other hand there is ample evidence that certain regular work had been discharged in the Chancery without special reference there, before the custom of making applications in matters of grace had become established. A case in 13 Edward II., in which a Defendant in the Chancery pleaded "non est factum," and the matter was sent into the King's Bench because it was not the custom to try pleas of that character in the Chancery; and another in 33 Edward I., where a "monstrans de droit" sent for trial, from the Chancery apparently, was referred to the Chancellor and Treasurer because of errors in the inquisition and pleadings which prevented the judges proceeding upon it, have been already cited[2].

Common Law in Chancery.

In the Year Book 12 and 13 Edward III. is a case of *scire facias* by Mareschal against Bambrighe[3], heard in the Chancery by certain of the judges, whether with or without the Chancellor does not appear, which seems to have been tried right through in the manner afterwards adopted in like cases. The Plaintiff had been accused of treason, and his lands were forfeited, and granted, by charter of the King, to one who aliened them to the Defendant. The Plaintiff, however, being restored to favour, obtained a *scire facias* against the Defendant, and a Com-

---

[1] 2 Cal. p. vi. c. p. *Sotehill v. Harrington*, 1 Cal. p. lxxxvi.
[2] *Abbreviatio Placitorum*, p. 336.
R. 1, and p. 256, R. 46, *ante*, p. 28.
[3] p. 96, and Introduction, p. civ.

mission, appointed to find the facts and make a return into Chancery, found there had been no forfeiture. On this the argument, of which the record is a report, took place, the Defendant's counsel beginning with a demurrer to the *scire facias*, and alleging that "this is only a place of office, wherefore we do not think that without a writ (of Right, or Novel Disseisin) you can put us to answer." The real objection was that by the procedure adopted the Defendant lost his warranty against his grantor. Fleta too, in the passage[1] quoted above, expressly states that *scire facias* on recognizances were taken in the Chancery as before the judges themselves, and he makes no suggestion of there being any difference in the procedure in that Court.

Stauneford[2], writing at the end of the 16th century, seems to have been in doubt whether the strictness of the rules of pleading at Common Law applied also to cases remitted for trial from the Chancery, and he cites two opinions of the judges of Edward IV., the first that a bad traverse is conclusive against the traverser, the other that this is not so, because it proceedeth in the Chancery, which is a Court of Conscience, and to the latter he adds the note, "but as to that a man may answer and say that a Chancellor hath two powers, the one absolute, the other ordinary, and this traverse is before him by an ordinary power, in which case, all things touching the same must proceed as it should happen before any other ordinary judge of the Common Law,"—and therefore the first opinion is right,—"*tamen quære.*"

The true inference to be drawn would seem to be that the oldest part of the Chancellor's jurisdiction, that relating to *scire facias*, recognizances, and claims affecting the King's rights, and the jurisdiction conferred upon him by statute[3] in respect of traverses of office upon escheats, was generally exercised by him according to Common Law rules, and with the Common Law Procedure, and that it was the custom when matters of fact were in dispute to send the case into the King's Bench for trial, but that in some

Conclusion.

[1] Fleta, 2. 13 (a).   [3] 36 Edward III. c. 13.
[2] See 1 *Law Quar. Review*, p. 454.

cases the procedure by bill and examination was adopted as in the case of the other matters dealt with by the Chancellor on application or reference to him.

On the other hand the case of *Hals v. Hyncley* shows that the Common Law procedure was adopted, sometimes at least, in cases not "touching the Office of the Chancellor," and this is supported by the terms of the references of many of the petitions by Parliament and the Council to the Chancellor[1] bidding the suppliant, "sue in the Chancery at Common Law," "habere remedium secundum legem terræ," and many times directing a writ to be issued to the Sheriff to find the facts by inquisition and to return it into the Chancery. The case of *Hals v. Hyncley* is an exceptional one. It arose in a peculiar way, for the Plaintiff was only prevented from suing at law by the King's command on going abroad, that there should be no assize of novel disseisin until his return, and the bill is quite unlike the bills in the Calendars, being framed upon the model of a *scire facias*, and asking that the Defendant should make answer to the Plaintiffs, and not, as usual, that he be examined by the Court. There is no record of pleadings at any length until the next reign, but when we do come to recorded answers, replies and so on, they none of them so closely follow the Common Law proceedings as those of this case, and the conclusion to the Country in it is, I believe, unique.

On the whole the statement of the older writers seems in the main correct, but with the qualification that, while the two procedures existed in the old Court of Chancery from its earliest establishment as a settled Court, and were specially appropriated to what afterwards were called respectively the Common Law and the Extraordinary Jurisdictions, they were not confined each to its proper side in every case, but that the application of the Common Law procedure to the extraordinary jurisdiction was far less common, and ceased at an earlier time, than that of the extraordinary procedure to the Common Law jurisdiction.

[1] Campbell, Vol. I. p. 207.

The next point to be considered is the constitution of the Court.

We have seen that the Equitable, and the greater part, at least, of the Common Law jurisdiction of the Chancellor arose from the frequent reference to him of Petitions directed to the Council and Parliament. These were referred sometimes to him alone, and sometimes to him and the judges, or other associates,—as the Treasurer or the Master of the Rolls,—and very often he was bidden to call in members of the Council to help him. The records show that the close connection between the Chancellor and the Council continued long after the bills had begun to be addressed to him directly and alone, and it would not be incorrect to describe the connection as it appears, as being that the Chancellor is the official representative and the acting Committee of the Council. Mr Pike[1] gives the following decrees as specimens of those recorded in the "County Placita." "Habita plena deliberatione cum toto Concilio domini Regis, videtur Curiæ" &c. "De advisamento Justiciariorum et Servientium ipsius domini Regis ad Legem, ac aliorum peritorum de Concilio ejusdem domini Regis in eadem Cancellaria ad tunc existentium, consideratum fuit quod literæ prædictæ revocentur et adnullentur." "De avisamento domini Cancellarii Angliæ, Justiciariorum, Servientium ad Legem et Attornati ipsus domini Regis consideratum est" &c. and these are precisely analogous to those found indorsed upon the bills in the Calendars. The frequent summons of the judges to aid in the discussions in Chancery was, as has already appeared, the subject of repeated complaint by the Commons; they continued to be called to assist the Chancellor down to the end of the 18th century.

The indorsement on one of the bills[2] remitted by Henry V. shows that the case was dismissed by the Lords of the Council, including the Chancellor, although committed by terms of the King's letter to the Chancellor alone. A writ issued on a bill to the Chancellor, of the reign of Richard II.[3] directs the

[1] 1 *Law Quar. Review*, p. 444.
[2] 1 Cal. xvi.
[3] 1 Cal. v. and 1 Cal. xii.

Defendants for certain causes, "propounded before us and our Council" to appear before "our said Council in our Chancery," and a bill of the same reign prays that the Defendant be arrested and brought before the Council, and in *Saundre v. Gaynesford*[1] in 29 Henry VI. is a decree by "the Lord Chancellor and other judges present."

In the reign of Edward IV. however the Court seems to have regularly given judgment upon its own authority, and the form of the endorsement of the decree is to this effect: "be it remembered (memorandum) that the Petition of the Plaintiff and the answer, reply &c., and the other examinations and proofs having been read, heard, and fully understood, on full and careful deliberation, it was considered and adjudged by the Chancellor and by the authority of the Court of Chancery that," &c.[2] In some cases the Chancellor is not mentioned[3], once only is there a decree by the Chancellor alone[4]. The judges were however still, as already said, occasionally called to the Chancellor's assistance, and decrees were made by their advice, possibly, as Edward IV. directed, in his instructions to Kirkeham, Master of the Rolls[5], and in accordance with the practice of later times, when a difficult point of law arose. Thus in a case in 14 Edward IV.[6] the widow of the Gaoler of Ludgate, and the late Sheriffs of London seek the Chancellor's aid and pray for a certiorari to the Mayor and Aldermen of London to bring into the Chancery an action before them at the Guildhall, in which the Defendants named in the bill are suing for damages for the escape of their debtor from the gaol, although he had been recaptured, and the Defendants had procured his escape themselves because he could not pay. In the reply the Plaintiffs added a new prayer for an injunction to stay the action. It was however "considered, adjudged and decreed" by the Lord Chancellor, with the advice of some of the judges, that the Defendants be dismissed "sine die."—In another case[7] where

[1] 2 Cal. xxviii.
[2] See 1 Cal. xci. xcvii. c. cix. (all Edward IV.)
[3] 1 Cal. lxviii. (3 Edward IV.) 1 Cal. cvii. (22 Edward IV.) 1 Cal. c. xiv. (1 R. III.)
[4] 1 Cal. xciv. (14 Edward IV.)
[5] post, p. 60.
[6] *Stokker v. Colyns*, 1 Cal. xcv.
[7] 1 Cal. lxxxv. (Edward IV.)

Henry Sotchill sued on behalf of the King, charging the Defendants with taking possession of the King's wards, the nieces of one of them, and asking, as usual, for a subpœna to them to appear and be examined, and also for an order to them to produce the wards, an order was made, in the Exchequer Chamber, "by the advice of the judges, serjeants, attorneys, and others of the King's Council," by the Chancellor committing the Defendants to the Fleet.

These cases are quite exceptional, so far as can be judged from the very few decrees found, and in them it is noticeable that the Chancellor makes the decree, and it may be taken as clear that, by the reign of Edward IV., the Chancellor himself conducted the judicial business of his Court and formulated its decrees.

The Masters in Chancery held an old and honourable office, dating from before the Conquest. Their position during the present period was sufficiently prominent to invite the attack of the Commons, who in 5 Richard II. complained that the Masters[1] were "over fatt both in boddie and purse, and over well furred in their benefices, and put the King to veiry great cost more than needed." They sat with the Chancellor on the bench, and acted as "Pedanei Judices," and the custom of recording the Chancellor's decree as that also of the Court may have arisen from the share taken by them in determining it before the growing judicial power and dignity of the Chancellor made their assent merely formal. The course of the Masters, unlike that of the Chancellor, was a downward one: present in the Witan as chief councillors, they remained as councillors also in the House of Lords, having precedence of all the serjeants until the unlucky presumption of one of their number in Elizabeth's reign lost them that dignity, and condemned them to perpetual silence in the House. Two of them in later times, until the present century, were always named with a judge to sit for the Chancellor, when he required a deputy, but, although at first cojudices with him, they ceased in the 17th and 18th centuries to be anything more than his advisers.

[1] Campbell, Vol. I. pp. 37, 305. See also the "Treatise on the Masters." Hargrave's Law Tracts, and Spence, Vol. I. pp. 238, 332, 357.

It is stated in the "Treatise on the Masters," written at the end of the 16th century, that the Masters at one time examined the witnesses on commissions, to the great assistance of the Court, for, says the author, "in wainge and consideringe of depositions the civilians and canonists holde that the countenance and irresolutenes of the deponents is speciallie to be regarded; of which point the masters, that should bothe take the depositions and assist the lord chaunceller at the hearing of the cause, might well informe him, which the commissioners" (whom it was the custom to appoint when the treatise was written) "cannot doe." It may well be that the Masters took the examinations which are recorded as taken in the Chancery in the 14th and 15th centuries, and a record headed[1], "These ben the proyntes and articles whiche that John Mathew squier praicth you that John Oxenbrigge squier may be examyned on before you in the chauncerye," which is followed by the result of examination, shows that the Master of the Rolls sometimes, at least, did so, but the commissions to take answers and evidence in the country were certainly not given to the Masters only, but to the nearest prominent Churchman, to an Abbot or a Bishop in most cases, or to judges, or to judges and laymen combined.

The Master of the Rolls had originally been merely the chief of the Masters, but before the reign of Edward II. he had attained a superior position, and, as we have seen, he had in that reign a petition referred to him by the Council. In the Calendars are two bills addressed to him directly, the first of which[2] is of the reign of Henry VI., and this would seem to show that he had already the power of hearing causes for the Chancellor which he exercised in and after the 17th century, and this inference is confirmed by the direction of Edward IV. to Kirkeham when he was appointed Master of the Rolls[3]. "The King willed and commanded there and then that all manner matters to be examined and discussed in the Court of Chancery should be directed and determined according to equity and conscience, and to the old course and

The Master of the Rolls.

---

[1] *Mathew v. Oxenbrigge*, 1 Cal. lix.
[2] *Goddard v. Ridmynton*, 1 Cal. lix.
[3] Campbell, Vol. I. p. 397. Cl. Roll 7 Edward IV.

laudable custom of the same court, so that if in any such matters any difficulty or question of law happen to rise, that he herein take the advice and counsel of some of the King's Justices; so that right and justice may be duly ministered to every man." He is referred to four times in the Calendars, twice in the addresses of bills, once with regard to an examination he was to take, and once when money is ordered to be lodged with him in Court[1].

The bills preserved are much alike in form. They are all addressed to the Chancellor, with the exception of about a dozen, which are either not addressed, or addressed to the King[2], the Keeper of the Seal[3] or the Master of the Rolls[4], and they humbly beseech him to grant the relief asked for, and to apply right and remedy to the suppliant, for the love of God and in work of charity. Between the opening words of address and the principal verb 'beseecheth,' or the like, of the single sentence which comprised the whole of the typical bill, is introduced an informal recital of the wrong complained of, generally showing or stating that the suppliant was without remedy at the Common Law. The specific relief, if any, asked for is extremely variable, but it almost always comprises a prayer that the Chancellor will cause the Defendant, under a great pain to be named by him, to come into the Chancery, and be examined upon the matter of the complaint. Often, in the earlier bills especially, no specific relief is suggested, but in those of Edward IV. and the later ones the prayer is generally precise; writs of *certiorari* to other courts, of *corpus cum causa* to bailiffs and gaolers, of *quibusdam causis*, of *supersedeas* to Commissioners, and of *procedendo*, being mentioned by name, and orders for delivery of the goods withheld, injunctions to restrain suits, and giving of sureties of the peace being asked for. Most of the bills have obviously been drawn by counsel, but there are some so ingenuous and inartistic in their wording as to leave no doubt that they were the productions of unprac-

The bills.

---

[1] *Mitchell v. Marunyen* (13 Edward IV.), 1 Cal. lxxxvii.
[2] 1 Cal. xvi.
[3] *Kirkeman v. Sheriff of London.*
1 Cal. xci. (Edward IV.)
[4] *Goddard v. Redmynton*, 1 Cal. lix. (Henry VI.)

tised draughtsmen. The following[1] is a translation of one of the earliest bills, and both its form and matter may be taken as typical.

"To the very honourable and very reverent Father in God, the Archbishop of York and Chancellor of England, Robert Briddecote showeth and grievously complaineth of John Forster. That whereas the said Robert was going in the peace of God and of our Lord the King, the Saturday next after the feast of St Barnabas on the highway on the other side of the town of Brentford, alone on foot, on a message to carry to Mr Piers de Besiles near Oxford; there the said John with divers persons unknown, all on horseback, met the said suppliant thus alone on foot without defence, and on him the said John cried with a loud voice in English 'slay slay the thief, shoot shoot the thief.' By force of which cry all the people there being, surrounded the said suppliant in great numbers, and some of them bent their bows; and some drew their swords and daggers to kill the said suppliant. Whereupon among others, a servant of the said John Forster shot the said suppliant with an arrow through all his cloaths into his arm, and thereupon he commanded the said servant to cut off his head, and the strangers there would not suffer him; Whereupon the said John Forster took a bow string, and threw it into water, and then tied his hands so tightly that the blood gushed out of his fingers; and so led him as a thief to the town of Brentford, and there in the presence of divers persons would have killed him with his dagger, if it had not been for certain esquires of my lord the Duke of York, when the said suppliant had no other expectation than of his death. And thus they brought him in such durance to London and there put him into a house, and went in haste to the Comptor of London, and there affirmed a false plaint of account upon the said suppliant of £1000, and thereupon he had two catchpoles assigned to him to arrest the said suppliant, being thus in custody he was delivered by the said John to the said two catchpoles, and by them brought to the said Compter tied by both hands as a thief, and there by force of the said plaint is to this day detained in strong and close

[1] *Briddicote v. Forster*, 1 Cal. iv. (Richard II.)

prison in despair of his life. May it please you for love of the Almighty to examine the said John on this matter, and to investigate his cause, thus to do and moreover to apply remedy and right to the said suppliant for God and in work of Charity."

This bill, as all those of Richard II. and several of those of Henry V., is in French. The following[1] is given in the original English.

"To a rev'ent fadur in God and a full g^acious Lorde my Lorde of Bathe the Chauncellor of Ingland.

Mekely besechith your pov'e oratryce Kat'yn that was the wyf of on John Danyell of Brambele, that hough here said husbond was sole seised in his demesne asof fee in c'teyn landes and teñ in Esthamme and Wolwych and died; so that the said landes and teñ come to the possession of on Richard Belyngburgh. And your said bedwoman for pov'te of here party and maintenaunce and overledying of the cuntre, be the peuryng of the monyfold gret mysdoers of the party of the said Richard, be this xxij yere last passed, myght nev' be suyt no be trety come to have resonable partie of the said landes and teñ, no nev' shall withowetyn your g^acious Lordship and socour; for your said oratrice for this mater is to the utterest empov'ed and destroed: so that in no wis she is of power to sewe the c̄oē lawe. Wherefore lyk yt to your gⁿce to send for the said Richard to apere to for you in the chancellar' ther to be examyned of the mater aforsaid so that by your g^acious Lord or your ordynaunce be trety or other wey your said orattrice may have fynale ende in the mater aforesaid in the werke of charite." (From the indorsement it appears that Richard came and confessed, and promised to give up 12 acres to the Plaintiff, and was then dismissed, by consent.)

The more technically expressed bills, especially the later ones, are too long to quote, but the following bill of the Archbishop of Canterbury may be taken as an example of their style, and also as illustrating the less cringing form of address adopted by suppliants of high position. It belongs to the reign of Edward IV.[2]

[1] *Danyell v. Belyngburgh*, 1 Cal. xxx. (temp. Henry VI.)
[2] 2 Cal. liii. (Edward IV.)

"Sheweth on to your Lordshyp Thomas cardinall and archebishop of Canterbure primate of all England, that where he was possessyd of CC.IIJ, li. VJ, s. VIIJ d, as of his propre money, and of an obligacōn contcynyng the summe of LXIIJ, li. VJ, s. VIIJ d, and so yeroff possessyd delivered the seid money and obligacōn to on William Durrant his servant, saveli to kepe on to his use, be vertu wheroff ye same William Durrant was theroff possessed on to ye use of the seyd cardinall, there com on John Derby, late alderman of London, draper, ymagynyng untreuly to trouble the seid cardinall, affermid a pleynit of dette of XIIIJ, li ayenst the same cardinall, as administrator of the goodys and catclx of Margarete late countesse of Shrewsbury, commyng on to the handys of the seid cardenall, as ordenary, before the maire and aldyrmen of London, and theruppon causyd XIIIJ li parcell of the seid CCIIJ li. VJ s. VIIJ d to be attached in the handys of the same William Durrant, supposing the seid CCIIIJ li to be the money of the seid late Countesse ye tyme of here deth, and hath causyd an enquest to be empanellyd of such as be of his affinite to find ye same, entendyng be suche sinister menes, ye said cardenall not knowyng thereof tyl it was don, to retorne the said XIIIJ li. contarie to all ryte and conscience. Wherfor please it your said lordshyppe, the premissis considered, to graunt a certiorari to be directe to ye seid maire and aldyrmen and shyrrefes of London, commaundyng them be the same to certyfie the same attachement before the king in his chauncerie atte a certeyn daye be your lordshype to be limited, there the cause theroff to be examinyd and revelyd as ryght and concience shall require."

The bills very rarely state any authority for the grant of the relief they ask. In one or two cases only are statutes referred to in them[1], and this is the more unexpected because several of the petitions seem to have been founded upon particular statutes, or at least are warranted by them. Thus relief against judgments fraudulently obtained in the Defendant's absence is within the Statute of Westminster the Second

---

[1] *Frebarn v. Davy*, 2 Cal. xxxvi. is an instance. The bill in *Guy atte Halle v. Goodbern*, 1 Cal. xlv. has a schedule of the grounds on which relief ought to be granted attached to it.

§ 10¹, and relief against a summons to answer for lands before a lord's Council is within 15 Richard II.² In the answers citations of statutes are more frequent, especially of the statute of Richard II. enabling the Chancellor to give damages, and in one case the statute 4 Henry IV., forbidding the questioning of judgments in Chancery, is cited and, apparently, with good effect³. In one case the bill asks for a remedy in accordance with the usage of the Court, and this suggests that some regard at least was paid to precedent; a point to which I shall return later on.

Several of the bills have reference to proceedings already commenced before the Court; thus a person who had been imprisoned by the Earl of Warwick as his neif, and had procured his liberty on giving bail in the Chancery to defend his freedom at law, applied to be released from the bail, "having regard that the father of the said suppliant, who is the principal, hath pleaded to issue of the country, that he is free⁴;" another instance is *Stavenre v. Bonyngton*⁵, where matters pending on a subpœna in Chancery had been referred for one David Marrys to report upon, or, at least, been adjourned until he should show the truth of them, and the said David, it was alleged, would gladly "knawelygge the treweth of the same matiers, bot he wald have a maundement from yowe for the cause that he shuld noght be haldyn parcaill in the same matier."

A good many of the bills pray for the dissolution of injunctions granted to stay actions in other courts, and one, a case of Henry VIII., alleges⁶ that the suppliant is too poor to sue in Chancery, and therefore prays a *procedendo*,—a plea that must have sounded odd indeed in a Court which specially promised to defend the weak, and in which, as a common form, the pleadings alleged the poverty of the party.

Cases of an amended bill⁷ and cross bills occur.

The bill is generally indorsed with the names of the pledges to prosecute, whom the Chancery borrowed, as it borrowed so

---

¹ *Armeburgh v. Bernard*, 2 Cal. xiv.
² *Freeman v. Poutrell*, 1 Cal. xlii.
³ *Beek v. Hesill*, 2 Cal. xii.
⁴ *Tregoys v. Warwick*, 1 Cal. ii.

⁵ 1 Cal. xix.
⁶ *Royall v. Garter*, 1 Cal. cxxx.
⁷ *Felbrigge v. Damme*, 2 Cal. xxiii. Hen. VI.

much of its procedure, from the Common Law Courts, and, in many cases, both before and after the statute 15 Henry VI., c. 4, there is an indorsement that *A* and *B* came into the Chancery on such a day and undertook for the within written Plaintiff to make satisfaction to the within written Defendant in case the Plaintiff shall not prove the Plaint.

The next step was the issue of the Writ asked for, generally, but, as already said, by no means always, a subpœna. The majority of the bills have no indorsement or note of further proceedings recorded with them, and it is impossible to gather from them whether the grant of the writs was a matter of form, or rather of price, as the petitions of the Commons suggest, or not. When Sir Thomas More was Chancellor it is said he refused to allow any step until he had considered the bill himself, and that this was at that time an alteration in the practice[1].

The writ.

If the Defendant did not appear on the subpœna he might be arrested[2], and in one or two cases his arrest is demanded in the first instance[3]; for example, one Trewonwall in the reign of Henry VI[4]. accuses the Defendant of sacking his house with Welshmen, Irishmen and Dutchmen, "unto the mooste utt'est destruccion of youre seid besecher," so that he "is not of power to sewe ayenste (the Defendant) at the cōō lawe," wherefore he prays the Chancellor to command a serjeant at arms to bring the Defendant into the Chancery, there to give security to keep the peace, and to be examined. In several cases, however, a second bill is brought, complaining of the failure of the first[5], and, if we can judge from what we know of the 16th century, such failure must have often occurred.

On the Defendant's appearance a day was given to the parties to be heard, and for the Defendant to answer. In early times he seems to have been examined straight away, *vivâ voce*. There is an account of the trial of one Thorpe[6] for heresy by the Chancellor, in 1407, from which

The Answer.

---

[1] Camp. Vol. I. p. 540.
[2] *George of Clay v. Aldeburg,* 2 Cal. lxii.
[3] *Sessay v. Beverneck,* 1 Cal. xii.
[4] 1 Cal. xlvii.
[5] *Queen Katherine v. Glover,* 1 Cal. xxiii.
[6] Camp. Vol. I. p. 314.

it appears that he took him "faste into a closett" and entered into an angry colloquy with him, and this, perhaps, represents the custom of the Chancellors of the time. By 21 Henry VI. however, written answers, corresponding to the written pleas which had been allowed at law since Edward III., were introduced, and these were apparently sworn to as in after times. The answers comprise demurrers, generally to the jurisdiction, pleas, and traverses, in the earlier cases, and in the amateur pleadings throughout, all mixed up together, along with the Defendant's own statement of the facts, and they usually conclude by asking for dismissal and costs. Under Henry VI. the answers, and in fact all the pleadings, become in several cases long and elaborate[1], the technical phrases of protestation against the sufficiency of the bill, and the introduction of the traverse of the Plaintiff's allegations, after the Defendant's own statement of his own, by the words 'without that the Defendant did' &c., pointing clearly enough to the model on which they were framed, the formal pleadings at law.

After the answer came the reply, which was very much like the answer. It generally realleged the matter of the bill, and concluded with a prayer, which was not infrequently different to that in the bill. *The Reply.* And then came further pleadings, often two or three more on each side, and of such character that one cannot imagine why, since their denials and counterdenials went on so long, they ever stopped at all. In some cases there is an offer to verify in such manner as the Court shall direct, but in none, so far as I am aware, a conclusion to the country, as at law; the case of *Hals v. Hyncley*[2] being, as already said, without a parallel in the Calendars.

When the pleadings stopped, the parties had a day given them to produce evidences and witnesses, and perhaps a further, and ultimately, if need be, a peremptory day[3].

If the parties, or one of them, or their witnesses, lived far away, a commission to take their answers, &c. and evidence was given to selected persons, judges and great churchmen being the usual commissioners, *Commission to take the evidence.*

---

[1] See *Scales v. Felbrigge*, 2 Cal. xxvi.

[2] Ante, p. 52.

[3] *Mayhewe v. Gardener*, 1 Cal. xcix.

by a writ of *dedimus potestatem*, which issued, sometimes before and sometimes after the pleadings subsequent to the bill were recorded. The writ directed the Commissioners to examine on the matters contained in the bill, or bill and pleadings and other documents, the parties and others who knew most about the matter, and the return generally states that the parties, and others whom it was thought proper to call, having been examined,—the laymen sworn on a book or on the Holy Gospels, and the Clergy sworn on their faith,—deposed the matters contained in the schedule to the return. This schedule contains merely a record that A said this, and B said that, sometimes adding that indifferent men made such a deposition, but it contains no report on the truth of the matter and nothing to guide the Chancellor through the conflicting statements to a proper conclusion. It possesses, in fact, the essential vices of the affidavit evidence of which it was the direct ancestor. The defect may have been corrected by the examiner sitting with the Chancellor, as suggested in the "Treatise on the Masters," but it seems unlikely he did so when he was, as he often was, a local dignitary placed at a distance from London[1].

Sometimes of course the Defendant confessed the truth, or the Plaintiff the falsity of the bill, and it would be surprising that so many cases were dismissed or adjudicated on by the consent of parties, if the mighty and unchecked power of the Chancellor were not taken into account: a power which attracted to his Court suppliants too weak to sue in the ordinary way may well have awed the petty tyrant of a village into an unwonted veracity.

A summary account of the proceedings in the great case of *Ardern v. Ardern*[2], will serve to illustrate what has been said, and to close this account of the early Chancery procedure.

In that case the bill alleges that the Plaintiff enfeoffed the Defendant of a Manor for life, on the understanding that he should take no profit during the Plaintiff's life, and the deed was committed to A and B to deliver to the Defendant after the Plaintiff's death. In breach of this trust, however, they

[1] See *Willebye v. Veyle*, 2 Cal. xvi. [2] 1 Cal. lxxii. 6 Edward IV.

delivered it at once, and the Defendant ejected the Plaintiff, and he had no remedy at the Common Law. By his answer the Defendant demurred, for that the Plaintiff should have sued (for the deed) in detinue, traversed the allegations of the bill, alleging that the Plaintiff gave one *H* a power of attorney to deliver seisin to him, and prayed dismissal of the suit with costs. The Plaintiff replied, and then a Commission to take depositions at Coventry was issued to Zerdeley, Abbot of Kenilworth. The Abbot reported that, on the day fixed, the Plaintiff brought some witnesses who were examined verbally by the Abbot, and that he said he had no more for lack of notice; that the proceedings were thereupon adjourned to the next Saturday when the Plaintiff brought no more witnesses, but brought letters and *testimonials*, and, as these did not refer to any one present, the Abbot advised the Plaintiff to have them in the Court of Chancery; that the Defendant then brought his witnesses, who were asked by the Abbot to depose in writing under their seals what they knew, and they made 'bills'; that one Agnes Lucy (one of the alleged trustees of the deed), being 30 miles from Coventry, and too ill to travel, sent her bill under her seal, and swore before the messenger, as he swore to the Abbot, that the statements in it were true; and that the Defendant also brought letters, and the Abbot gave him the same advice with regard to them as he had given the Plaintiff. This is the whole report. Finally, the matter was settled in the Plaintiff's favour.

It appears that there was no cross examination, and that exceedingly loose practice in regard to evidence was allowed.

The forms taken by the decrees have already been indicated. Of the small number recorded a large proportion are dismissals,—the Defendants to go 'without a day,'—and, in some of them, the Plaintiff is ordered to pay the costs of the Defendant, or an assessed sum in lieu thereof, and sometimes, in addition, to be committed to prison[1]. In the cases turning on trusts, however, the Plaintiff appears to have generally succeeded, the Defendant being ordered to 'make a sufficient estate,' but in these cases the real dispute was nearly

The decrees.

[1] *Reed v. Prior of Launceston*, 1 Cal. cxiv. (Rich. III.)

always over the terms of the will for the purposes of which the trust existed. Allusion has been made to the frequency of compromises, and with these may be compared a few cases in which the parties agreed to refer the matter to the decision of the Chancellor, or some other person[1]. The detailed enquiry, the direction for accounts, and the complex and apportioned decree, so characteristic of the Court in the 18th and present centuries, was as yet entirely unknown.

Section II.

The Relief sought.

Turning from the procedure of the Court to the subject-matters of the bills we find that these range over a very extensive field: the description of the scope of the jurisdiction by Coke, as comprising trusts, fraud and accident only, is quite inadequate, and the view that outrage and maintenance were the only wrongs which brought parties into the Chancery is equally incorrect.

I propose to divide the cases in the following manner:

(A) where the Common Law remedy could not be obtained;

(B) where Common Law process was being used oppressively or fraudulently;

(C) where forgery or duress formed the ground of complaint;

(D) where no remedy was contemplated by the Common Law; and

(E) cases specially within the jurisdiction of the Chancellor.

The last head may be disposed of at once, it comprises a very few bills only, and those of early date, referring to cases of the King's claim or his wardships, or cases concerning ships, witchcraft, heresy, and the assumption of jurisdiction by the Council of a lord[2].

[1] *Beek v. Hesill*, 2 Cal. xii. [2] 1 Cal. pp. xii. xxiv. xxv.

(A) The poverty, illness or imprisonment of the Plaintiff, his fear of the Defendant, who in such cases is generally roundly charged with maintenance, 'overlaying the country,' barratry and outrage, and the mightiness of the Defendant and of his party compared with the weakness of the Plaintiff and his, are, in the earlier cases at any rate, the most frequent of the reasons alleged for the lack of remedy at the Common Law[1], and with these may be classed those cases where the Defendant is a local official, as a Sheriff, or a King's officer, whom it would be hopeless to sue in the local court, or before a jury of his own selection[2]. A system of popular justice is likely to work exceedingly ill where one of the parties has lost the good wishes of his neighbours, and a perusal of these bills forcibly illustrates this danger, and shows how urgent was the need in mediæval England for a great judge, who, being also a great executive officer and constantly in possession of the King's ear, could bring to book offenders who safely braved the terrors of the Common Law.

Where the Common Law remedy could not be obtained.

The matters complained of in the above cases are generally disseisins, thefts and outrages, and the bills frequently ask, besides the examination of the Defendant, that he may find sufficient surety of the peace[3].

Much allowance must be made for the gross exaggeration of petitioners, who felt it necessary to found the jurisdiction of the Court by showing that the ordinary remedies were useless to them, but still the picture of anarchy and insecurity of life and property which the bills paint is a most melancholy one. The poor widow and the helpless old man are attacked and beaten, their houses broken into, and their chattels swept away by bands of marauders, whose leaders were known to the whole countryside, and who made no attempt to conceal their identity since

---

[1] 1 Cal. pp. iv. v. vii. xx. xxx. et passim.

[2] *Quyncy v. Landasdale*, 1 Cal. xxxi. et passim.

[3] 2 Cal. pp. xxix. xxxii. The Writ of Supplicavit, which only became obsolete in the last century, was sued regularly out of the Chancery, and is mentioned in the Natura Brevium. It was granted upon the exhibition of sworn 'Articles of the Peace' of which these bills are the ancestors.

[4] Spence, I. p. 690.

retribution, save at the hands of the distant Chancellor, was little likely to overtake them.

(B) The second head includes applications which are closely analogous to those just mentioned, and which still further illustrate the liability to abuse of the local court, and the 'jury of the vicinage.' The proceedings here complained of are in most cases, not those of the King's Courts, but those of the minor courts of the Sheriffs, or the franchise courts of the towns, but this is not always so. It must be borne in mind, that almost all the Common Law actions had to be tried, that is, their venue had to be laid in the county where the wrong was alleged to have taken place, so that the parties' neighbours might find the facts. There was indeed a remedy provided by the law to avoid the danger of a prejudiced jury, and new trials with other juries, or challenges to the panel, were allowed if the sheriff or bailiff who had summoned the jurors were related to the Plaintiff, or were the 'capital enemy' of the Defendant[1], but these protections were quite inadequate, especially when the action was brought in a subordinate Court.

Where Common Law process was being used oppressively or fraudulently.

The following bill is a good instance of the present class[2]. The Earl of Kent alleges that he had for a year or two resorted to the tavern of Walter ap Rice in London, allowing him to keep the reckoning, and giving him from time to time orders on his receivers and farmers, who paid what was due; that now the said Walter is suing the Plaintiff before one of the Sheriffs for £84, as for his reckoning, a most preposterous sum, and will not confess his receipts, seeing that the servants of the Plaintiff are not ready to prove them, and is like to succeed "by favour of certayne juryours of the same citie with whome he is of speciall acquaintaunce," and so the Plaintiff prays a subpœna to examine the Defendant, and a *certiorari* to remove the suit.

A large number of the later bills are for writs of *certiorari* or *corpus cum causa* to bring up 'feigned actions' before Sheriffs

---

[1] *Abbreviatio Placitorum*, pp. 114. R. 30 (2), 323. R. 84, 340. R. 22.

[2] *Grey v. Rice*, 1 Cal. cxxv. (temp. Henry VII.)

and others[1], many of these arising out of trade disputes. Such is the case of Damico, a silk weaver[2], who had set up in London under the patronage of the King, Edward IV. The Defendants, the Plaintiff says, to stop his trade, have brought actions against him for sums so large that he cannot find bail, and he is therefore like to remain in prison all his life.

Other bills charge that the Defendant has coerced the jury, or has brought his suit in a foreign court, before a jury of his affinity, or has got judgment in the Plaintiff's absence, and pray for *certiorari* or injunction, and, generally, for the examination of the Defendant also. Several instances of the last charge occur, and they show that the provision of the Statute of Westminster II. c. 10, requiring the Justices in Eyre to fix days after which no writs should be received, was not observed. The recital in the Statute exactly tallies with the bill in *Armeburgh v. Bernard*[3]. There the Plaintiff attended at Warwick Assizes, and asked the Sheriff's deputy, the Clerk of the Rolls, and others if there were any writ against him, and was told there was none. Then he went away, and the Defendant produced a writ and got judgment, and by his bill the Plaintiff prayed that execution on the judgment might be stayed till after the examination of the Defendant in the Chancellor's presence.

Under this head come also a few heterogeneous complaints of abuse of the Common Law and other process, including sometimes that of the Chancery itself. Thus in *Wele v. Courtenay*[4], the bill alleges that one of the defendants had sued out of the Chancery a commission of oyer and terminer to certain commissioners, including two judges, to adjudicate upon a claim of his Co-defendant, but without his authority, against the Plaintiff and one Taillour, and that Taillour intended to confess judgment, and so let the Plaintiff in for heavy damages.

(C) The first two divisions have dealt with cases where the Common Law at least contemplated a remedy, the fourth deals with cases where none was contemplated by it: that now

---

[1] 1 Cal. lxxxviii. xci. ci. civ. cv. xxxiii. (temp. Henry VI.)
[2] *Damico v. Burdican*, 1 Cal. ciii. [3] 2 Cal. xiv.
cf. *Quyncy v. Landasdale*, 1 Cal. [4] 2 Cal. viii. (Henry V.)

to be considered stands between the former and the latter. Forgery, fraud and duress could always be pleaded in defence at law, but preventive measures could not be taken there, nor had the action on the 'Common Courts' yet been developed, as it was during the 18th century, so as to enable a Plaintiff to recover money which the Defendant had improperly deprived him of, or which he had been compelled to pay under circumstances which made it just and right that the Defendant should repay it. In consequence of this want there were numerous complaints to the Chancellor alleging that the Defendant by a forged power of attorney had obtained payment of the Plaintiff's debt, or payment from the Plaintiff of money due to another, or that the Defendant had sued or was suing the Plaintiff upon a forged charter[1].

Complaints resting on forgery or duress.

Analogous to these are cases where the Defendant, being the Plaintiff's debtor, has obtained a release from him or his joint creditor, by fraud, and where the Defendant has obtained, by the like means, an obligation, upon which he is suing the Plaintiff, or title-deeds under which he claims an estate[2]. A bill of the last kind is remarkable both for the ingenuousness of its wording and the peculiarity of its prayer, which it will be seen asks for "cancellation and delivery up," a prayer often present in modern Chancery bills. The bill relates that the Defendant came to the Plaintiff's house and got him to execute a bond and conveyance by making him drunk. "And y as a man withoute counsayll, for drede dude as he badde me," and "so my wyff and I had ful evel rest that nyght," the poor suppliant adds, and he begs the Chancellor, considering "that I am of grete age, that my discresion many tymes and for the most pt ys passed awey fro me," and that "I was owte of myselff and also with owte my wyff, frende or eny con"...(sic) to order the Defendant to deliver up the charter and to annul the acknowledgment[3]. The bill concludes with the appoint-

---

[1] *Bief v. Dyer*, 1 Cal. xi. *Walker v. William*, 2 Cal. xxx.
[2] *Hulkere v. Alcote*, 2 Cal. xv. *Cobblethorn v. Williams*, 1 Cal. li. *Box v. Bank*, 2 Cal. lxx.
[3] *Stonehouse v. Stanshawe*, 1 Cal. xxx. (Henry VI.)

ment of an Attorney to sue "as well tofore the Kynge and his counseil as in (Chancery)."

A few cases of frauds of a different kind occur; thus, one Slefeld bought an Exchequer tally for £100 from one who had bought it of the Defendant, and the bill alleges that, during the absence of Slefield abroad, the Defendant obtained an 'innovate' from the Exchequer, saying he had lost the tally. Slefield had given the Defendant notice of his title, but had no record of the sale, and he was, he said, without remedy at Common Law. The answer traversed the allegations of fact in the bill, and submitted moreover that it was matter for the Common Law, and the bill was dismissed[1].

The Chancellor had in some cases a statutory jurisdiction to relieve against obligations obtained by duress, under 31 Henry VI. c. 9. The Statute throws some light upon the procedure of the Court at the time, but, as already said, the Calendars do not afford any instances of commissions being issued to try causes, the commissions being always directed to examine the parties and their witnesses, and to return the result into Chancery[2]. The Statute recites that "divers persons of great power, moved with insatiable covetousness against all right, humanity, integrity and good conscience," had seized ladies and compelled them to enter into obligations, and it enacts "that in all such cases aforesaid the party bound may have a writ out of the Chancery, containing the matter of their unreasonable intreaty, directed to the Sheriff of the County where any such offences were done, or after shall be done, commanding him that he by force of this writ make proclamation in the full country, and in the next County Court, after the receipt of the said writ that the person or persons contained in the said writ shall appear at a certain day and place prefixed in the said writ, before the Chancellor of England for the time being, or otherwise before the Justices of Assize in the county where the said offences

---

[1] *Slefeld v. Grafton*, 1 Cal. xcvii. (temp. Edward IV.)

[2] Directions to try the facts by a commission, which should make a return into the Chancery, were very common in the original references of Petitions by Parliament to the Chancellor. See the account of the year 19 Edward II. in the Parl. Rolls.

were done; or else before some other notable person to be assigned by the Chancellor," and the Chancellor, justice or commissioner, "by virtue of this ordinance shall duly examine the said parties upon the premises," and if they find the obligations were made as aforesaid, "then the said obligations and all process and execution sued or to be pursued thereon shall be void." There does not appear to be any peculiarity in the bills, or, where there are any, the other proceedings in the cases charging duress, nor is reference ever made to this statute, and the Plaintiffs are in many cases not women but men. The Statute can therefore only be regarded as a partial recognition, but coming as it did, with the assent of a hostile House of Commons, a striking one, of a larger jurisdiction independently exercised by the Court.

The subpœna was sometimes passed through the Sheriff's hands[1], as the Statute suggests, but the ordinary course was for it to be sent straight to the Defendant.

One of the earliest cases of this class, which occurred about the middle of Henry VI.'s reign, is a curious one[2]. The Plaintiff alleges that the Mayor of London (acting, no doubt, judicially) compelled him, by duress, to lodge an obligation with the Defendant, the City Clerk. The Defendant, when sworn and examined, admitted that there was such an obligation, but said he could not deal with it without the consent of the Alderman. Unfortunately one cannot tell whether this irregular manner of appeal was allowed to succeed or not.

The relief prayed in these cases is sometimes that the Defendant be made to appear in the Chancery and bring the obligation; sometimes, where he has commenced to sue upon it, a *certiorari* to bring the action before the Chancellor.

(D) It remains to consider those cases where the relief prayed for could not in any event be obtained at Common Law. Under this head come applications based on the superior machinery of the Chancery with its examination of the Defendant upon oath, including the recovery of chattels which the Plaintiff could not specifically describe, (in almost every case

Where no remedy was contemplated by the Common Law.

[1] *Bief v. Dier*, 1 Cal. xi.   [2] *Pickering v. Tonge*, 1 Cal. xliv.

muniments of title not "contained in a bagge, boxe or cheste or other thynge enseled¹'") so that he could not sue in detinue, and cases where the Defendant, being sued in *debt*, had waged his law, or where, the debtor being dead, his executors could not be sued, because, had their testator lived, he might have availed himself of this defence².

The earliest case of discovery among these bills is of the reign of Henry VI., but applications had long before been made to the Chancellor for this purpose³. The bill in the case referred to is by a customary heir against his ancestor's executor and it asks that the executor may be examined, so that the Plaintiff may know for what goods "he maye conceve hys accon att the lawe"..."consideryng that wythoute soch examinacon hadde your saide besecher ys withoute remedye⁴." Soon after there occurs a case to which several parallels might be found in the collection⁵. The Plaintiff alleges that he is cousin and heir of Watier Shiryngton, who, with other feoffees, was seised of lands to his own use, and who died without a will, and that the late Lord Say induced the cofeoffees to sell him the lands, and by duress compelled the Plaintiff to release his claim "and aft'ward the same Lord Say, knowyng hymself to be putte to deth by that horrible and crewell tretour Jakke Cade opunly knowlechid among other extorcions this mater," charging his confessor to urge Lady Say, the Defendant, to redress the wrong. And he prays the examination of the confessor. Another case where discovery and relief are asked for is *Cullyer v. Knyvett*, in which the Plaintiffs allege that they are copyholders on the Defendant's manor and have replevied a distress against him, and that, the replevy having been removed into the Common Pleas, they are likely to lose their lands as the only evidence of their title is the Court Roll which is in the Defendant's possession⁶.

Closely allied to bills for discovery are bills for the preser-

---

¹ *Reed v. Prior of Launceston*, 1 Cal. cxiv. (Richard III.)
² *Giglis v. Welby*, 1 Cal. cxx. (7 Henry VII.)
³ See 3 *Rot. Parl.* 79, No. 24. 3 Richard II.
⁴ *Polgrenn v. Feara*, 1 Cal. xxxix.
⁵ *Brown v. Say*, 1 Cal. xlvii.
⁶ 1 Cal. cxxxvii. (temp. Edward VI.)

vation of testimony of which examples are to be found from the reign of Henry VI. onwards. The earliest case[1] being to take and record the examination of the brother-in-law of the Plaintiff, who had confessed, in the presence of certain notaries, that a feoffment made by the Plaintiff's wife, since dead, had been procured by the Defendant's duress, and had subsequently retracted the confession. The relief asked for was granted by the issue of a Commission to examine the brother-in-law and the notaries also.

By far the most important cases under the present head are the cases of uses or trusts. The work of the Chancery in connection with these became, from the end of the reign of Henry VI., so prominent a part of its jurisdiction that, by the middle of the following century, the idea had already gained ground that the Chancellor's equitable jurisdiction had been originally constructed for the purpose of protecting them.

Trusts.

The common explanation of the origin of uses is, that they were introduced by the Clergy, who were well acquainted with the dual ownerships of the Roman Law,—quiritarian and 'in bonis,' and dominium and usufruct, and fidei commissa, —in order to avoid the restrictions on gifts into Mortmain[2]. Mr Justice Holmes has lately[3] traced their origin to a different source, and he finds in the Teutonic 'Salman' the ancestor of the mediæval feoffee to uses: each was a person to whom property was transferred in order that he might make a conveyance according to his grantor's directions, and the essence of the relation, in each case, was the *fiducia* of the grantee. The executor was originally a salman whose duty it was to distribute the estate, and, though his interest became confined to the personalty, under the early Plantagenets, when devises of land were no longer generally allowed, yet under Edward I., where, by custom, lands were subject to the will, the executor was still put into possession of them before or immediately after the death. Edward III. himself made a feoffment to his executors of lands of his pur-

[1] *Lewis John v. Earl of Oxford*, 1 Cal. xxvii. (6 Henry VI.)
[2] Blackstone, Vol. II. p. 271. History *of Real Property*, Digby, 271. Vin. Ab. *Uses*.
[3] 1 *Law Quarterly Review*, 163.

chase, and afterwards gave the executors verbal directions how to dispose of them, which however the Judges advised they were not bound to obey[1].

Again, "if the remedies of the ancient popular Courts had been preserved in England it may be conjectured that a *cestui que use* in possession would have been protected by the Common Law. It was not, because at an early date the Common Law was cut down to that portion of the ancient customs which was enforced in the Courts of the King. The recognitions (assizes) which were characteristic of the royal tribunals, were only granted to persons who stood in a feudal relation to the King, and to create such a relation by the tenure of the land something more was needed than de facto possession or pernancy of profits." The meaning of the word scisin became limited to such possession as was protected by the assizes, but ultimately "a series of statutes more and more likened the pernancy of profits to a legal estate in respect of liability and power, until at last the statute of Henry VIII. brought back uses to the Courts of Common Law[2]."

The more important of the statutes referred to are 50 Edward III. c. 6, giving creditors execution against lands and chattels in spite of gifts made in fraud of them; 7 Richard II. c. 12 forbidding aliens, and 15 Richard II. c. 5 forbidding spiritual persons or corporations (who, says the statute, are as perpetual as the others) to hold lands by way of use; 1 Richard II. c. 1, making all grants by, and executions against a seller or grantor of lands binding upon his heirs and upon feoffees to his or their use; and 3 Henry VII. c. 4, avoiding deeds of gift on trust, made to defraud creditors[3].

The position of the cestui que use in remainder was different; he was a stranger both to the possession and to the covenant, and his remedy originally was found in the jurisdiction of the Courts Christian in case of *fidei læsio*, over which there was so long a struggle between the lay and ecclesiastical courts, and subsequently the ecclesiastics who sat in the Chancery carried out there, as secular judges, the principles which their

[1] *Rot. Parl.* III. 61 (26).
[2] Holmes, *loc. cit.* p. 167.
[3] See 1 *Law Quar. Rev.* p. 167 n. (3), p. 168 n. (3).

predecessors had striven to enforce in their own tribunals under the authority of the Church.

Whatever be thought of this striking theory, it is clear that by the reign of Edward III. feoffments to uses were already well known, and attempts were made to enforce them in the Common Law Courts, on the one hand by the aid of conditions in favour of the intended beneficiaries[1], and on the other by the series of statutes in restraint of fraudulent feoffments referred to above.

In the third year of Richard II. there is a petition to Parliament by the heirs of William de Cantelow[2] complaining that they have been impleaded in the Chancery, by Thomas, son of Robert de Roos, of certain lands of which their ancestor, before he went over the sea, made a feoffment to feoffees on conditions in the Indentures appearing; that the feoffees have been examined before the Chancellor and the Lords and others of the Council then present in the Chancery, and that the Seneschal of de Cantelow, who was in his confidence, has been examined also; that afterwards, at the suit of the said Robert, who sued on his son's behalf, and suggested that the examination and the writing of it did not show the truth, a commission was issued to one R. R., clerk, and others to examine one of the feoffees afresh; that the examinations were taken, and by them it was found that the feoffment was made under conditions and other circumstances which tended for the saving of the Plaintiff's rights, and the examinations are of record in the Chancery; but that Robert nevertheless is seeking to try the case before a Jury, intending to aver that the feoffment was made without any condition, against good faith, conscience and truth. The Petitioners therefore pray that the indentures and examinations and matters may be shown in Parliament by the Serjeants, who have cognizance of them, and that the rights of the Petitioners may be saved.

Thereupon Parliament issued an 'injunction' to the Chief Justices and others to examine the parties and to return the

---

[1] In the Year Book 19 Henry VI. Mich. 72, there is a discussion as to whether, if A enfeoff B that he may enfeoff C, and C refuse the feoffment, A can enter upon B.

[2] 3 *Rot. Parl.* 79, (24).

result into Parliament. The record, which gives the topics of examination as well as what the deponents said, states that the examination was taken before certain judges, serjeants and others, and that, *inter alia*, one deponent said that de Cantelow, after coming back from abroad, required the feoffees to reinfeoff him, and, if they did not, to infeoff Thomas son of Robert de Roos, and the heirs of his body, and if Thomas died without heirs of his body that the lands should remain to his own right heirs, and that, if they did not infeoff Thomas, it should be lawful for the said Thomas to enter. Robert de Roos said he had had a part (counterpart) of the indenture containing these uses (described as conditions), but that he had given it up to the feoffor at his request. There is no record of any further proceedings after the report of the examination.

I have quoted this petition and the proceedings at length because they show, in a most interesting manner, how the feoffment to uses, or as they are here called conditions (the first known mention[1] of a 'use' being in 7 Richard II. cap. 12), was used to reintroduce the will of freeholds, in a manner recalling the conveyance to the 'familiae emptor' in old Rome. It is noticeable that the declaration of the will is made after the feoffment as in the previous case of the will of Edward III., which the judges had declared to be of no effect. In the subsequent cases in Chancery, or rather, in the earlier of them, a promise 'of great trust,' at the time of the feoffment, to perform the will is usually alleged. The petition incidentally shows that at its date the Chancery was already in full operation, and was resorted to for discovery in aid of proceedings at law.

Uses, being driven in all cases[2] into the Chancery for enforcement, and there protected by the characteristic remedy of a 'subpœna' and decree binding the person, came to be regarded as mere choses in action, and were so described by the lawyers, but the protection afforded to cestuis que trust was soon extended beyond that accorded to ordinary rights *in personam*[3]. In the reign of Henry VI. we find a bill against

---

[1] Digby, p. (274). Soon after the term became very common, see for example *Rot. Parl.* III. p. 297 (15 Rich. II.).

[2] 1 *Law Quarterly Review*, p. 170.

[3] See Digby, p. 282 et seq.

the heirs (in gavelkind) of one of several feoffees who held to the uses of the marriage settlement of the Plaintiff's wife, and by their answer the Defendants allege that they have conveyed to her son by an earlier marriage than that with the Plaintiff, who was the proper cestui que use, and they do not suggest that they are not bound by the trust[1]. The judges in the next reign denied that the heirs were bound[2], but it is clear the Chancellor had already held the contrary. On the other hand, a use was not property in the full sense, for from the terms of the bills which complain of conveyance by the feoffees to a stranger it appears that, as in the case of a modern trust, only purchasers with notice were bound, and that they were bound the judges held in 5 Edward IV.[3] Moreover the lord claiming on an escheat, the creditor on an elegit, and the consort in curtesy or dower, were not bound by the use as yet.

The following cases from the Year Books show that, under Edward IV., both the existence of the use, and that it was protected only in Chancery, were recognised by the judges, although in 7 Henry VI. a judge said[4] "that if one enfeoffed another with a proviso that the feoffor should take the profits, the feoffee would nevertheless have them as the proviso was entirely void." In 37 Henry VI. Lord Chancellor Waynflete consulted the judges[5], and they resolved that, if the intent of the feoffor were expressed *in writing*, the feoffee must fulfil it, and if the feoffor devised to one for life, with remainder to another, the remainderman, in Chancery, even during the life of the life tenant, might compel a conveyance. In 4 Edward IV.[6] to a writ of trespass, the Defendant pleaded that the Plaintiff held to his use, and that he occupied by sufferance and at the will of the Plaintiff. The Plaintiff's counsel replied that the Defendant must plead a lease. Moile, J., said the plea

---

[1] *Goold v. Petit*, 2 Cal. xxxix. (35 Henry VI.)

[2] Digby, p. 282, Year Book, 8 Edward IV. (6) and 22 (6). See Rowe's *Bacon on Uses*, n. 39.

[3] Year Book, 7 (*b*). Spence 1. p. 445.

[4] Campbell, Vol. 1, p. 376. Year Book, 7 Henry VI., Trin. (21)

[5] Camp. *loc. cit.* citing Bro. Ab. Garde 5, but query.

[6] Year Book 4 Ed. IV. (8) translated in Digby, p. 294.

was good ground to allege in Chancery, "for the Defendant there shall aver the intent and purpose upon such a feoffment, in the Chancery a man shall have remedy according to conscience upon the intent of such a feoffment, but here, by course of the Common Law, in the Common Pleas or King's Bench, it is otherwise, for the feoffee shall have the land; and the feoffor shall not justify contrary to his own feoffment, that the feoffment was made in confidence, or the contrary." The Defendant's counsel suggested that the law of the Chancery was the Common Law of the land, but the judge replied that on the point in question it was not so.

In 7 Edward IV. there occurred a case[1] in the Exchequer Chamber before the Chancellor and all the judges, adjourned thither by the Chancellor, no doubt, as we have seen cases often were adjourned, for the consideration of the judges.—There had been a feoffment to the use of a woman who afterwards married, and she and her husband sold, and the feoffee to uses conveyed at her request. After her husband's death the woman sued a subpœna against the feoffee, who pleaded the circumstances, and the wife thereupon demurred. The Chancellor, treating the case as a 'cui in vita,' said the Plaintiff could not consent to the conveyance, and, in response to the request of her counsel that the feoffee be attached until he made satisfaction, he said, "You can have a subpœna against the Vendee who is in possession, and recover the land against him." If, added Yelverton, J. "he knew of the deceit and wrong done to the woman, then a subpœna lies against him, otherwise not." "He knew," said the Chancellor, "that she was married." The Plaintiff's counsel decided to take the attachment against the feoffee and to consider whether they would attack the Vendee or not. It is noticeable here that the Common Law judge founded the liability of the vendee on his concurrence in a wrong, but the Chancellor put it on his notice of the weakness of his own title. Neither suggested, as it would be ruled in the case of a modern trust, that, once notice of the trust brought home to the vendee, he would be bound to prove an effective conveyance to him of the equitable estate, and that his know-

[1] Year Book (8), translated in Digby, p. 297.

ledge of the coverture of the beneficiary, or of the deceit practised upon her would be immaterial.

Returning to the Bills in the Calendars, we find that the first which turns upon a trust[1] was presented in one of the first four years of Henry V. It alleges a feoffment of land and chattels, in trust during the Plaintiff's absence, and that the Defendants, the feoffees, had put the land to farm without the Plaintiff's assent and refused to redeliver the chattels. After this the cases of trust become very numerous. In the earlier ones the feoffment is on trust to 'make an estate' to the feoffor or his nominee upon the happening of some event, as the demand of the feoffor, or his death, and where there is a change of title the new cestuis que use request the feoffees not to convey to them immediately, but to continue the uses, the feoffee being, in fact, extremely like the Salman to whom Mr Justice Holmes compares him, but later on, it is evident, a continuance of the dual ownership was often contemplated, when, under Edward VI., uses became the rule, and possession with seisin the exception. From the first, several feoffees are employed, and appointments of new trustees by a feoffment by the surviving trustees to a third person, and a refeoffment by him to the continuing and the new trustees occur[2].

In the case last cited the uses were declared by a will under seal, and the feoffees, by deed also, undertook to make an estate to the Plaintiff according to the will, but writing in either case is very rarely alleged in the bills, and, in spite of the opinions of the judges upon the will of Edward III. and the opinion of Waynflete in 37 Henry VI., already quoted, nuncupative wills were regularly enforced[3], in fact the whole contest in the majority of the trust cases of which a record remains was as to what last declaration of his wishes the feoffor actually made. Nothing could show more forcibly the dangers informal wills invite than a perusal of such cases as *Felbrigge v. Damme*[4], in this collection, where the Plaintiff alleged one will,

---

[1] *Dodde v. Browning*, 1 Cal. xiii.
[2] *Rothenhale v. Wychingham* (8 or 9 Henry V.) 2 Cal. iii.
[3] 2 Cal. xxi. *Myrfyn v. Fallan* (24 Henry VI.)
[4] 2 Cal. xxiii. cf. *Withe v. Mullesworth*, 2 Cal. xxxvii.

the Defendant another, and by amended bill the Plaintiff charged the Defendant with having altered the testator's will three days after the testator last spoke, and with producing yet another will after the proof of the first, and the case of unwritten wills was even worse.

The common prayer asks, besides the ancillary examination, that the Defendant be ordered to make an estate, and there is a case in 29 Henry VI. in which the Chancellor, with the advice of the judges present, after the examination of the Defendant, ordered him to convey on the spot and make and seal a power of attorney to one to deliver seisin to the Plaintiff[1]: a method of summary execution which must have made the Chancery remedy 'against the person' no whit less beneficial than the legal judgment binding the estate.

Occasionally in the cases of disputed wills the feoffees interpleaded[2], but generally they had identified themselves with one side or other by making, or refusing to make, a conveyance. In one of the former cases[3], a party who had been "ruled by the Court to enterplede with the seide Johan," (the Plaintiff) sets out his title in detail.

After the bills to enforce trusts, and in most cases, as I have shown, really to recover devises, the most common of those dealing with trusts are, applications against feoffees who have fraudulently released debtors to the estate whom the cestuique-use has sued in their names[4].

The means employed to carry out a will of lands were used also where chattels were to be disposed of, the feoffee being a trustee for the executors, put into possession, as the executors themselves had been in Glanvil's time, during the life. Thus under Henry VI. we find a bill[5] alleging a deed of gift of chattels in trust to perform the donor's will. The donor made

[1] *Saundre v. Gaynesford*, 2 Cal. xxviii.
[2] *Flykke v. Banyard*, 1 Cal. cxv. (Rich. III.)
[3] *Saundre v. Saundre*, 2 Cal. lvi. (Ed. IV.)
[4] *Gross v. Depeham*, 1 Cal. xlviii. (32—3 Hen. VI.). There is a petition

to Parliament of 15 Rich. II. (*Rot. Parl.* III. p. 297) in which the suppliant says that one who is trustee for her refuses to enforce a covenant against the debtor. Bro. Ab. Conscience, (7) (9).
[5] *Wilflete v. Cassyn*, 2 Cal. xxxiii.

one of the Plaintiffs the 'surveyoure' of his estate and the others his executors, and the donees, other than the Defendant, were willing to assign the chattels to the Plaintiffs, but the Defendant refused, wherefore the Plaintiffs dared not take up the administration of the will, and it was likely never to be performed. It is difficult to see the utility of employing a trustee when executors were appointed, for executors, since the time of Edward I., had had universal succession to the personalty, unless indeed a fraud were intended, such as that alleged in the bill in *Mayhewe v. Gardener*[1], where a parson complained that his predecessor had made a gift of all his goods to the Defendant, and died intestate, so that the Plaintiff could sue no one for his dilapidations. Here the Plaintiff actually recovered his damages. The statutes of Edward III. and Richard II. cited above[2], were directed against frauds such as these.

Besides wills, feoffments in trust were employed to carry out arrangements made upon sales, and to secure the payment of purchase money, and the performance of conditions which were intended to be precedent to the vesting of the estate in the ultimate takers, buyers or others[3]. The feoffment alleged in *Clay v. Aldeburgh*[4] is an example of this. There an advowson was conveyed to the Defendants to secure the next presentation to one of them.

The deeds of feoffment to uses, and releases relating to them, were frequently recorded in the Chancery for safe keeping, and references to such records occasionally occur[5].

Another important class of applications to the Chancellor was for the enforcement of verbal contracts. At law the action of covenant had during the reign of Edward I. become restricted to cases where there was a writing, which at that time meant a deed under seal, and the action of debt had come to lie only for money due on a promise, although it had originally lain for chattels also[6], and it was open to the

Contracts.

[1] 1 Cal. xcix. (Ed. IV.). Bro. Ab. Conscience (20), relief given in such cases in Chancery.
[2] Ante, p. 79.
[3] *Ardern v. Ardern*, 1 Cal. lxxii.,
Edlington v. Everard, 2 Cal. xxxi.
[4] 2 Cal. lxii. (Ed. IV.)
[5] *Rope v. Rollyng*, 2 Cal. xix.
[6] See History of Contract: Salmon, *Law Quar. Rev.* 3, p. 167.

serious danger that the Defendant might 'wage his law,' and, moreover, as a consequence of this possibility, it did not avail against the executors of the debtor[1]. Consequently the creditor on a verbal contract often had, as the bills allege, no remedy at law at all, and therefore made application to the Chancellor. Later on, after the action of assumpsit, a form of the action on the case, allowed already under Edward III. and Richard II. for breaches of contract by malfeasance, was extended under Henry VII. to breaches by nonfeasance also, a competent remedy being provided in the Common Law Courts, this part of the jurisdiction of the Chancellor fell into abeyance.

The earliest bill of this class[2] complains that the Defendant agreed to assure a reversion to the Plaintiff, and, to make him suppose he would keep the agreement, gave him all the deeds. The Plaintiff, relying on the affiance of the Defendant, went to London to see his Counsel on the matter, and spent 40/- in so doing, and then the Defendant refused to perform his promise, and the Plaintiff having "no special or other writing of the covenant" was without remedy at Common Law. Wherefore he prayed the Chancellor to grant a subpœna to the Defendant "to answer him of the deceit aforesaid, and according to his answer to give your judgment according to that which loyalty, good faith and conscience, demand..."

In this case a pledge of faith (affiance) is alleged, and it seems that the jurisdiction of the Chancellors in contracts was at first based upon the presence of this pledge[3]. There had been three methods of making a binding promise in the two centuries after the Conquest, by writing, oath, and pledge of faith, the contract in the last case being enforced in the Ecclesiastical Courts[4]. These Courts were however repeatedly forbidden to interfere in questions arising on contracts between laymen, even though faith were pledged, under Henry II. and subsequent

---

[1] *Vavasour v. Chadworth*, 1 Cal. xcii. (Ed. IV.)
[2] *Wheler v. Huchynden*, 2 Cal. ii. (Rich. II.)
[3] Holmes, J., Early English Equity,
Law Quar. Rev. I. p. 173. Fry, L. J., Specific performance and Læsio Fidei, 5 (*ibid*), p. 235. Year Book, 9 Ed. IV. (11).
[4] Spence, I. p. 118.

kings, and the judges restrained their interferences by prohibition, and ultimately, as in the case of trusts, the Chancellors took under their protection in the Chancery what they could no longer protect in their Spiritual Courts. The *fides* however soon dropped out of sight, and the promise of the Defendant, supported in most cases by a part performance, is the allegation on which the bills rely.

In the *Diversité des Courtes*[1] it is said that "a man shall have remedy in Chancery for covenants made without specialty, if the party have sufficient witness to prove the covenants." The contrary appears however to have been decided soon after the date of the treatise, but then, under Henry VIII., a competent remedy already existed at law.

Although the action of assumpsit took away ordinary claims on contracts from Chancery, one form of relief based upon agreements, already granted there in the present period, was never, after the reign of Edward III., obtainable at law, and so became an important branch of the equitable jurisdiction,—the enforcement of specific performance.

There are several bills in the collection claiming specific performance in cases where executors and trustees had agreed to sell with the assent of their cestuis-que-use, and others where the cestuis-que-use had themselves made the agreement. They all allege payment or part payment by the Plaintiff, and, no doubt, the analogy of the position of one who has paid his money under agreement for conveyance to him to that of a cestui-que-use, which was afterwards the foundation of the conveyance by "bargain and sale," was already recognised.

Specific performance.

There are several bills dealing with pledges and mortgages, but the relief sought is not the special relief afterwards given in such cases[3], but redress where the defendant has had an absolute instead of a conditional deed made, or, after the day for repayment is passed, is suing at law,

Mortgages.

---

[1] *Law Quar. Rev.* p. 172.
[2] *Scales v. Felbrigge*, 2 Cal. xxvi. (Hen. VI.). *Furby v. Mostyn*, 2 Cal.
xi. *Senyng v. Grangeman*, 2 Cal. xlviii.
[3] *Broddesworth v. Coke*, 1 Cal. lxvii.

or has refused to accept tender of the money upon the day fixed and claims nevertheless under the forfeiture[1]. Nor is there, as yet, any trace of the relief against penalties in Chancery, although a case occurs where the Chancellor stayed by injunction an action on a bond of which the condition was not pleadable at law[2].

The administration of the estates of deceased persons was at this time peculiarly within the cognizance of the Spiritual Courts, but the jurisdiction of the Chancellor in cases of trust naturally led applications to be made to him in the allied cases of claims against executors, who, as we have seen, were often also feoffees to uses[3], but no special jurisdiction in regard to them had as yet arisen. *Executors.*

Amongst miscellaneous applications to Chancery in default of a remedy at Common Law are several to compel arbitrators, to whom parties have committed disputed claims, to give awards, and to enforce the awards of such arbitrators when given[4].

In the exercise of his jurisdiction the Chancellor had for the most part the full concurrence of the judges, who in many cases, assisted him at the hearing, and often referred parties to his Court, but when the Chancellor claimed to arrest the fruits of an unconscionable judgment, the seeds of a contest between "the two sides of Westminster Hall" were sown. The judges having held, as already stated, that Equity could only bind the person[5], injunctions similar to those previously issued by the King and Parliament were resorted to by the Chancellor, where he found it necessary to interfere, to forbid a party suing at law or enforcing a judgment there obtained. *Injunction.*

The judges from the first refused to bow to these injunctions. In 22 Edward IV. they urged the Plaintiff at law to take judgment in contempt of the Chancellor's order, telling him that if the Chancellor should fine him the fine could not be

---

[1] *Shakespeare v. Lambert*, 1 Cal. cxlv. (Eliz.).
[2] *Astel v. Causton*, 1 Cal. cviii.
[3] *Fitzharry v. Lyngen*, 1 Cal. xlviii. *Wilflete v. Cassyn*, 2 Cal. xxxiii.
[4] *Hoton v. Hardewyn*, 2 Cal. xv. (Hen. VI.). *Blower v. Luke* (Ed. IV.).
[5] Campbell, Vol. I. p. 377. Year Book, 36 Henry VI. 13, 4 *Inst.* 84.

levied at law, and if he should imprison him, they would release him by writ of *habeas corpus*. The year before the judges had given the Plaintiff at law, whose action had been temporarily stayed by an injunction, the costs occasioned by the delay[1].

A number of applications for injunctions from the time of Henry VI. onwards occur in the calendars. The earliest case is that of *Beek* v. *Hesill*[2], in which the Plaintiff alleges that, the Defendant having laid claim to her land and sued a *cessavit* against her, the then Chancellor, by consent, took the matter into his 'governance and ordinance,' and ordered the Defendant to 'leve his sute of the seid cessavit.' He had, however, continued it, and recovered judgment in the Plaintiff's absence, leaving her no remedy, "saf by a writ of right, the which writ is the utmost suyt in lawe." On this the Defendant pleaded his judgment, and the Statute 4 Henry IV. against reopening judgments, and was dismissed *sine die*.

Instances of injunctions being granted are; where the Defendant had been seized by the Plaintiffs as the villain regardant of the Bishop of Ely, who had fled and lost all the evidences of his (the Bishop's) title, and the Defendant had commenced an action at Common Law[3]; where the Plaintiffs were suing in the Sheriff's Court, on the case, against a pretended surgeon for failure to cure, and injuries, and the Chancellor's servant came into Court and delivered an injunction[4]; and the much discussed case of the bond paid but not released, and then sued on again. In the last case it was held by the Chancellor and judges under Edward IV. that the obligee should not sue again[5], but that in the case of a statute staple, because it was of record, the debtor should have no protection.

The latter proposition is stated (in the case of judgments satisfied without acquittance), in the "*Diversité des Courtes*[6]," and the former in the "*Doctor and Student*[7]."

The statement of the 'Student' called forth a pamphlet[8] by

[1] Bro. Ab. Conscience (16), (22).
[2] 2 Cal. xii. (early in Henry VI.)
[3] *Edyall* v. *Hunston*, 1 Cal. cxiii. (Rich. III.)
[4] *Royall* v. *Gartner*, 1 Cal. cxxx. (Henry VIII.)
[5] Year Book, 22 Ed. IV. (6). See Bro. Ab. Conscience.
[6] (circ. 21 Henry VIII.)
[7] (1518).
[8] Hargrave's *Tracts*, p. 325.

a 'Serjeant,' who stoutly objects that no injunction ought to go in such case, for the Common Law should not be overthrown by the folly of an individual. "I mervaile moche," says the writer, "what authorite the chancellor hath to make soche a writ (of injunction) in the Kinge's name, and howe he dare presume to make soche a writ to let the Kinge's subjects to sue his lawes." The Chancellors, he says, "have done this thing through ignorance of the goodness of the Common Law," and, he adds, "in my conceite in this case I may liken my lord chaunceller, which is not learned in the lawes of the realme, to him, that stands in the Vale of Whitehorse farre from the horse and (be)holdeth the horse; and the horse seemeth and appeereth to him a goodly horse and well proportioned in every poincte, and that if he come neere to the place wher the horse is, he can perceave no horse nor proportion of any horse," and so when the Chancellor knows the Common Law he will see the matter is not fit to be reformed in the Chancery, certainly not on the plea of conscience, for "the lawe of the realme is a sufficient rule to order you and your conscience what ye shall do in everie thinge and what you shall not do."

The worthy Serjeant's metaphor would have been a dangerous one a century later, when people were found to suggest that a lawyer might look so closely at the propositions of his books as to lose sight of the outlines of reason, and might rule his conscience so straitly by the law of the realm that it should bear no resemblance at all to the consciences of his neighbours.

The Serjeant's pamphlet was answered by a "Little treatise on the Subpœna," evidently written by a Chancery lawyer, which is a valuable statement of the equitable jurisdiction of the Chancery early in the reign of Henry VIII. and I shall therefore shortly summarise its contents [1].

The Chancellor, says the writer, gives relief, where, because certainty of pleading is impossible, none is obtainable at Common Law, as in the common case of claims to recover title-deeds (evidences); where an incorporeal hereditament

---

[1] Hargrave's *Tracts*, p. 331. (It is, so far as I am aware, the earliest account extant of the jurisdiction of Chancery, other than the bare references of the two books just referred to.)

(lying at law 'in grant') is granted for a *quid pro quo* but without writing; where a rent is reserved, but there is no reversion; where an obligation is paid and no acquittance given; and in the cases of uses. These last, he states, were so many it would take a special treatise to declare them.

<small>The jurisdiction of Equity at the beginning of the reign of Henry VIII.</small>

The writer then gives a list of cases where, though there is a right in conscience, there is no remedy at Common Law, and none by subpœna either. Several of them may be generally described as cases of estoppel. Where on a replevin by a tenant by knight's service the lord 'avows' on a tenure in socage, he cannot afterwards sue the heir for his marriage or wardship; where the owner, having no notice, is barred by a fine and nonclaim, "for there is no subpœna directlie against a Statute, nor directlie against the maxims of the lawe"; where there is procured a collateral warranty against the right of another and the estate descends upon him, and he is barred; where the grand jury in attaint affirm a false verdict of the petty jury, for if a subpœna were allowed the law would have no end, and it would be against 4 Henry IV. c. 23; where in debt the Defendant 'wages his law,' or executors, whose testator might have waged his law, are sued; where a woman induces her husband to sell her lands and to convert the money to her greater profit than the land, and of her own free will promises further assurance, but after her husband's death sues a '*cui in vita*'; and where two are joint tenants and one takes the whole profits. And no Subpœna lies, he says: For waste by the tenant for life of a term; for offences done by a man's servant without his assent, although the Master is in conscience bound to repair them[1]; or where a lessee for life covenants to leave the ground in good condition, and sudden tempest or strange enemies destroy the woods without his fault. And the Chancellor must rule his conscience by the law, so that if a man *seised* of lands make a will of them, he must hold it void, and if a son buy land and die, leaving a father and an uncle so that the uncle inherits, and dies, and the lands pass to the purchaser's younger brother, "and if the matter come in variance

[1] The modern opinion is that the Common Law has outrun the demands of conscience on this head.

in the Chancery, for evidence or otherwise," the Chancellor is bound to give his judgment according to the law, i.e. for the younger brother, not the father. The author throws some light on procedure also, for, in cautioning the Chancellor as to what he is bound in conscience to observe, he reminds him that a subpœna should not be issued without sureties, or after judgment, and that he should only allow further pleading after the proofs are brought in, in a very special case. "Also he may suffer the parties to change their demurrer, and that is a greate favour, for they shall not be admitted thereto in none other Courte of the Kinge; also in the Chaunceric a double plea, ne a departure from his plea, ne two pleas wher the one goeth to the whole shall not condemn him that pleadeth it; but the verie trothe in conscience is to be searched, and that trothe cannot be searched by conjectures, as me seemeth."

Comparing the sketch given of the Chancery in this pamphlet with the review previously made of the records in the Calendars, and the few cases in the Year Books, it appears that the contents of the equitable jurisdiction were, at the beginning of the reign of Henry VIII., by no means extensive. The earlier cases of outrage and violence had passed from the Chancery and gone over to the Star Chamber, the business in regard to uses had attained a very great extension, and the correction of the injustice wrought through the inferior Courts, which had so much occupied the Chancellors in the 15th century, was now, through the fading importance of those Courts, and the supervision exercised over them by the King's Bench, no longer the subject of application to the Chancellor, but it had a parallel in the correction which the Chancellor had long before claimed to make of the injustice wrought by the rigid rules of the King's Courts themselves. It is during the next period that Equity, as a later system modifying an earlier, which in part no longer agreed with current morality, becomes really important, and the establishment of the right to grant injunctions against suits at law, and against the enforcement of judgments there obtained, early in the 17th century, was the foundation of the great structure erected by the later Chancellors.

Summary.

CHAPTER VI.

FROM WOLSEY TO THE COMMONWEALTH. THE CHANCELLORS.

DOWN to the appointment of More in 1529 the Chancellors
The Ecclesiastical Chancellors. had been, with few and unimportant exceptions, unacquainted with the Common Law. They were for the most part Churchmen, bishops or archbishops, well versed indeed in the Civil Law and its descendant the Canon Law, as all great ecclesiastics of the later Middle Ages were, and furnished by these with a repertory of principles and maxims which they used as a guide in the cases of conscience which came before them, but they were chosen for office, not because of their skill as civilians or canonists, but entirely on political grounds. Like the Chief Justiciars whom they succeeded, the Chancellors were the greatest political officers of the realm, and their judicial work, though by the end of the 15th century of great importance and prominence, was merely subsidiary and quite subordinate to their political labours and occupations. Several common lawyers of high reputation had indeed held the Great Seal under Edward III., and the creation of beneficial rules has been attributed to them by common law writers, whose confidence in their own order has supplied the lack of authentic information, but their rule, in fact, left no impression upon the jurisdiction of Chancery, nor, in the absence of reports, could it have done so.

The work of the Ecclesiastical Chancellors was an exceedingly beneficial one, for it may well be doubted whether judges trained in the practice of the Common Law would ever have possessed the courage to interfere with its rules, in the face of the professional opinion of their brethren, or indeed have been sufficiently detached in mind to discover that the rules stood in need of correction. It were better, the judges held, in the case of actions on bonds paid without acquittance taken, that an individual should pay twice than that the law be changed, and it is certain that none but a great officer, wielding all the power of the King, could ever have enforced his decrees as the Chancellor did. The judges had comparatively little dignity or power. They eked out a miserable stipend by the suitors' fees, and were subject to removal at any time if they offended the King or the reigning favourite, but my Lord Chancellor, while his term of office lasted, was the greatest man, next the King, in the country, and in a time of lawlessness and anarchy often his orders alone could command respect.

Wolsey, the last of the race of political and ecclesiastical Chancellors, is also the typical example of the class. He was Prime Minister and keeper of the Royal conscience, and, secure in the former office, he ventured in the latter to lengths beyond any of his predecessors, but he fell upon a time of changing conditions. The rise of the middle classes, following upon the fall of the great Barons, had greatly strengthened the position of the lawyer class, and, on the other hand, the pacification of the country, and the consolidation of the central power had made the extraordinary interferences of the Chancery less needed. The contrast between the arbitrary decision of an untrained judge in Chancery, tempered no doubt by "the old course and laudable custom of the same Court[1]," and the decisions of the judges of Common Law, moulded and controlled by the precedents in the Year Books, now first digested in Fitzherbert's Abridgement and the early text-books, become more and more striking, and, at least to the lawyers, more and more distasteful. In fact, when the ordinary law became settled, scientifically studied, and in a way popularised, it became necessary that equity also should be administered in a regular fashion on settled principles, and during the present period many steps were taken in this direction, of which the most important was the introduction of the practice of having great lawyers as Chancellors, which commenced with the

Wolsey.

[1] Edward IV.'s direction to Kirkeman, M. R., quoted above, p. 60.

appointment of More, and was regularly adhered to after the time of Lord Coventry. Wolsey is charged with having extended the jurisdiction of his Court in a very arbitrary manner, and in his time the applications to it increased so much that he erected no less than four Commission Courts to sit for him, one of which, that of the Master of the Rolls, has continued ever since as an assistant Chancery Court[1]. In a controversy with a Common Law judge he very distinctly claimed the power, as representing the King, " to execute justice with clemency where conscience is opposed to the rigour of the law," "and to command the high ministers of the Common Law to spare execution and judgement where conscience hath most effect," for " laus est facere quod decet non quod licet[2]." After his fall the articles of his impeachment[3] charged him with misusing, altering and subverting the laws, with issuing injunctions to parties to actions to stay their actions, and, after judgment, to stay execution, and often without any bill having been presented, and even with sending for the judges and expressly, with threats, commanding them to defer judgment; and with calling, by writ of *Certiorari*, actions against his own officers, into Chancery. "And by such means," it was alleged, "he hath brought the more party of suitors of this your realm before himself, whereby he, and divers of his servants, have gotten much riches, and your subjects suffered great wrongs."

Wolsey was succeeded by Sir Thomas More, a lawyer of great reputation, and, moreover, a man of culture and liberality of mind. Though he had taken a prominent part in the impeachment of his predecessor, he also found it necessary to grant injunctions to stay actions at law condemned by equity as against conscience, but, according to the well-known tale, he did not do this until he had called upon the judges to grant the relief in their own Courts, and they, anxious as the Chancellor thought to cast all responsibility upon the jury, had refused to do so[4]. More sat but two years

Sir T. More.

---

[1] (That is until 1881, when the M. R. was made a judge of the Court of Appeal. The M. R., as stated above, had exercised judicial functions, oc-casionally, at an earlier period.)
[2] Camp. I. p. 499.
[3] Coke, 4th Inst. p. 89.
[4] Camp. I. p. 542.

and a half, and in that time succeeded in removing the arrear of causes which had already commenced to be an abuse in the Chancery, and of which, after his death, with a few brief intervals, there was a continuous complaint until modern times. The hopes excited by More's advancement, that the seals would be henceforth held by a good lawyer, were not fully realised for another century, but that special knowledge was now considered necessary to satisfactory performance of the duties of the Chancellor is shown by the pains which Wriothesley, the last Chancellor of Henry VIII., Hatton, who held office under Elizabeth, and Williams, who succeeded Lord Bacon under James I., took to qualify themselves for an office for which they had had no previous training, while the success which, according to their contemporaries, they attained, shows, on the other hand, the meagreness of the code they had to administer, and the freedom of discretion allowed them. The men who followed More were of no special mark until, during the conservative reaction under Mary, Bishop Gardiner was given the Seals. Elizabeth's first Lord Keeper, Sir N. Bacon, was an accomplished lawyer, and during a careful administration of twenty years of office, he must have done much to consolidate and settle the practice and doctrines of his Court. During his time an Act was passed to give the Lord Keeper the same jurisdiction as the Chancellor had, so that the Queen's reluctance to confer the greater dignity and reputation of the Chancellor's office might not curtail the powers of the Court. "The business of the Court of Chancery," says Lord Campbell[1], "had now so much increased that to dispose of it satisfactorily required a judge regularly trained to the profession of the law, and willing to devote to it all his energy and industry. The Statute of Wills, the Statute of Uses, the new modes of conveyancing introduced for avoiding transmutation of possession, the questions which arose respecting the property of the dissolved monasteries, and the great increase of commerce and wealth in the nation brought such a number of important suits into the Court of Chancery that the holder of the Great Seal could no longer

Increase of business in the Chancery.

[1] Vol. 2, p. 87.

satisfy the public by occasionally stealing a few hours from his political occupations to dispose of bills and petitions." Lord Keeper Bacon in fact sat, during term time, at his own house in the afternoon, as well as at Westminster Hall in the morning, and sat also frequently in Vacations, as his predecessor More had done, and the custom became permanent that the Chancery should be always open for the relief of suitors.

Notwithstanding these changes one of Bacon's successors in the same reign, Sir Christopher Hatton, owed his preferment not to his legal acquirements, for he was only nominally a Student of Law, but to the Queen's personal favour, won, it is said, by his skill as a dancer, and yet with the assistance of a learned civilian, Dr Swale, and the Masters of the Court, whom by one of his orders he required to be in constant attendance upon him, he satisfied his contemporaries, and quieted the revolt of his Bar, who had at first refused to practise before him. A speech of his in calling a Serjeant, in 1587, shows that, if no lawyer, he yet professed a great respect for the Common Law. Referring to bills to quiet possession, which the Chancellors had introduced, and which had formed one of the subjects of complaint against Wolsey, he said, "I find that many are called hither and much money spent, and in the end their causes are sent to law, where they might have been begun at the first, if the parties had been well advised and counselled. We sit here to help the rigour and extremities of the law. The holy conscience of the Queen for matters of equity is, by Her Majesty's goodness, in some sort committed to me ; but the law is the inheritance of all men[1]".

Elizabeth did not repeat the experiment of choosing an outsider again after Hatton's death, and Puckering, Egerton (created Lord Ellesmere by James I.) and Francis Bacon formed a succession of holders of the Seals as well qualified for their position as any who have presided in the Court.

Lord Ellesmere is practically the first Chancellor whose decisions have come down to us, and few of his remain. He has the reputation of having been the first to establish equity upon the basis that

Ellesmere.
Chancellor
1596.

[1] Spence, I. p. 693.

its jurisdiction was to be found in and guided by the cases already decided and the principles to be extracted from them[1], and he certainly did much to settle the practice of his Court, for almost all the decisions referred to in the sketch of Chancery procedure prefixed to the "Choice Cases in Chancery," published in 1672, but evidently written much earlier, are his decisions. The larger claim must however be allowed with much reservation. To precedents he no doubt frequently referred[2], and he directed the Masters to search for them in particular cases. But, it is clear, he added many new doctrines to equity and gave relief in many new cases, as his successors did after him. He certainly did not regard himself as entitled only to administer rights ascertained by positive law, which, when once discovered, could neither be diminished nor enlarged by his discretion, and he allowed appeals to be made, not only to his judgment, but also to his feelings. "The pitiful cries of the father and mother dying as aforesaid" (they had died of the plague) "and of the poor orphans called to God for relief, and moved the heart of the Chancellor to take compassion upon them, and to take such order as he hath done," is the reported reason[3] for his decision in one case, and this instance of vicarious charity stands by no means alone in the records of the time. Sir N. Bacon, for instance, let off an unsuccessful Plaintiff without costs, because he was "a very poor boy in very simple clothes and bare legged, and under the age of 12 years[4]." And another case[5] Lord Ellesmere himself decided on its special circumstances, with the proviso that his decision was not to be a precedent. The judges, his contemporaries, had made no scruple of appealing to the compassion of one of his immediate predecessors in recommending him to grant a decree for quiet possession to a woman who had recovered her dower at Common Law[6]. In the great case of the Earl of Oxford, decided shortly

---

[1] (It must be added that he shares this reputation with several of his successors.)

[2] As his predecessors sometimes did, see an order of Sir N. Bacon, *Acta Cancellariæ*. Munro, p. 423, et passim.

[3] Proceedings in Parliament &c. C. P. Cooper, p. 5.

[4] Munro, p. 433.

[5] *ibid.* p. 687.

[6] *ibid.* p. 506, Bromley L. K. 1581.

before his death, Lord Ellesmere plainly claimed power to determine new cases on new principles, even against the law, and to legislate on individual rights[1]. "The Chancellor is by his place under his Majesty to supply that power (i. e. of Parliament) until it may be had in all matters of *meum* and *tuum* between party and party," and "the cause why there is a Chancery," he said, "is for that men's actions are so divers and infinite that it is impossible to make any general law, which may aptly meet every particular act, and not fail in some circumstances."

The question how far precedent was regarded as binding on the Court and as limiting its jurisdiction under the early Chancellors and during the present period has excited much discussion. The more popular view is that of Blackstone and Lord Campbell, which Selden and Coke, Lord Ellesmere's contemporaries, held, and which made Whitelock, when offered the Great Seal under the Commonwealth, object to the responsibility, for, he said, "the judges of the Common Law have certain fixed rules to guide them; a Keeper of the Seal has nothing but his own conscience to direct him, and that is oftentimes deceitful. The proceedings in Chancery are 'secundum arbitrium boni viri,' and this *arbitrium* differs as much in several men as their countenances differ[2]." Spence[3], on the other hand, has ably argued for the opposite conclusion. If the popular opinion be correct, he says, "it is a little extraordinary that causes" (under the Clerical Chancellors) "should have been brought to a hearing and heard with so much of ceremony and of regard to regularity" as the records exhibit. In his opinion the Clerical Chancellors, and, to a less extent, their lay successors, introduced the doctrines of the Civil Law, and were chiefly guided by adherence to its rules, and he shows how much similarity there is between many of its doctrines and the doctrines of equity as established by the end of the present period. But the importance of this similarity may, I suspect, be much overrated. Granting that the process of discovery by

Sidenote: The influence of precedents.

---

[1] *Leading cases*, W. and T. 2, p. 644.
[2] See the chapter on the Common-wealth, post.
[3] Vol. I. p. 367.

the oath of the Defendant, which the Chancery borrowed from
the Canon Law, and of injunction to quiet possession, which
Wolsey is charged with having introduced, bear close analogies
to forms of procedure allowed at Rome, it is not clear that any
of the doctrines of early equity can be traced to the Civil Law,
although, when the construction of legacies and gifts *mortis
causa*, at a later date, were taken over by Equity from the
Ecclesiastical Courts, no doubt the Civil Law rules in regard to
them were taken also. The Civil Law, as I have already said,
was referred to as a repertory of moral principles, and, as such,
it was accepted, not only in our Court of Chancery, but
throughout the Western World. The Law of Nature to which
the publicists of a later age constantly referred was nothing
more than the Civil Law denuded of its technicalities, and
modified occasionally by contrast with the positive morality of
the Christian system. In this sense the Ecclesiastical Chancellors perhaps referred to the Civil Law, and guided their
discretion by its rules, but in this alone. The protection of
trusts may have been suggested by the double ownerships of the
older code, but such ownerships, as already shown, were known
apart from it, and the wording of the earlier bills in Chancery
would suggest that it was due to the simple principle of compelling a Trustee to give up what he had only received on an
express undertaking to do so. The great doctrine of Specific
Performance of obligations both arising *ex contractu*, and apart
from agreement, is wholly without warrant from the Roman
Law.

But if there be no reason to suppose that the early Chancellors
restrained their discretion by the rules of the Civil Law, it is
clear they attached much force to the practice and usage of
their own Court. The direction to this effect to Kirkeham,
M. R., several times cited above, the record of cases on *subpœna*
and *conscience* in the Year Books, and the express declarations
in the tracts already referred to are sufficient to establish this.
On the other hand, in the absence of reported cases, this
practice and usage must have been uncertain and variable, and
the precedents recorded down to Lord Ellesmere's time were
exceedingly few, so much so that Mr Norburie, at the beginning

of the 17th century[1], lamenting their paucity, suggests that the judges should make some, and those that existed were not invariably followed, as may be seen by the contradictory decisions in Tothill's book. The actual state of the matter seems to be that where they could be found and cited, precedents were generally followed, while in their absence the tradition of the Court, as reported by the Masters, or as known to the Chancellor, was generally adhered to, and this to a greater and greater degree, especially during the long Chancellorships of Lord Ellesmere and of Lord Cov entry, but neither the traditions nor the precedents were of bin ding authority if the presiding Chancellor was satisfied that a new or a special rule ought to be adopted in a given case.

The last years of Lord Ellesmere's Chancellorship were marked by the crisis in the long struggle over the claim of the Chancellors to issue injunctions against proceedings at Common Law, and to stay executions on judgments there, and by the successful establishment of their right to do so. To this subject I shall return later on.

Lord Bacon, who succeeded Ellesmere in 1616, had been chiefly instrumental in securing this great victory, and in his opening speech on taking his seat he showed that he had conceived a high idea of the dignity of his new office and fully intended to preserve and develope its jurisdiction.

He compared the Chancellor to the Roman Prætor, and, as the Prætor issued his Edict on taking office, he proposed, he said, to state in his speech[2], the principles which would guide him in his administration of equity, and what orders and resolutions he had taken in conformity with the King's charge, so that the Bar might know what to expect, and not move for anything against his rules. "It is no more," he declared, "I will not, but I cannot after this declaration," and, he continued, "this I do under three cautions. The first is that there be some things of a more secret and council-like nature, more fit to be acted than published,"—referring perhaps to the private directions which he received from James and his favourite, his

Bacon's speech on taking his seat as Chancellor.

[1] Hargrave's *Tracts*, p. 431.   [2] Works (Ed. 1827), vol. 7, p. 244.

obsequiousness to which, as well as his corruption by more direct bribes, disgraced his rule in the Court. The second caution referred to details, and the third was "that these imperatives, which I have made but to myself and my times, be without prejudice to the authority of the Court, or to wiser men that may succeed me." The King's charge, he said, "rested on four heads. The first was, that I should contain the jurisdiction of the Court within its true and due limits, without swelling or excess,...the third that I should retrench all unnecessary delays, that the subject might find that he did enjoy the same remedy against the fainting of the soul and the consumption of the estate, which was speedy justice, 'Bis dat qui cito dat.'"

He then divided the excess of the Court into five natures.

"The first is when the Court doth embrace and retain causes both in matter and circumstance merely determinable and fit for the common law; for, my Lords, the Chancery is ordained to supply the law, not to subvert the law;" and, in guarding the jurisdiction, he promised that he would determine demurrers himself, or at least, the Master of the Rolls should, instead of referring them to the Masters (as Lord Ellesmere had done), a promise which he carried out by his order that they should be heard in Court[1].

"The second point concerneth the time of the complaint, and the late comers into Chancery; which stay till a judgment be passed against them at the common law, and then complain: wherein your lordships may have heard a great rattle and a noise of a *præmunire* and I cannot tell what. But that question the King hath settled according to the ancient precedents at all times continued....My rule shall be...that in case of complaints after judgments, except the judgments be upon *nihil dicit*, and cases which are but disguises of judgments, as that they be judgments obtained in contempt of a preceding order of this Court, yea, and after verdicts also, I will have the party complainant enter into good bond to prove his suggestion: so that if he will be relieved against a judgment at common law upon matter of equity, he shall do it 'tanquam in vinculis,' at

[1] O. 45.

his peril,"—thus re-introducing in this case the condition which the Statute of Henry VI. had required to be fulfilled before the issuing of any subpœna, but which had quite fallen into disuse.

The speech goes on to promise that the Chancellor would not rely too much on the reports of the Master, or delay his decisions after the hearing until he had forgotten the argument, and then re-hear the case, as his predecessors were said to have done, and that he would abolish prolixity, punishing the party and fining the offending counsel.

Lord Bacon's orders as to the practice of his Court were published soon after, and they are described as the first attempt to systematise and settle the procedure, but as we have seen, Lord Ellesmere's decisions had done much in this direction, and a few other general orders had been issued before Lord Bacon's. The orders are carefully framed to carry into effect the promises of the speech. They introduced or adopted many beneficial rules which remained in force down to the procedure reforms of the present century. Some of these will be discussed later on, in a review of the practice of the Court in the present period. "Although they have been varied in detail, I only find in them one principle which would not now be recognised," says Lord Campbell[1], namely: that "no decrees shall be made upon pretence of equity against the express petition of an Act of Parliament" (so far so well) "nevertheless, if the construction of such an Act of Parliament hath for a time gone one way in general opinion and reputation, and by a later judgment hath been controlled, then relief may be given upon matter of equity for cases arising before the said judgment, because the subject was in no default." But this was a very mild suggestion in comparison with Lord Ellesmere's claim to legislate upon "matters of meum and tuum between party and party," and to declare, as he did in the Earl of Oxford's case, that to be a good lease which an Act of Elizabeth had declared the lessor might not make. The judges themselves of this age did not regard statutes as necessarily binding, if opposed to fundamental principles of the Common Law, especially where they were old.

[1] Vol. 2, p. 421 n. Order (6).

Lord Bacon promised to use generously the fruits of his victory over the common law lawyers, and it is said he discussed the matter of injunctions with the judges as Sir Thomas More had done, taking however a somewhat higher ground, for the predominance of the Chancellors was now once more established within the legal, though not in the political sphere[1], and told them that, if they would acquaint him with any proceedings of the Chancery which seemed to be exordinate or inordinate, he and they would soon agree, or if not, the King would settle their differences. He held the seals for four years only. What he might have done for Equity had he held them as long as his predecessor it is idle to speculate upon. Of all men of his age he was probably best fitted to devise new principles, and to rationalise the old ones, and his mighty reputation and transcendent genius, if unsullied by the shame of his degradation, would probably have preserved for long the fabric he perfected, but no man of his age could have devised a system fitted to the new social wants, and to ideas liberated, thanks in a great degree to Bacon's own labours, from the tyranny of the scholastic philosophy, which were so soon to come, but of which there then was no anticipation.

A churchman, Dr Williams, was chosen to succeed Bacon, and deeming some knowledge of Equity useful to a Chancellor, and being quite ignorant of Equity, he set to work to study the rules he was to administer. On his first appearance in Court he reminded his bar that "it may be that the continual practice of strict law, without a special mixture of other knowledge, makes a man corrupt and underhand for a Court of Equity." But, notwithstanding his varied acquirements, he does not seem to have worked any noticeable improvement in the doctrines or practice of his Court, and many of his decrees were overruled by his successor, Lord Coventry.

Lord Hardwick, in his celebrated letter to Lord Kames on English Equity, dates the establishment of general rules of Equity "so far as it has been judged the nature of things would admit, especially from the time of my Lord Keeper Coventry[2]," and certainly a great number of the

Lord Coventry.

[1] Camp. II. p. 364. [2] (1625 to 1639.)

principles of Equity, some of which have been re-discovered in comparatively modern times, are to be found illustrated in the "Reports in Chancery" of his time. Many of the cases were decided "on view of precedents," and with the assistance of the judges, and they are somewhat better reported than the decisions of Lord Ellesmere, of which we have generally only the Registrar's notes, but otherwise I can find little difference between the decisions of Lord Coventry's and those of Lord Ellesmere's time.

Lord Coventry, with the assistance of Sir Julius Cæsar, the Master of the Rolls, issued some orders which were afterwards embodied in Lord Clarendon's, and of which Mr Spence wrote[1] as still, in his day, forming the basis of the practice of the Court with regard to interrogatories and the examination of witnesses, and which introduced the practice of putting particular interrogatories to the different witnesses, and made other alterations with a view to shorten pleadings and facilitate procedure. He gained further renown by clearing off an arrear of 500 causes which had accumulated under his predecessor.

[1] Spence, I. p. 402.

CHAPTER VII.

THE STRUGGLE FOR PRE-EMINENCE.

WHEN two rival systems of judicature exist in the same country and profess to administer the rights of the same litigants according to different rules, some understanding must be arrived at to determine which is to prevail at the last resort; this was, of course, plain from the first, and, as I have already shown, injunctions had been granted from the reign of Henry VI. prohibiting Plaintiffs from proceeding with actions at common law or issuing executions on judgments there obtained, in cases where, in the Chancellor's opinion, their legal claims were against conscience. This had not occurred without some objection on the part of the judges, who feared that all suitors would be drawn into Chancery if the power of the Chancellor to override or intercept their decisions became established, and much discussion had taken place over the case of the paid but unreleased bond, apparently with different results under different Chancellors. The controversy raised by the publication of the 'Doctor and Student' at the beginning of the reign of Henry VIII. seems to show that it was the settled practice to issue these injunctions in some few cases, although the right to do so was bitterly denied by the lawyers[1]. Wolsey however was then Chancellor, and the judge would have been unusually bold who would have ventured to disregard his decree, or to advise the Plaintiff at law, as the judges under Edward IV. did, to proceed with his action and ask for judgment in contempt of the Chancellor's order.

Injunctions.

[1] Ante, p. 89.

It was made a charge against Wolsey after his fall that he had interposed to prevent judgment at law, and had questioned judgments when given, but his successor, Sir T. More, although identified with the common law Bar as the son of a judge, and for long a successful practitioner, continued the practice.

All through the reign of Elizabeth the dispute over the Chancellor's claims continued. The judges, on the one hand, were now men of better standing and position, and, on the other, the Chancellors were no longer ministers whom it was dangerous to offend, and hopeless to defeat so long as the Royal favour continued. A considerable improvement moreover had been effected in the Common Law, both by its development by the judges, to a great extent under the incitement of a well-grounded fear that if they gave no remedy the Chancery would do so, and also by statute. The action of 'assumpsit' had been, by the beginning of this period, so expanded that it offered a fairly complete protection in all cases of simple contract, the action of ejectment had begun to be employed to try questions of title by means of fictitious leases in place of the difficult and expensive writ of right[1], the statute of Uses had for a time greatly diminished the number of double ownerships, the statutes of Wills[2] had restored the right of devising without the need of having recourse to a trust, and several statutes of Elizabeth had been passed for the 'expedition of justice' and the improvement of common law procedure. The most important of the statutes last referred to were 27 Elizabeth, c. 5, which provided that the judges should "proceed and give judgment according as the very right of the cause and matter of law shall appear unto them, without regarding any imperfection, defect or want of form," in any pleadings or proceedings except those specially set down in a demurrer, and that, with the same exception, the Courts might amend all such imperfections from time to time; and 27 Elizabeth, c. 8, which, reciting that erroneous judgments in the King's Bench were

Improvement of the common law.

---

[1] Throcmorton's case, 4 Inst. 86.
[2] A short account of these statutes will be given in reviewing the growth of equity during this period: Chap. ix. below.

only reformable in Parliament, which did not sit so often as formerly, enacted that a party might sue out a writ of error to examine a judgment of the King's Bench in the Exchequer Chamber before the judges of the other Courts, who should have power to reverse the judgment for errors other than want of jurisdiction or of form. The position of the judges was therefore a strong one, and there seemed much probability of their ultimately prevailing, at least upon the question of staying execution after judgment had been obtained at law, for comparatively little objection was now made to injunctions against actions on forfeitures caused by accident, as, for instance, the rise of the river preventing a debtor from reaching his creditor in time to pay on the day, or by the fraud of the Plaintiff at law himself. Even Coke admits 'accident' as a head of Equity jurisdiction. The contest over injunctions[1].

Coke cites the following case in which, at the end of Elizabeth's reign, the Chancellor's injunction seems to have been defeated[2].

The Plaintiff in Equity claimed a lease against the Defendant, Sir Moyl Finch, who pleaded that he had made a lease to one privileged to sue in the Court of Exchequer, for the purpose of recovering in ejectment on an alleged forfeiture, and that his lessee had recovered judgment, and the judgment had been affirmed on appeal. The Plaintiff however showed clear matter in equity to be relieved against the pretended forfeiture, and Lord Keeper Egerton[3] ordered the Defendant to answer the bill, with a view, no doubt, to granting an injunction against the ejectment if the Plaintiff proved his case. The Defendant appealed to the Queen, and she referred the matter to all the judges. It was argued for the Plaintiff that he did not question the judgments, but, confessing them, claimed equitable relief on grounds which could not have been pleaded at law against them, and precedents of the last three reigns were shown to support the right to do this, but the judges allowed the plea, "for though the Lord Chancellor......

---

[1] See Spence, I. p. 673, Camp. II. p. 235, Hallam, *Const. Hist.* I. p. 469.
[2] 4 Inst. 86, Throcmorton's case (39 and 40 Eliz.).
[3] Lord Ellesmere.

would not examine the judgment, yet he would by his decree take away the effect of the judgment: and for the precedents, they were grounded on the sole opinion of the Lord Chancellor, and passed *sub silentio.*" In fact the question in dispute being referred to one of the parties was naturally decided in that party's favour, and small importance was attached to earlier examples of the other's claims.

Coke cites other cases to show that the judges not only regarded Equity as altogether barred by a judgment at law, but that they denied its jurisdiction to determine the right to freeholds, in every case, just as the petitions of the Commons had denied it at an earlier time. No subpœna lay, the judges resolved, in another case against the same Defendant two years after the case just cited, because the right of inheritance was determinable at Common Law and not in Chancery, and they further resolved that, when any freehold, or other matter determinable at the Common Law, came incidentally in question in Chancery, the same could not be decided there, but ought to be sent for trial to the Common Law, where the party grieved might be relieved by error, attaint or by action of higher nature.

Lord Ellesmere did not, however, abandon his claim to determine suits affecting either judgments at law or rights to freehold, and about 10 and 11 James I. the dispute came to a crisis. In 1614 the case of *Courtney v. Glanvil*[1] occurred. The Defendant had sold to the Plaintiff a jewel worth £20, which he pretended was worth £350, and other jewels worth £100, for £600, taking a bond in payment, and had got judgment (in the first instance by consent) upon the bond, and the judgment had been affirmed on appeal. The Plaintiff then filed his bill in Equity, and it was decreed that the Defendant should take back the £20 jewel and be paid £100, and should release the judgment. He refused to obey and was committed to prison. The judges then granted a Habeas Corpus to release him, and Coke said the decree and imprisonment were unlawful.

[1] Cro. Jac. p. 343.

THE EARL OF OXFORD'S CASE.   111

Two years later the great case of the Earl of Oxford[1] came before Lord Ellesmere. Magdalen College had granted a lease for 72 years of the Covent Garden at £9 a year, and when 50 years of the term were expired they conveyed the fee to the lessee under a license from Elizabeth, by way of grant to her, on condition to grant to the lessee. The consideration for the conveyance was £15 a year, and the profit to the College on the transaction was therefore considerable. After the conveyance had been in peace forty years, and £10,000 had been spent on the land in building under it, the Master of the College, alleging that the conveyance was void under the statute of 13 Elizabeth against alienations of ecclesiastical and college lands, took possession of part of the land, and a lessee, claiming through the Earl of Oxford, the then owner under the disputed conveyance, brought an action of ejectment on fictitious leases to try the validity of the Earl's title. The jury found a special verdict, and before the matter could be debated by the judges the leases of the nominal parties to the litigation, or one of them, ran out, and the action thereupon discontinued. The judges however delivered their opinions[2], deciding that the conveyance was void, and that no act of the Master could bar the title of the Fellows or of his successors. Upon this the Earl filed his bill for relief, and the plea and demurrer of the Defendants being reported against by two of the Masters, the Defendants, who still refused to answer, were committed to prison. The matter then came before Lord Ellesmere on a motion to sequester their property until they did answer, and he delivered a careful judgment upon the jurisdiction of Chancery to interfere with judgments at law. The judgment is of great interest for the insight it gives into the nature of the arguments adopted in Equity Courts of the day, and of the principles by which their decisions were ruled.

By the Law of God, said the Chancellor[3], he that builds a house ought to dwell in it, and yet here in this case, such is the conscience of the doctor, the Defendant, that he would have the houses, gardens and orchards, which he neither built nor

[1] 2 W. and T. 642.   [2] 11 Rep. 66.   [3] (Citing Biblical authority.)

planted. Equity and good conscience were wholly for the Plaintiff, for Equity speaks as the law of God speaks. And as to there being a judgment at law, this, he said, was not in fact the case, for there was only a discontinuance of the suit, which gave no possession, but, he added, "take it as a judgment to all intents, then I answer, that in this case there is no opposition to the judgment, neither will the truth or justice of the judgment be examined in this Court...and therefore a judgment is no let to examine it in Equity so as the truth of the judgment, &c., be not examined." He then went through some of the precedents, and stated the conclusion to be drawn from them thus: "When a judgment is obtained by oppression, wrong, and a hard conscience, the Chancellor will frustrate and set it aside, not for any error or defect in the judgment, but for the hard conscience of the party." A second objection was made that this judgment was grounded upon a statute, but this also the Lord Chancellor overruled, claiming, in a passage already quoted, the power to legislate on private rights in particular cases. The judges themselves, he said[1], claimed power to adjudge as void statutes repugnant to the Common Law, and he adduced several instances where the letter of a statute had been departed from by the Courts. Finally, the law of the land was not against the jurisdiction, for cases in the Year Books recognised it and there was no statute to retain it. The statute 4 Henry IV., c. 23, providing that "after judgment given in the Courts of Our Lord the King, the parties and their heirs shall be thereof in peace" until the judgment be reversed, on which the attack upon the injunctions now chiefly turned, and which (as has already appeared) had once been allowed as a good answer in the Chancery itself, he explained away by the suggestion that it refers to legal proceedings only, and was intended to secure that the judges "should be constant and certain in their own judgments, and not play fast and loose,"—an explanation which is not only false historically, but directly contrary to the recital of the statute, for the King himself, his Council and Parliament are

---

[1] Citing 8 Coke's Reports, 118.

mentioned as the authorities to whom applications to upset judgments were made.

Other statutes which had been cited on the Defendants' part, and which were less directly in point, the Chancellor disposed of on the ground that they referred to the Ecclesiastical interferences with the Common Law, not to that of the Chancery.

Soon after this case the judges, led by Coke, the Chief Justice, made a determined attempt to put an end to the Chancellor's interference. The opportunity was seized when Lord Ellesmere was ill, and it was thought unlikely that he would recover[1]. A judgment at law had been obtained, it was said, by the Plaintiff inveigling the Defendant's witnesses into an alehouse while the hearing was going on, and the Chancellor had granted an injunction to stay proceedings upon it. On this Coke recommended the Plaintiff's Attorney to indict the Defendant, his counsel and all concerned in obtaining the injunction of a præmunire under 27 Edward III., for impeaching a judgment; and in the following term he persuaded Choke, J., in charging the Grand Jury, to tell them to enquire, among other things, of such persons as questioned judgments by bill, and he himself strongly pressed the Jury to find true bills against one such person, but they, having a wholesome fear that to be employed as a weapon in the contest between the Chancellor and the Chief Justice would bring but little profit and much danger, altogether declined to follow his advice. The Chief Justice, moreover, announced that any counsel who signed a bill praying an enquiry into the circumstances of a judgment would find his mouth closed for ever in the King's Courts, an even more severe measure than the imprisonment by which a barrister in Elizabeth's reign had been driven to humble apologies[2] for the same offence, for, until centuries afterwards, there was no separate Chancery Bar.

The Lord Chancellor appealed to the King, and he referred the matter to Bacon (then Attorney-General) and other lawyers[3],

[1] Camp. II. p. 236.
[2] Spence, I. p. 675.
[3] (Their reports are given in Cary, and in the Reports in Chancery. The first report, at least, is obviously Bacon's workmanship.)

to report upon the instances on record of "complaints made in the Chancery, there to be relieved according to equity and conscience after judgments in the Courts of the Common Laws, in cases wherein the judges of the common law could not," because of their oaths, grant relief themselves. The referees reported that there was a "strong current of practice of proceeding in Chancery after judgment," from the beginning of the reign of Henry VII., "in cases where there is no remedy for the subject by the strict course of the common law, unto which the judges are sworn," and that this was, in most cases, upon matters of equity precedent to the judgments, and not matter of agreement after. They found, they said, "in the said cases, not only the bill preferred, but motions, orders injunctions and decrees thereupon, for the discharging and releasing the judgments, or abiding the possession thereupon obtained, and sometimes for the mesne profits and the release of the costs." The judges themselves moreover, they reported, had directed parties to seek relief in Chancery, and sitting there, "in the vacancy or absence of the Chancellor," had granted it, and the hands of "sundry principal Counsellors at Law, whereof divers of them are now judges, and some in chief place," had appeared in bills of the kind in dispute.

A second report drawn up by the same learned persons and the Attorney of the Prince of Wales, stated that Chancery was not restrained by any Statute of Præmunire from giving relief after judgment, but had given it for six score years, not only under the Bishops, who, said the Referees, "might be thought less skilfull or lesse affectionate towards the laws of the land, but also by divers great Lawyers, which could not but know and honour the law, as the means of their advancement." They then argued that the Statute 27 Edward III. against appeals '*in aliena curia,*' not, as they say, '*in alia curia*[1]', does not apply to an English Court, and that the Statute 4 Henry IV. c. 23, does not either, first, because the Chancery, being unnamed, must be taken to be outside its purview (a better answer than Lord Ellesmere's); secondly, because it was made on

---

[1] (The words in the French are "qi suent en autri court a deffaire ou empescher les juggementz renduz en court le Roi".)

one of two petitions of which the other, not the one it was founded on, attacked the Chancery; and thirdly, because in restraining parties from proceeding in judgments there is no 'answering anew,' such as the statute forbids, but matters are discussed which could never be relevant to the trial at law.

After these reports James decided in favour of the Chancellor's contention. "Now, forasmuch," his Decree runs, "as mercy and justice be the true supports of our Royal Throne; and it properly belongeth to our princely office to take care and provide that our subjects have equal and indifferent justice ministered to them; and that when their case deserveth to be relieved in course of equity by suit in our Court of Chancery, they should not be abandoned and exposed to perish under the rigor and extremity of our laws, we...do approve, ratifie and confirm, as well the practice of our Court of Chancery expressed in the first certificate as the opinions for the law on the statutes." *The King's decree 14 July, 1616.*

Coke bowed, at the time, to the King's decision, but his bold attempt cost him his place, and afterwards when he wrote his third Institute[1] he questioned the authority of the decree, for, he said, it was obtained by importunity, and the jurisdiction of the King over the law obtains so far only as he decides judicially. His contemporary Jenkyns, too, in his *Eight Centuries of Reports*, reckoned among the abuses of the law "the excess of Jurisdiction in Chancery, in examining Judgments at Common Law." That Court, he said, ought to do nothing else but compel the execution of trusts and moderate the rigour of Forfeitures[2].

An attempt was made to revive the controversy at the end of the 17th century, and Sir Robert Atkyns, late Chief Baron, published a book attacking the jurisdiction to grant these injunctions[3], but nothing came of it, and from the time of Lord Bacon down to the Judicature Acts the 'common injunction' was regularly issued, although, of course, after the settlement of equitable jurisdiction it assumed quite a different aspect to that it had borne while the common law was still supposed to mark the limits of every man's civil rights. Coke disliked it, not only as an insult to his own Court, but also as a deliberate

[1] p. 125. [2] p. vii. [3] See below p. 172.

interference with property, upon the security of which against arbitrary power the happiness of the community depends, but when once the injunction in given cases became common form, it had, of course, to be included in the consideration of every question of ownership. Lord Bacon when he succeeded Lord Ellesmere in the chancellorship used his success generously, and, by his orders published in January 1618, he made careful provision[1] to prevent injunctions to stay actions being used for mere delay, or being otherwise abused. Such injunctions were not, he directed, to be granted upon priority of suit or mere surmise in the Plaintiff's bill, but upon matter confessed in the answer, or of record, or in writing plainly appearing, or where the defendant was in contempt or was claiming an old long sleeping debt, or the debtor or creditor was dead some good time before the suit was brought, and in any case only upon security for costs.

An almost immediate consequence of the victory now gained was the extension of the interference of Chancery to cases, not only where a judgment had been obtained by fraud, or by the defendant's accidental default, but in some instances where a right deliberately granted and secured by the Common Law was being enforced by unexceptional means. The creation of rights in Equity in substantive opposition to rights at law, of which perhaps the case of the right to redeem a forfeited mortgage is the earliest and most striking example, dates from about this time.

Besides the cases of conflicting rights, the 'common injunction' went on suggestion of fraud and other matters destructive of the defendant's equitable right to sue at law, and it continued to do so long after the improvement of legal procedure and of the spirit of its administration, and especially the introduction, in the reign of Charles II., of the grant of new trials with reference to the merits of the evidence[2], made this but rarely necessary, and this vehicle of so much improvement in our law, once the valued remedy against outrageous evils, became a standing nuisance. Sir J. Mansfield, C. J., in 1809, stated[3] that he

[1] Orders, 21—25.
[2] Spence, I, p. 700.
[3] *Goldschmidt v. Marryat*, 1 Camp. Rep. 559. The particular reference in

thought it highly desirable that some steps should be taken to check the growing practice of seeking for injunctions against proceeding to trial at law, and, in more recent times, Lord Cottenham, admitting the necessity for their existence, stated his opinion that the power to issue them practically did as much injustice as it promoted justice[1].

that case was to injunctions issued by the Court of Exchequer.
[1] *Brown v. Newell*, 2 My. and Cr. 570. 1837. Both cases are cited in Warren's *Law Studies*.

CHAPTER VIII.

FROM WOLSEY TO THE COMMONWEALTH. PROCEDURE AND PRACTICE.

THE regular session of the Court under professional chancellors for over a century gave birth, as would be anticipated, to a formal and ordered system of procedure. For the regulation of this, orders were from time to time issued, and, from Lord Ellesmere's Chancellorship, we find established a practice of the Court which, in the main, lasted down to the Chancery reforms of the present century, and in it the presence of some of the evils that disgraced the Court so long is already apparent, and formed, in the time of the Commonwealth, the subject of bitter complaint.

Sir Thomas More had refused to allow a subpœna to issue until the bill had been approved, and this course had been recommended in the 'Treatise on the Masters'[1], at the beginning of the period, but the practice was soon settled the other way, and the issue of a subpœna became a matter of course. The requirement of security for the expenses of the defendant in case the plaintiff failed had also fallen into disuse in ordinary cases, as appears from Lord Bacon's direction that this should be made a condition precedent to the grant of an injunction to stay proceedings upon a judgment.

The bill was signed by Counsel and filed, and it, as also the other pleadings and the interrogatories, might be objected to, for scandal[2], for multifariousness, if it joined together different causes of complaint by different plaintiffs[3], for undue prolixity, and on other grounds, one of which

The Bill.

[1] Hargrave's *Tracts*, p. 301.
[2] Monro, p. 632.
[3] Toth., p. 26; Ch. Cas. p. 6.

was derogation of the settled authority of any Court, and this, if supported, entailed the punishment of the party and his Counsel[1]. Prolixity seems to have been a crying evil: it is mentioned in nearly all the codes of orders, notwithstanding that offenders were severely treated, one Mylward, for instance, in 1596, for drawing a replication on six score sheets of paper which might have been well contrived on sixteen, was directed to have a hole cut in the said replication and to be shown at the bar of each of the Courts in Westminster Hall with his head put through the hole, and to be fined £10 and 20 nobles costs[2].

In early days the main object of the subpœna had been to compel the personal attendance of the defendant for examination by the Chancellor himself or the Master of the Rolls, and after written answers, and, early in the 16th century, attornies[3] were allowed, his appearance and answer were still necessary to enable the plaintiff to obtain relief, for his default or other contumacy was not sufficient to establish the claim. "If a man should allege by his bill that one had done him wrong, and the defendant should answer nothing, yet if it should appear to us that the defendant had done no wrong to the plaintiff he shall not recover[4]," is the very reasonable declaration of a Chancellor under Edward IV., but although in the "Choice Cases[5]" an order in 18 Elizabeth, admitting the plaintiff to proof on the defendant's refusal to answer, is cited, and the author says that "of late orders have been granted to take the bill pro confesso," these were clearly exceptional cases. Most stringent means were taken to compel appearance and answer, extending not only to committal to the Fleet, but, from the end of the 16th century, to a commission of Rebellion, equivalent to an outlawry of the contumacious defendant, and sequestration of his property[6], the plaintiff being put into possession of such of the property as was claimed by him, until the defendant should purge his contempt.

---

[1] Bacon, Ord. 56.
[2] Monro, p. 692.
[3] (The attornies at this time were officials of the Court, 'the six clerks'.)
[4] Ed. IV. 14 (9) cited Spence, I. 376.
[5] p. 10.
[6] Bacon, Order 29, and see Beames' note.

In case of transmission of title by death or marriage of the plaintiff, *pendente lite*, it was necessary that a bill of Reviver should be filed to continue the suit.

The answer. The defendant's answer to the interrogatories attached to the bill was due eight days after the bill was filed, unless he required to see evidences or confer with parties 20 miles away from London, or unless he were over 70 years of age or too ill to travel, and in the latter cases he might have a 'dedimus potestatem' to take his answer. The first answer was however rarely deemed sufficient, and second, third, fourth and further answers might be ordered on the Master's Certificate, the defendant paying, as appears from an entry of 1594 in the Registrar's Books[1], costs as ordered, in that case 20s. on each of four insufficient answers and 40s. on a fifth. Bacon's orders[2], however, provide that double costs should be paid on a second insufficient answer, treble on a third, and quadruple on a fourth, after which the defendant might be committed, and examined by interrogatories on the points as to which the answer was insufficient. But it by no means followed that the process of extracting a sufficient answer from a stubborn defendant commenced at once, he might demur to the

Demurrers and pleas. bill or jurisdiction, or plead, or both[3]. The common practice was to refer demurrers and pleas, as indeed most other interlocutory matters, to the Masters, and many reports on them occur in Mr Monro's collection, but Lord Bacon[4] promised to hear demurrers (upon which the whole legal question in the suit would often turn) himself, in open Court. When the demurrer was decided against the defendant he generally abandoned it, having indeed in later times no option but to do so, and Lord Keeper Egerton in a case[5] where the defendant persisted, in spite of an adverse decision, in pressing his demurrer, gave a final decree for the plaintiff. No costs were given, in any event, upon demurrer, for the truth of the matters in question was not tried[6]; this must often have worked great hardship to defendants, for a speculative plaintiff

[1] Monro, p. 647.
[2] Order, 61.
[3] Bacon, Orders, 58.
[4] Speech (ante) and Order 45.
[5] Ch. Cas. p. 13.
[6] *Year Book*, 7 Ed. IV. 146.

might find out on the interlocutory discussion that he had no chance, and then, under a rule which lasted down to Lord Chancellor Jefferies, dismiss his suit on payment of 20s. costs only.

When pleas and demurrers were disposed of, and a sufficient answer obtained, the plaintiff in the same term, or at least the next term, put in his Reply, which *The Reply.* might not be a new departure or contain new matter, and then, on subpœna to rejoin and join in a commission to examine witnesses, the defendant rejoined[1]. The pleadings went no further, the old extravagances of rebutters, and surrejoinders being, early in the present period, abandoned, and what of their work was necessary being done by amendments. Even the rejoinder was probably already rare at the end of the 16th century.

The examination of witnesses might take place at any time after the answer, or on special grounds before it, one case being given in Monro[2] where it preceded the bill. In London the examination was con- *The Examination of witnesses.* ducted by the official examiners, in the country by commissioners named by the parties. It was always private, and the examiners or commissioners took the witnesses in turn through a list of interrogatories supplied to them, having no discretion to judge of the pertinency of the questions, and no power to frame new questions after hearing the examination on behalf of the other side. The order to examine ran, (according to a rule introduced, it seems, by Lord Keeper Egerton, for the earlier Chancellors and Commissioners had been unrestricted in their examination,) *super interrogationibus inclusis* not *administrandis*[3], so that, in effect, the evidence resembled modern affidavit evidence, save that a party could examine, but not cross-examine, an opponent's witnesses. The answers of the defendant were taken before the Masters, if sworn in, or within 3 (afterwards extended to 5) miles of London, in other cases before the Masters Extraordinary, or, if sworn more than 20 miles from London, before commissioners. Evidence by affidavit

[1] Ch. Cas. p. 14.
[2] p. 518.
[3] Ch. Cas. pp. 16, 69. Beames, p. 30.

was allowed for some purposes, for example, on motions, but, according to express orders, it was never accepted in proof of title, or on other important issues[1]. The next step was the 'publication' of the evidence, after which, except in special cases, no further evidence could be taken on the same matters[2], though it was allowed on matters springing out of them, and no deposition could be amended.

Publication.

The delays allowed before one party could force another, if unwilling, to take these necessary steps of examination and publication, are astounding, and after considering them, and considering the references to the Masters on pleas, on demurrers, as to the sufficiency of answers and the relevancy of replies, and for enquiries, the delays of commissions and the frequent rehearings, one's wonder ceases that causes should be found five, ten and even twenty years in arrear, as the contemporary records complain. Surely the claim to be the "Great Sanctuary of Plain Dealings and Honesty[3]" must have sounded odd in a Court which permitted this, and whose method of getting at truth was no more effective than a hole-and-corner examination of the alleged knave and his friends, upon questions framed by themselves, or framed by the other side, in complete ignorance of the tale intended to be set up, except so far as the answer disclosed it, and the discussion of the evidence produced by such examination before a judge who had no opportunity of deriving assistance from the demeanour of the deponents or their manner of giving their answers. Yet this course was pursued by the Court of Chancery for centuries, and in a modified form continues to work injustice in its successor, the Chancery Division[4].

The dilatoriness of procedure.

It is true disputed rights were sometimes sent to be tried at law, where a more rational system of examination prevailed, and references were also made to the Masters who saw the

[1] Bacon, Ord. 75, 76.
[2] Ch. Cas. p. 17. Monro, p. 32.
[3] Preface to "Cases in Chancery."
[4] (Witness the piles of contradictory affidavits, carefully drafted by counsel to set the facts in their best possible light, or such of them as it is deemed advisable to state, which are put before the Court on contested motions. The power of cross-examining upon the affidavits does something to mitigate the evil, though it involves great expense and delay.)

parties and their witnesses[1], and occasionally, by special order or by consent, witnesses were examined, as in every case where the facts were in dispute they should have been, at the hearing, but the normal course was that I have described[2]. An extraordinary practice, grounded upon the peculiar responsibility of the Chancellor's position as judge of conscience without appeal, was sometimes resorted to. After publication of the evidence taken by the parties, new witnesses, or those who had already made their depositions, were privately examined 'ad informandum conscientiam judicis,' and the evidence so obtained was reserved for the judge's eye alone unless he chose to disclose it[3]. Great improvements were effected in the manner of taking evidence and the rules in regard to it by Lord Coventry's orders of 1635, chiefly in the direction of abolishing unnecessary interrogatories and restricting the evidence to the matters which the bill and answer really left in dispute. And it was enjoined on plaintiffs and their counsel that in every case they should consider whether they could not proceed to the hearing upon these last materials alone, a practice which is also referred to in Lord Bacon's Orders.

Evidence.

An interesting letter to a country client from Lord Ellesmere, when he was at the Bar, advising on a case then pending, which Lord Campbell has published[4], throws some light upon the manner in which the hearing was conducted, and depicts it as a leisurely proceeding in which the opposing counsel put in their evidence, criticised that of their opponents, and made their points alternately, and it would seem that the formal speeches which the presence of the jury fostered in the common law Courts never obtained in the rival forum.

The Decree is described[5] as "a final sentence or order of the Court, pronounced upon the hearing and understanding of the cause, which decree being drawn up by the pleadings, and the final order so pronounced, by one

The decree.

---

[1] (In the 17th century they also ceased to hear the parties and proceeded on affidavit evidence only.)
[2] Ch. Cas. p. 19; Toth., p. 190.
[3] Bac. Ord. 74.
[4] Vol. 2, p. 177.
[5] Ch. Cas. p. 21.

of the Six Clerks, and signed by the Chancellor, and enrolled of record may not be altered upon any Motion or Order, but the party is put to his Bill of Review if he have good cause," but until so signed it was an interlocutory order merely, and open to reconsideration.

The decrees of the present period, so far as can be judged from the records, were simple orders that the plaintiff have quiet possession, recover the property asked for, or the like; and Spence seems to have attributed to the flexibility and complexity which characterised Chancery decrees at a later time, too early a date when contrasting these decrees with the judgments at Common Law[1]. Cross bills by the defendant were however already well known in the preceding period, and the rule is now found that though no such bill could be allowed after 'publication,' in a proper case a decree could be made for the defendant at the hearing, without it, and this must have often tended to complicate the decree[2]. The only mode of appeal from a decree drawn up and signed by the Chancellor was by way of a Bill of Review, or by a petition to the King. The former is said to have been introduced in the time of Henry VIII.[3], and under Lord Ellesmere it was, nominally, only admitted upon new matter occurred since decree or on matter of record, or contained in writing and not used before. Lord Bacon introduced some valuable improvements in regard to these bills, especially by requiring obedience to the decree questioned, (unless it entailed the extinguishment of the Appellant's right at common law, as if the cancellation of a bond were ordered,) before the bill was admitted, and requiring the appellant to give security for costs, and the damages occasioned by delay[4].

Motions, that is to say, summary applications to the Chancellor, in interlocutory matters, had become exceedingly frequent—"more than needful, and not tending to the end of the course: (they) are many times the cause of long and tedious suits in Chancery." "Some have conceived," adds the writer[5], "that there needs but one Motion

Motions.

[1] Spence, 1, p. 390.
[2] Ch. Cas. 22.
[3] Spence, 1, p. 394.
[4] Orders, 1—5.
[5] Ch. Cas. p. 30.

in a cause, viz., for an injunction for quiet possession as at the time of the bill exhibited, and for staying of suits at the common law in the meantime till the cause be determined here." Common injunctions, objections to answers and pleadings, injunctions to stay waste and cutting of timber, applications for security, and applications in regard to the conduct of commissions and taking the evidence, the latter of which were generally referred to the four of the six clerks not concerned in the cause, were all the subject of motions, and the frequency of these gave rise to the generations upon generations of orders, amounting sometimes to 500 orders in a cause, among which, according to the Commonwealth reformers, at times counsel, parties and judges alike lost themselves and lost sight of the original cause of dispute. It was found necessary to provide that any order made without the Court being informed of the last material order before it should be void[1].

References of the cause for report on particular issues, and upon the whole case, were another cause of frequent complaint, especially those of the latter kind, and they were repeatedly forbidden by Lord Ellesmere, and by Bacon's Orders[2] they were directed to be 'sparingly granted,' but they nevertheless constantly occurred, and often a plaintiff eight or nine years after the reference would find himself, it is asserted[3], obliged to return to Court and go on again where he left off. These abuses mark the latter end of the present period chiefly, for the reports of the Masters under Elizabeth do not seem to have been much delayed; thus a certificate of Masters Lambard and Hobarte[4], stating that an account referred to them is long, and that the defendant seeks to rip it all up again, and praying that, as they have no time for it in term, and are going into the country for the Vacation, a single arbitrator with more leisure may be appointed instead of them, would not have been made if such monstrous delays as those alleged had already become familiar.

References.

One subject of such references seems often to have been to settle the dispute by the Master's arbitration, as many disputes

[1] Bac. Ord. 86.
[2] Ord. 47.
[3] Ch. Cas. p. 34.
[4] Monro, p. 15 (1597).

were settled in Court by the good offices of the Chancellor himself. An instance of this appears in the certificate of Master Tyndal in 1610, which reports that the Master had done his best to reduce the parties to peace but without success, and he prays he may be no more troubled about the matter[1].

Petitions.   Besides the regular procedure upon bill and answer, the more summary mode of procedure by petition had been introduced in a few cases, the petition being an informal statement of the case, as the bill originally was, without interrogatories attached to it. Bacon's Orders give a list of things which could not be done upon petition, including the grant of injunctions, making of final orders and overruling demurrers. Generally petitions seem to have been used only for more or less formal applications, and in addition to these, it is interesting to note that applications to reverse the decrees of Charity Commissioners were made by petition 'containing only matter fundamental'[2], offering a precedent, to some extent, for what Lord Redesdale thought the dangerous innovations of Sir S. Romilly's Charity Act at the beginning of the present century.

Suits in *formâ pauperis*.   Suits in *formâ pauperis* were already allowed by special leave, which Lord Ellesmere refused if the suit were already begun, but which was subsequently granted, on the intended plaintiff's oath that he was not worth £5, without reference to this rule. If in such a suit the plaintiff failed, as he paid no costs, he was sometimes ordered to be whipped or pilloried as a warning against similar abuses, or in deference to the once well-received maxim that he who cannot pay with his purse should pay with his body. By an order of 1623[3], a certificate both of the 'likely good of the merits of the cause,' as also of the mean and weak state of the intended plaintiff, was required.

The Decrees were, as we have seen, taken to bind the party only, and were enforced by process against him, imprisonment (which, being 'in the nature of an execution,' was to be close), and, in case of obstinacy, fines, and, if the decree were for pos-

---

[1] Monro, p. 129, see also p. 622.   [3] Beames, p. 49.
[2] Ch. Cas. p. 23.

session, then successively, if need be, a Commission of Rebellion against the offender, and a Commission to the Sheriff to put the plaintiff into the possession of the lands adjudged to him[1].

An important addition to the working power of the Court was made by the establishment of the Master of the Rolls as a regular judge to hear causes, which is commonly dated from the time of Tunstall, M. R. in Wolsey's Chancellorship, although, as has already appeared, he had exercised some judicial duties, at least occasionally, and had attained a higher position than that of the other Masters in the preceding period. He sat in the Rolls to hear causes referred to him by the Chancellor, when the Chancellor was not himself sitting[2]. Considerable discussion took place as to his judicial authority, and though it was well established, and regularly acquiesced in, the controversy did not cease until an Act of George II.[3], was passed to put an end to it. In the reign of Elizabeth he seems to have assisted the Chancellor in Equity matters somewhat by way of concession: the Chancellor "moved the Master of the Rolls to hear the cause, which at his Lordship's motion the said Master of the Rolls was content to do" is the recital in an order[4] of 1579, but in the reign of Charles I. his position as one of the rulers of the Equity Court was so thoroughly settled that he issued many general orders for the regulation of its practice[5].

The Master of the Rolls.

The importance which the Master's offices had now attained in regard to the equitable jurisdiction of the Court, may be gathered from the references already made to them. It is to this period that the earliest development of the great administrative system of the later Chancery, which was carried out in these offices, with its enquiries, accounts and reports, must be traced. Matters of account, say Bacon's Orders[6], unless in very weighty cases, are not fit for the Court, but to be prepared by reference, with perhaps directions as to taking the account given at the hearing, and so examinations of Court Rolls, upon customs and copies are to be referred, and if the

The Masters.

---

[1] Bacon's Orders, 7—10.
[2] Ch. Cas. p. 64.
[3] 3 Geo. II. c. 20.
[4] Monro, p. 468, cf. pp. 439, 518.
[5] Beames, p. 49, et passim.
[6] Orders, 50, 51, 53.

defendant by his answer, confess a trust, then there is no need for a hearing, but the reference can take place at once.

The Masters continued to take acknowledgments of deeds, oaths of witnesses, answers and affidavits and similar business in London; and orders were made by Lord Chancellor Hatton that the Masters Extraordinary, then lately constituted, should not interfere in this business within three miles, extended by an order of 1622 to five miles, from the town, their work lying apparently outside this district, but within a radius of twenty miles, beyond which limit commissions were issued, but they continually infringed the privileges of their more dignified fellows[1].

Another class of officers attached to the Court were the Six Clerks, who were supposed to supervise the steps taken in every cause, one of them always appearing, in early times really, but from the end of the present period only nominally, on each side, as the party's attorney[2]. And by repeated orders of the reign of Charles I. it was provided that no subpœna 'ad audiendum judicium' should be issued to secure the attendance of the persons intended to be bound by the decree until the Six Clerks engaged were satisfied that the cause was ready for hearing. These officials made great profits from the copies of proceedings their clients were bound to take from them, and for which they charged exorbitant fees. No complaint during the 17th century against the Court was more frequent than that excited by these extortionate payments for work, which was generally unnecessary, made to men who performed it by underpaid deputies.

[1] Beames, p. 48.
[2] Solicitors, but not professional solicitors, were already known. See an order that the plaintiff's servant who had acted as his solicitor was not to be examined by the defendant as a witness. Monro, p. 519 (1583).

CHAPTER IX.

FROM WOLSEY TO THE COMMONWEALTH. THE MATTERS DEALT
WITH BY THE COURT AND THE RELIEF GIVEN.

IN the collections of Tothill and Cary, the "Choice cases," which are chiefly decisions of the reign of Elizabeth, and the "Reports in Chancery[1]" of the time of Lord Keeper Coventry, material is to be found from which some idea of the matters dealt with during this period by the Court, and the relief afforded by it can be obtained. The reports are however exceedingly meagre, and rarely give any clue to the grounds of the decisions, or the lines of the arguments adopted, and often contain only the barest statement of the facts of the case and the Court's decision. Still, almost all the great heads of equity can here be traced in embryo, and the precedents recorded were the authorities referred to, so far as any authorities were, in the great constructive period which commenced directly after the Restoration, and it will therefore be useful to briefly indicate their nature. In doing this I propose to follow chiefly the excellent summary of Spence, but to discard the inferences which he has drawn from the course of the Court in later times, as it seems exceedingly dangerous to accept the rulings of the Chancellors at the end of the 17th century, when they were adopting new rules and determining new questions on the largest scale, as any guide to the course of the Court fifty or a hundred years before.

(1) The Chancery enforced rights which were unrecognised at Common Law, *trusts* were peculiarly its care, and the sub-

---

[1] First published in the years 1649, 1650, 1672 and 1697 respectively. Bridgman's *Legal Bibliography*, p. 57.

jects of *administrations, charities, separate estate,* and *equities of redemption* were closely connected with the preservation of trusts; (2) as a Court of Conscience it interfered where a legal advantage had been unjustly gained by *fraud, accident,* or *mistake,* and granted relief according to the true intent of the parties, as it understood it, in cases of joint indebtedness and suretyship by its doctrine of *contribution;* (3) and where a right was recognised at law, but was there imperfectly protected or secured, it stepped in to decree *specific performance,* to take *accounts,* to allow *set off,* to enforce *dower* or *partition,* and to quiet and end rival claims, by *interpleader* and *bill of peace,* by its *injunction* to secure *quiet possession* and to afford protection from threatened wrongs, and by *discovery* to give assistance in aid of proceedings at law, and to perpetuate testimony in danger of being lost.

I. *Trusts.*

Before the present period trusts or uses were fully established[1], and conveyances by way of use had become so common that the rule was adopted that on a feoffment without valuable consideration, and where the feoffee was not a near blood-relation of the feoffor, unless the use were otherwise declared, it should result to the feoffor. " Because purchases were things notorious, and uses were things secret, the Chancellor thought it more convenient to put the purchaser to prove his consideration, or the purpose of the grant than the feoffor and his heirs to prove the trust[2]". So where the owner agreed to sell or lease, or undertook to stand seised for another, for valuable consideration, the Chancellor declared that he should hold to the other's use. The agreement or undertaking under the early Chancellors might have been by parol, but, after uses fell within the cognizance of the judges, they declared that " a man cannot raise an use by parol in the nature of a covenant to stand seised without feoffment, by natural affection, for it would be mischievous if one without any ceremony in law could raise an use without a settled resolution manifested by a deed." Where, however, there was valuable consideration,

---

[1] Ante, p. 79 *et seq.* [2] Bacon, *Reading on Uses.*

marriage for instance, they subsequently determined to support even a parol declaration of use[1].

And, on the same principle, relief was given in cases where the legal estate had been conveyed, or not conveyed, by or through fraud or accident, by declaring a constructive use for the party deemed by the Chancellor to be entitled.

It had been settled that uses should descend to the heir like freehold estates, and that they could be alienated by any direction to the feoffee, even, as appeared in the numerous cases of nuncupative wills in the Calendars, though given verbally only. It was settled also that, the creation of uses being freed from the restrictive rules of the common law, they could be made to commence *in futuro* or to cease by matter subsequent; could be declared in favour of the grantor himself, or of his wife; and were not subject to defeat by the ouster of the cestui-que-use. Other instances, says Spence[2], "might be cited, showing how little the rule that '*Aequitas sequitur legem*' was adhered to where it would have interfered with the determination which the clerical Chancellors appear to have entertained, of making property subservient, through the medium of uses and trusts, to all the legitimate objects of family arrangements, and for the purposes of commerce." But in this passage, as elsewhere in his book, I think the learned author is attributing too early a date to principles found in operation, not in the 15th century, or the first half of the 16th, but in the latter half of the 16th, and the following centuries. The clerical Chancellors refused to allow a trustee to betray his trust, and cared nothing for legal rules of which they knew little, but one may suspect that in dealing with the settlements, by will or deed, that were brought before them, which to judge from the Calendars were exceedingly simple in character, they had in view no wide-reaching plan for the improvement of their country's institutions.

The use rested on 'confidence in the person' of the feoffee, and therefore a corporation or the King could not hold to uses, but, though on this ground the judges under Edward IV. had

---

[1] *Collard v. Collard* (Mary) 2 Rolle, Ab. 788, and *Corbyn v. Corbyn* (37–8 Eliz.) 2 Rolle Ab. 784.
[2] Vol. 1, p. 456.

advised the Chancellor that the feoffee's heir was not bound, this ruling had been reversed before the present period. So the purchaser for value without notice of the use was not bound by it. It rested also on 'privity of estate,' and, as a consequence, neither tenant by the curtesy, nor tenant in dower, nor tenant by elegit, claiming through the feoffee but without his act, nor the lord on escheat, nor a disseisor, abator or intruder who had expelled the feoffee, was bound by it. On the other hand, though, as already said, the use descended to the heir of the cestui-que-use or passed to his assign, neither curtesy nor dower could be had out of it, it could neither be escheated nor forfeited, and the creditors of the cestui-que-use could not have execution against it for their debts.

A series of statutes, as we have seen[1], had been passed with a view to preventing the frauds perpetrated under this immunity of the use from execution, and to protecting the feudal claims of the lords. For example, uses had been declared liable to wardships and reliefs by 4 Henry VII. c. 17, to execution by 19 Henry VII. c. 15, and to forfeiture by 26 Henry VIII. c. 13. These statutes altogether failed to meet the evils which the existence of uses was alleged to create, and after the fall of Wolsey and of More the temporary triumph of the common lawyers was marked by a statute[2] which was intended to sweep away uses, root and branch, to abolish devises and all the other facilities for transferring interests in land which had grown up by their aid, and to reinstate "the Common Laws of this Realm," whereby, as the preamble to the statute stated, "lands, tenements and hereditaments be not devisable by testament, nor ought to be transferred from one to another, but by solemn livery and seisin, matter of record (or) writing sufficient, made *bona fide.*"

The preamble complains that by secret conveyances and by wills made " by nude parolx and words, sometimes by signs and tokens, and sometimes by writing" (made for the most part by persons *in extremis*, with) " scantly any good memory or remembrance," and " provoked by greedy and covetuous persons lying

[1] Ante, p. (79).   [2] The Statute of Uses, 27 Hen. VIII. c. 10.

in wait about them," many persons indiscretely disposed of their inheritances, whereby heirs lost their lands, and lords their rights, and purchasers were made insecure; men lost their tenancies by curtesy, and women their dowers, perjuries were encouraged, and the King was deprived of his profits on attainders, and on purchases by aliens; and many other inconveniences happened,—to the "utter subversion of the ancient Common Laws of this Realm." The statute provides "for the exterping and extinguishment" of these errors, that "where any person or persons stand or be seised...of and in any...lands, tenements...or other hereditaments to the use, confidence or trust of any other person or persons or any body publick, by reason of any bargain, sale, feoffment, fine, recovery, covenant, contract, agreement, will or otherwise,...all and every such person and persons and bodies politick that have...any such use, confidence or trust in fee simple,...or otherwise,...or in remainder, or in reverter...shall stand and be seised and adjudged in lawful seisin, estate and possession of and in the same lands (&c.)...of and in such like estates as they had...on use, trust or confidence of or in the same." Sections 4 to 7 deal with the case of freehold jointures settled by way of use, and provide that where a woman had such a jointure she should not claim dower if it were settled before marriage, and if settled after she should elect between her dower and her jointure. And section 11 provides that wills of lands made before the statute, in the manner in use within the last 40 years, should be "taken and accepted good and effectual in the law."

The immediate effect of the statute was to convert such uses as it operated upon into legal estates, and to import into the common law (if the judges allowed the same latitude to the creation and transfer of uses as the Chancellors had, and this, in effect, they ultimately did), the varied interests commencing *in futuro*, and upon matter subsequent which had previously been created by way of use only, and also to introduce new methods of conveyance of the legal estate characterised by the same secrecy as had attended the transfer of the use. The Statute of Enrolments[1] passed in the same session required

---

[1] 27 Hen. VIII. c. 16.

that bargains and sales of freehold interests should be enrolled, but it was evaded by the device of conveying by a lease, which the Statute of Uses executed in possession, followed by a release of the reversion, and this became the common form of conveyance down to the present century.

An even more important consequence of the Statute of Uses, was the abolition, except where local custom allowed, and in the case of copyholds, to which the statute did not apply, of the power of devising, now enjoyed for over a century. It is not worth while to speculate whether on the construction of the statute, but in defiance of its expressed intention, or under cover of the trusts which escaped its operation, devises would have been reintroduced when the pressure of the demand for them was felt, had not Parliament interfered. The attempt to suppress them excited an outcry so loud that the Court party, who had fathered the restraining statute, five years afterwards brought in the Statute of Wills to undo their previous work.

This statute[1] recites that the King's subjects, for want of the power of devising, "cannot use or exercise themselves according to their estates, degrees, faculties and qualities," maintain hospitalities, bring up "their lawful generations, which, in this realm, (laud be to God) is in all parts very great and abundant," pay their debts or advance their children, and therefore, with a great show of royal generosity, but the utmost care that the King and the overlords shall lose nothing by the concession (except possibly a chance of escheat), the power is granted for[2] anyone to devise the whole of his socage lands and two-thirds of his lands held by knight's service.

The history of uses so far as they were within the Statute of Uses, and of wills of real property, does not belong to the subject of this essay. They passed into the jurisdiction of the ordinary Courts, and thus a great portion of the earlier business of the Court of Chancery was swept away. The statute however did not touch many of the uses, or, as they are from this time commonly called, the trusts which the Chancellors had protected. Trusts raised out of chattels, or chattel interests in

---

[1] 32 Hen. VIII. c. 1.
[2] (In effect, taking the statute and the amending statute 34 and 35 Henry VIII. c. 5, together.)

realty were from the first clearly outside it, and gained therefore no protection at law by its aid. It was held, soon after the statute was passed, that special trusts, which cast some duty upon the trustee, remained unexecuted by it also, since where they existed the use was partly, at least, in the trustee. A more important exception was made by the narrow construction put by the judges upon the terms of the statute. In *Tyrell's* case, which came before the Court of Wards in the reign of Philip and Mary, it was declared[1] that limitations to uses contained in a bargain and sale, which itself operated under the statute, were void: "because an use cannot be springing, drawn or reserved out of an use, as appears *prima facie.*" The Chancery, following its former course of preserving to a grantee rights which were intended to be passed by the grant, stepped in and supported as trusts, identical in character with the old uses, the trusts or uses which the law refused to recognise, and these are the trusts so familiar in later equity.

It would seem that the statute did, nevertheless, greatly diminish for a time the prevalence of dual ownerships: the power of devising had been granted without the creation of a use being necessary, except as to copyholds, which were devised by way of surrender to the use of the surrendor's will until the present century, and forfeitures had become comparatively rare, the feudal claims of the King indeed remained over lands held by knight's service, but the claims of the mesne lords had for the most part been forgotten, and there was therefore little inducement to separate anew the legal and beneficial ownerships. It is probable that for a long time after these statutes the Chancellor's court had little to do with trusts. A few cases however occur in the books of the reign of Elizabeth, and at the beginning of the seventeenth century this branch of the jurisdiction of Chancery was completely reestablished. This is well shown by the remarks of Coke, C. J., in a case[2] in 12 James I. The action was "on the case" against the lord of a manor to whom a surrender to the use of the plaintiff for life had been made, and who refused to admit him. The Chief Justice compared it to an action against feoffees in trust who

[1] Dyer, 155 (*a*)   [2] *Foorde v. Hoskins*, 1. Bulst. 337.

would not perform their trust: "if the cestui-que-use desires the feoffees to make an estate over, and they so to do refuse, for this refusal an action on the case lieth not," he said, "because for this he hath his proper remedy by subpœna in the Chancery;" and again, "he which hath the trust, hath no remedy by way of action, against the other who hath the interest; for a trust is not assets, nor yet forfeitable by attainder, and so in effect, the same is nothing," and the action was dismissed.

By Lord Bacon's time, suits in regard to trusts were again so common, that by his orders he provided that, where an answer confessed a trust, the matter should be at once referred to a Master to take the trustee's accounts without any hearing being required[1].

The old rules with regard to uses were applied, in the main, to trusts, so that they were governed in most things by the same law as legal estates, the analogy being in some cases more closely followed than in later times. Thus it was held in 6 Charles I. that the wife of a trustee was entitled to dower out of the trust estate[2],—a judgment which was overruled after the Restoration. And where in a marriage settlement trusts of a term were declared for the heirs of the body of the husband, the judges, to whom the case was referred, advised that, as no cestui-que-trust under this declaration was in being at the date of the deed, the trust for the heirs was void, and that the whole term belonged to the husband's executors, and ought to be sold to pay his debts[3].

[1] O. 53 (1618).
[2] *Nash v. Preston*, Cro. Cas. 190. This is a curious case. One who was seised in fee, wishing to mortgage the reversion on his own and his wife's lives in the land, conveyed to the mortgagee on condition that should he immediately demise to the mortgagor and his wife for their lives, and that the conveyance should be void if the money were repaid at the end of 20 years. The mortgagee died and his wife claimed dower against the mortgagor, on the ground that, by the conveyance the fee simple had been vested in her husband. The judges, to whom the case was referred from the Chancery, thought the claim unjust, but clearly good at law, and equity, they said, ought to follow the law: "and it was (the mortgagor's) folly that he did not conjoin another with (the mortgagee) as is the ancient course in mortgages."

[3] *Lyddal v. Venlore*. Rep. in Chy. 5. (The note of this case in Toth.

On the other hand, trusts were not considered to be within the Statute *De Donis*, and, during the present period, it was held that entails in trust estates could be barred by a mere conveyance without fine. Entails indeed were little favoured in Equity. *De Donis*, Lord Ellesmere declared, was "an ambitious statute, let it help him (the plaintiff) at law as it may[1]".

Towards the end of the present period a case occurred which shows that the question of the liability of a trustee for the safe keeping of the property subject to the trust had arisen, and its importance was already recognised[2].

A trustee had been ordered to account for all the rents and profits raised out of an infant's lands under a trust, which, so far as they were not already accounted for, had been received by his co-trustee. The case was reheard by Lord Coventry, who directed a search to be made for precedents, and called in the judges to advise: "whereby some course might be settled that parties trusted might not be too much punished, lest it should dishearten men to take any trust, which would be inconvenient on the one side, nor that too much liberty should be given to parties trusted, lest they should be emboldened to break the trust imposed on them, and so be as much prejudiced on the other side." Several precedents, both in the Court of Equity and in the Court of Wards, for charging trustees on their several receipts were found, but no others, and the Chancellor and judges resolved that, "unless there be *dolus malus*, or any evil practice, fraud or ill intent in him that permitted his companion to receive the whole profits," a trustee should be liable only for what he himself received.

The employment of old terms of years to protect the legal owner from subsequent charges on his estate, by assigning them to trustees to 'attend the inheritance,' which became so important in later conveyancing, was already familiar, and it was settled that such terms would not be allowed to prejudice

---

(p. 187) is "look into it, how to remove a trust made for use of children."
[1] Ch. Cas. p. 49.

[2] *Townley v. Sherborne* (9 Car. I.), 2 W. and T. 960.

any other rights than those they were created or assigned to bar[1]. They were employed in Equity "to protect property and keep it in the right channel," and were "moulded according to the uses, estates and charges which the owner of the inheritance declares or carves out of the fee[2]." And a clear distinction was drawn between them and long terms 'in gross,' which equity regarded as frauds on the king and overlords[3].

Successive interests in chattels, which until the time of Coke were not permitted at law, were protected when created by way of trusts, or by the limitations being construed in Equity as limitations of the use only[4]. And a case occurred under Charles I. where the life tenant of the chattels was compelled to give security for their delivery upon his death[5]. In the same way assignments of possibilities[6], and assignments of choses in action, of which Coke says[7] "the great wisdom and policy of the sages and founders of our law have provided that no possibility, right, title or thing in action shall be granted or assigned to strangers, for that would be occasion of multiplying of contentions and suits, of great oppression of the people, and chiefly of terre-tenants, and the subversion of the due and equal execution of justice," were nevertheless allowed and protected in Equity, where the assignor was regarded as trustee for the assignee, if valuable consideration were given. The practice in the case of choses in action dated at least from Edward IV[8]. The reason why the assignee was not recognised by the judges was, no doubt, because they regarded the obligation as a strictly personal bond between the debtor and creditor[9], and, on the same ground, they advised the Chancellor under Elizabeth that a trust of a term could not be assigned, but this ruling, if ever

---

[1] *Huddlestone v. Lamplough* (5 Car. I.), Rep. in Chy. 19.
[2] Lord Hardwicke in *Willoughby v. Willoughby*, 1 T. R. 763.
[3] Ch. Cas. p. 49. Bacon, Order, 15.
[4] Spence, I. p. 458 (f), *Game v. Hone* (4 Car. I.), Rep. in Chy. p. 15, and per Lord Nottingham in *Seaman v. Warman*, 1 Free, 306.
[5] *Bracken v. Bentley*, Rep. in Chy. 59.
[6] *Warmsley v. Tanfield* (4 Car. I.), Rep. in Chy. 16; *Wiseman v. Roper* (21 Car. I.), Rep. in Chy. p. 85.
[7] 10 Rep. 48.
[8] Spence, I. p. 457 (b).
[9] Pollock on Contracts, 4th ed. p. 206 and note G.

followed, was not adhered to in the 17th century or subsequently.

In administering trusts, as in much of the other work of the Court, questions of legal rights and the construction of instruments often arose. The same rules of construction were generally followed as at law, though great license was still allowed in interpreting, by extrinsic evidence, what was thought to be the intent of the parties. Points of law were often sent to be determined in the common law Courts, and questions of fact too, especially of title, were occasionally sent there with, in some cases, directions as to the conduct of the trial.

Administration. The administration of the estates of deceased persons, which afterwards fell wholly upon the Court, was already the subject of its care. The grant of administration and the recovery of legacies were the special business of the Ecclesiastical Courts, but the jurisdiction of these Courts was a very lame one. By a statute of Edward III.[1] administrators had been made accountable to the Ordinary as executors already were, but though a legatee could question the accounts rendered by them, a creditor could not. And by 21 Henry VII.[2] executors and administrators were required to make an inventory of the goods of the testator or intestate. The facilities for obtaining discovery in Chancery naturally led legatees and creditors to seek the aid of that Court, and many cases occurred, during this period, in which an executor or administrator was ordered to make an inventory on his honour or oath[3]. Applications, as already stated, had frequently been made to the Ecclesiastical Chancellors for aid in recovering from his executor a simple contract debt of the testator, for the executor could not be successfully sued in 'debt,' because the testator, it was said[4], might have "waged his law," and creditors continued to apply in Chancery after this difficulty disappeared. There is a reported case[5] of 40 Elizabeth in

[1] 31 Ed. III. st. I. c. 11.
[2] c. 5, secs. 2, 6.
[3] The executor was considered a trustee to pay debts and legacies. Cary, p. 28, and see Monro, p. 300, as to the power of one executor to sue another in equity. Toth. pp. 86—9.
[4] *Vavasour v. Chadworth,* 1, Cal. 93.
[5] Cary, p. 11.

which the Plaintiff after having been defeated at law, filed a bill against the executors of his father-in-law for a marriage portion promised by him, and when it was found by the Master's Report that the executors had assets for funerals, debts and legacies, with a good overplus to satisfy the complainant, a decree was made for payment of the portion. From this it appears the creditor's right to sue was settled, and the machinery of an enquiry into the amount of the assets and of the charges upon them was already adopted. Under James I. in several cases the executor was compelled to distribute the residue among the relatives, although by the Common Law, after paying the debts and legacies, he was entitled to retain it[1]. The Court always regarded such distribution as probably in accordance with the testator's intention, and in later times it seized the smallest indication of such intention in the will to enforce it. In 5 Car. I. in a suit for administration a time was fixed for the next of kin, among whom the surplus was decreed by the Court to be distributed, to bring in their claims[2].

Some of the doctrines which the Court afterwards adopted in administrations are already traceable. Thus, under Charles I., it was held that a charge of debts upon land did not prevent the personalty being primarily liable, a point settled, after much consideration, by Lord Thurlow[3]. It was also held, in the same reign, that the appointment of a creditor as executor, which put an end to the debt at law, would not be allowed to do so in equity[4].

There was some doubt down to the Chancellorship of Lord Ellesmere whether bills would lie for simple legacies. He sometimes sent the Plaintiffs to the Spiritual Courts, but often allowed the suits, and, it seems, with more latitude than a report on a demurrer to a bill for recovery of legacies, an inventory, and an account against an executor, in 1607, would

---

[1] Anciently he was bound to account for the surplus to the Ordinary *in pios usus*, and this is stated to be still the rule in Cary, p. 29 (1602).
[2] Toth. 129.
[3] *Smith v. Hopton* (18 Car. I.), Rep. in Chy. 82. *Ancaster v. Mayer*, 1 W. and T. 723.
[4] *Askwith v. Chamberlain*, Rep. in Chy. 73.

indicate, for there it is said the demurrer was good, unless trusts were alleged in the bill[1]. After his time the jurisdiction was fully established, Equity adopting from the Ecclesiastical Courts the Civil Law Rules by which, in those Courts, the construction of legacies was governed. Among other rules adopted was that avoiding conditions or legacies in restraint of marriage[2].

Wills of lands had passed from the cognizance of the equity courts, but wills of personalty, in the manner described, had practically come to be there exclusively construed and administered, and in regard to them there seemed a strong probability that the doctrine of inofficiousness would be introduced with other rules from the Civil Law. Several cases on this point of the reign of Charles I. occur in the Reports in Chancery. In one the Plaintiff's father had made a will giving all his property to his executors in trust for the Defendant, whom he had intended to marry. The trust, which seems to have been verbal, was disputed, and a judge, to whom the cause was referred, certified that it was not proved, and that the Defendant was a lewd woman, but the decision of the Court is reported thus: The Court, "much disliking that the estate (of the testator) should be given away from his own child" to (the Defendant) dismissed the Defendant's cross-bill and decreed for the Plaintiff[3]. In another case the will was actually set aside as inofficious, but there it was suggested that the draftsman had not carried out the testator's intentions[4]. There is a note in Tothill of two cases which seem to have involved the same point. In the first, the Court, it is said, "was assisted with bishops and noblemen at the hearing of a cause in Chancery, in July, 5 or 8 Jac., upon a point of disinherison," and the other is "a disinherison, and a decree for confirmation, yet after twenty years the decree reversed and disinherison avoided in 8 Car.[5]" The doctrine however did not become established, and full liberty of bequest became and remains the rule of our land.

[1] Monro, p. 109, and see pp. 10, 425, 761.
[2] Toth. p. 129.
[3] Answorth v. Pollard, p. 54 (11
Car. I.).
[4] Maundy v. Maundy, p. 66.
[5] Toth. p. 81.

142   CHARITIES AND SEPARATE ESTATE.

Charities. Charities had always been peculiarly the subject of the Chancellor's care, and accordingly the statute[1] of Elizabeth put the appointment of Commissioners to enquire into abuses of charities into his hands, and directed the appeal from their judgments to lie to his Court. After the statute there seems to have been a constant reference to the Court in charity cases, and special favour was extended to trusts for charitable purposes, neither the incapacity in law of the donees to take, nor the absence of a devisee in trust being allowed to prejudice the charity, and, in spite of the general refusal to enforce nuncupative wills, parol devises for charities were supported[2].

It was always the boast of the Court that the poor and helpless there found redress, and as it protected charities for their relief, so it often admitted bills by them which were otherwise demurrable, as, for instance, if the amount claimed were smaller than the sum, fixed by Bacon at £10, regarded as the lowest the dignity of the Court should allow it to be concerned with[3].

Separate Estate. By the Common Law the property of a married woman is wholly vested in her husband, and consequently she can neither sue nor be sued without him. In Equity however she was, according to the rules ultimately adopted, entitled to hold her 'separate estate,' and deal with it, as a feme sole. During the present period not only was a wife's separate estate protected against her husband, but, in some cases, a married woman was admitted to sue the trustees of it alone, and in her own name, and even to sue her husband[4]. In the reign of Charles I. however, we find her suing strangers in the name of a friend, and it was decided that husband and wife could not sue each other[5].

Separate estate could be created out of the woman's own savings, or by property being given to trustees for her use,

[1] 43 Eliz. c. 4.
[2] Bacon, Ord. 15. Toth. *Charitable Uses*, p. 29.
[3] Monro, p. 108, and see p. 355, a suit for a *shirt and a coif*, and a suit for a *swarm of bees*, dismissed.
[4] Toth. p. 94, *Sanky v. Golding*; Cary, p. 124 (21-2 Eliz.).
[5] *Danby v. Peele*, (13 Car. I.) Toth. p. 96. *Simpson v. Simpson* (3 Car. I.), Toth. p. 97.

and the Court was "clear of opinion, and so declared, that for things in action, or upon a trust, a feme covert might by will dispose of the same without the assent of her husband[1]."

Mortgages. The interests hitherto considered were protected in Equity, although void at law, in pursuance of the intention of their creators, but in the case of mortgages the Court took from the legal owner, not only what the law gave him, but what the express agreement of the parties had provided should be his. Though other forms of mortgage were known, that commonly employed in England at and before this period was an absolute conveyance of the land with a proviso for reconveyance if the money secured were paid by a fixed day and, as in the analogous mortgage of the Roman Law, the "*fiduciæ contractus,*" if the day were not kept the mortgagor's estate became absolutely forfeited, but as Constantine abolished this rule at Rome, so Equity practically destroyed its effect in England. The security of the debt was the main object of the transaction, and if this were attained, if repayment of principal, interest and costs were offered, current morality demanded that the mortgagee should abandon his hold on the land, and this Equity ultimately enforced.

The establishment of the right to redeem dates from the reign of James I. Before that time, and it seems from the time of Edward IV. where the default happened through accident, or if there were any other acknowledged equitable ground, as a collateral agreement that, notwithstanding the forfeiture, the mortgagor might redeem, or if any fraud or practice of the mortgagee prevented payment on the day, the Chancellor gave relief, but in no other case[2]. From 9 James I. onwards, however, cases occurred where redemption was allowed after the day, and in 4 Charles I. there occurred a case of *How v. Vigures* which shows that the right was then settled[3]. The suit was for foreclosure, and from the presence of the allegations as to the Plaintiff's position, and the hardship that the refusal of relief would entail, it seems probable that this is the first case

[1] *Gorge v. Chansey* (15 Car. I.), Rep. in Chy. p. 67.

[2] Spence, I. p. 602, citing *Year Book*, 9 Ed. IV. 25, Cary, p. 1, and cases in the Calendars, ante p. (88).

[3] Toth. p. 132, et seq.; Rep. in Chy. p. 18.

of foreclosure that occurred. A reversion had been mortgaged, and devised by the mortgagee to the Plaintiff, and the day was past. "The Plaintiff, being a merchant, and his livelihood consisting in the returns of money, and the consideration in the said deed of mortgage being £340 disbursed in 18 Jac... upon a dry reversion," the Plaintiff prayed the Chancellor to order repayment of his money, or a sale. The decree was that the Defendant pay the principal "with damages," i.e., interest, or in default the property be adjudged to the Plaintiff to be sold:—"this was *nisi causa*, but none showed."

Eleven years later[1] the Court asserted the right of redemption in very emphatic terms. "The Court will relieve a mortgage to the tenth generation, though the purchaser had no notice, because it is supposed that he cannot purchase, but it must be derived from the mortgage, and (it will also relieve) in some cases where the mortgagee will suddenly bestow unnecessary costs upon the mortgaged lands, of purpose to clogg the lands, to prevent the mortgagor's redemption."

Tothill reports that there were decisions as to whether the executor or heir of the mortgagee was entitled to the mortgage money, but does not state their result, and the point remained to be decided by Lord Nottingham. The Court, however, constantly refused to allow claims on old and forgotten mortgages to be set up, and, as it gave relief against actions at law for old debts "long slept upon," so, within its own jurisdiction, it enforced the maxim "vigilantibus non dormientibus jura subveniunt."

II. *Fraud.* The cases under the second head of Jurisdiction may be summed up more briefly. To give relief against all kinds of fraud had from the first been one of the objects of the Court, and its power of searching the conscience of the defendant, and of decreeing '*restitutio in integrum,*' in place of mere damages ascertained by the rough assessment of a jury, gave to the relief it offered, in many cases, a peculiarly beneficial character. Moreover, fraud was already, as in later times, understood in equity in a far more extensive sense than at law,

[1] *Bacon v. Bacon*, Toth. p. 133 (15 Car. I.).

FRAUD AND ACCIDENT. 145

as the dictum that "in Chancery fraud may be inferred from attendant circumstances; at law it must be proved or be apparent from the intrinsic nature of the transaction[1]," shows. The two Statutes of Elizabeth[2] against fraudulent Conveyances extended the powers of the Common Law Courts to defeat such devices, but recourse continued to be had to the Chancery to set aside settlements in fraud of creditors[3], and to recover property colourably transferred to defeat their claims. The Court declined to interfere in such cases on behalf of the transferor for "fraus non est fallere fallentem," but did so to protect the rights of innocent third persons[4]. The extensive relief offered by equity in modern times in cases of instruments obtained by undue influence, or other unconscientious means, is found foreshadowed in that given in the present period against deeds "gotten by threats and practice," and leases and bonds obtained from "simple" lessors and obligors[5].

Accident. Accident had been an important occasion of the interference of the Court under the Ecclesiastical Chancellors, and it continued to invite that of their successors. Where a copyhold was mortgaged without a surrender[6], a bargain and sale for value not inrolled, a feoffment made without livery, or a penalty incurred through the rising of a river over which the debtor must pass to effect his payment in time, or through similar unavoidable mischance, the Court forbad the enforcement of the legal rights retained or acquired thereby. In the old cases too of lost or unacquitted bonds the relief had become a common form, and when equity expanded its rules in this direction, by staying actions on old and sleeping debts or claims, upon the presumption that they had been paid or discharged, the benefits of limitation were in some measure secured. About the beginning of the 17th century a step further was taken, and where a penalty was incurred by a man's own neglect, if the neglect were trifling and unintended, relief was granted against it. But no trace is yet to be found of the veto after-

[1] Spence, 1, p. 625, citing Tothill.
[2] 13 Eliz. c. 5, 27 Eliz. c. 4.
[3] *Naylor v. Baldwin* (13 Car. I.), Rep. in Chy. 69.
[4] Cary, p. 18.
[5] Toth. p. 170.
[6] Toth. pp. 54, 170; Ch. Cas. p. 106.

K. 10

wards put upon the exaction of penalties wherever compensation could be given[1].

Mistake. Mistakes in the drafting of legal instruments, whereby they were avoided or caused to have an effect other than that intended, were readily corrected by a Court which paid so much regard to intention, and so little to the legal doctrine of estoppel as the Chancery of this age. Instances of it are recorded in the calendars[2], and many occur under Elizabeth and her successors. The following may be taken as an example. A lease was to be made excepting the woods, but the clerk drew the deed so that it made no mention of woods, though it did refer to some exception, and on the lessee commencing to cut, he was enjoined not to do so[3].

Suretyship. The contract of suretyship in the mercantile community of London, during the 15th and the two following centuries, was a very important one, offering as it did, in many cases, the only available security upon which money could be borrowed, and from the earliest time, equity insisted that the surety, who generally enters gratuitously into a dangerous obligation, should be treated by the creditor with the utmost fairness. A case occurred as early as Edward IV. where the Chancellor released a surety because the executor of the creditor had given time to the debtor[4], and similar relief was given, under James I., where the creditor delayed to get paid for many years, the surety not being aware of the continuance of the bond, but thinking that payment had been made[5]. There is a decision recorded in Tothill[6] which seems however to favour the surety to the extent of defeating the very purpose of his contract: "One becoming bound with sureties," says the Reporter, "and afterwards bankrupt, the creditors sued the sureties, because they were remediless as against the bankrupt, yet ordered not to take any advantage." It is difficult to tell precisely to whom the pronouns refer, but it would appear that it was the

[1] *Underwood v. Swan* (1649), Rep. in Chy. p. 85. *Bidlake v. Phillips* (9 Car. 1), Rep. in Chy. 50.
[2] *Astel v. Causton*, 1 Cal. 108 (Ed. IV.).
[3] Toth. p. 131 (37 Eliz.).
[4] Spence, 1, 638 (a).
[5] *Saunders v. Churchill* (10 Jac.), Toth. p. 181.
[6] *Johnson v. Pudicott*, p. 181 (10 Jac. I.).

creditors' claims which were the subject of the injunction. Perhaps the Chancellor in this case proceeded in the high handed manner adopted in another[1] reported by the same authority, where the creditors were ordered to make terms with an insolvent debtor instead of suing his sureties, or perhaps he gave his decision on special grounds to which the report yields no clue.

Cary[2] states that in his day it was usual to allow nothing more than the debt and damages to be taken from the surety, that is to relieve him against the penalty of his bond, and this[3] is said to have been the first step towards the grant of the relief to the mortgagor, of which the development has already been traced. Cary thought the rule very objectionable. Sureties were not only protected against the creditor, but as between themselves, they were compelled to bear the obligation equally. Several cases of contribution among sureties of the reign of Charles I. are reported[4]. This however was an application of a larger principle adopted by the Court, extending to all joint liabilities. "If a man grant a rent-charge out of all his lands and afterwards selleth his lands by parcels to divers persons," writes Cary[5], "and the grantee of the rent will from time to time levy the whole rent upon one of the purchasers only, he shall be eased in the Chancery by a contribution from the rest of the purchasers; and the grantee shall be restrained by order to charge the same upon him only."

III. *Specific Performance.* The more complete relief offered in Chancery for the enforcement of rights recognised at Common Law is illustrated by the grant of specific performance of which many cases occurred before the present period, as we have already seen. To the report of the case in 21 Henry VII. which decided that assumpsit should lie for non-performance of a contract Brooke adds this note[6]: "by this he will get nothing but damages, but by subpœna the Chancery can compel him (the defendant) to convey the estate, or imprison him, *ut*

---

[1] *Mildmay v. Wentworth* (11 Jac.), p. 47.
[2] p. 17 (1601).
[3] Spence, 1, p. 602.
[4] Toth. p. 41.
[5] p. 3.
[6] Cited by Fry, L.J., *Specific Performance*, 2nd ed. p. 9.

dicitur." Coke[1] objected to the grant of specific performance on the ground that it was not contemplated by the parties, the covenantor understanding that it was his election either to lose damages or make a lease, a view of contract which still finds favour in America[2], but the jurisdiction was well established in the time of Elizabeth. The restrictions afterwards imposed upon the grant of this relief are not yet traceable, and it was extended to other cases than those of promises to convey land, for instance, to an agreement to make a licence to use a patent, but causes were sometimes dismissed as "meet for common law[3]."

The enforcement of the performance of obligation was extended beyond those arising out of contract; awards, for example, were frequently decreed to be carried out, and the delivery of chattels in specie to their owner was directed[4].

Accounts. An action of account lay at common law against a guardian, bailiff or receiver, and for one merchant against another, the account being taken before appointed auditors, but Chancery even in these cases gave a more beneficial assistance by its process of discovery, and its permanent administrative officials, the Masters, and it extended relief to all cases where the taking of accounts was necessary to determine mutual rights and obligations. We have already seen that the Masters under Elizabeth were constantly employed in this work, and that special directions were made by the orders of the Court[5] as to how and when accounts were to be taken. The newer relief, as time went on, entirely superseded the elder, even where that could be had, but though account became practically, it never was nominally, an exclusive subject of equity jurisdiction, and it is curious to find that Lord Hardwicke dismissed a cause because it was very much entangled, and the transactions of long standing, preferring rather to leave the plaintiff to his action at law than to direct an account before the Master[6].

[1] *Broniage v. Jennings,* Rolle Rep. 368 (14 Jac. I.), also cited by Fry, L.J.
[2] (See Anson on Contracts, early editions, note to Chap. 1.)
[3] Spence, 1, page 646. *Greville v. Bowker,* Cary, p. 135 (22 Eliz.).
[4] Cary, p. 80 (19 Eliz.) and p. 47, (Phil. and Mary), *Church v. Roper,* Rep. in Chy. p. 75.
[5] Monro '*accounts*' in index. Bacon's orders.
[6] *Sturt v. Mellish,* 2 Atk. 610.

INJUNCTION. 149

The facilities for accounting in Chancery naturally brought questions between partners to that Court for determination also, and, ultimately, partnership law was there exclusively administered.

Partition. Commissions to effect partitions[1], in some cases where none could have been obtained at law, to set out dower[2], and suits to determine boundaries[3], are also found in the present period.

Set-off. The "Set-off" of what was due to the Defendant was of course allowed without difficulty where the defendant had the right to file a cross-bill, or, without one, to have his claims considered in the decree[4].

Bills of Peace. "Bills of Peace[5]" to establish a general right on behalf of, or against numerous claimants or defendants (as commoners, for instance), which the strict rules of the Common Law as to parties made it difficult or impossible to bring as actions, were of frequent occurrence under Elizabeth and her immediate successors, and the analogous "Bill of Interpleader" by a Plaintiff indebted to one of several rival claimants, who brought the debt into Chancery and was thereon protected against any future process on account of its payment, is found as early as the second year of Elizabeth[6].

Injunctions. Injunctions to quiet possession, in some instances founded upon the advice of the judges[7], granted sometimes until trial at law, sometimes until the hearing in Chancery, and sometimes, after the right had been established in one way or the other, in perpetuity, are found in many cases during this period, and they formed one of the matters in contest in the great dispute between the Chancellors and the judges. It was by the aid of the last kind of injunction that the effectiveness of the possessory action of ejectment to decide the title to lands was secured[8].

---

[1] Toth. 155.
[2] *Huddleston v. Lamplough* (5 Car. I.), Rep. in Chy. p. 19.
[3] Cary, p. 107 (21 Eliz.).
[4] Spence, 1, p. 651.
[5] Spence, 1, 656, Cary, p. 30.
[6] Cary, 65.

[7] Monro, pp. 348 (1564), 431 (1575), 506 (1581).
[8] Spence, 1, p. 658 (but the learned author is wrong in supposing its use was suggested by the Chancellors. See the case of the Earl of Oxford stated in Chap. VII. ante).

The grant of injunctions in all cases of threatened wrongs formed one of the chief branches of the Court's business, and, as appeared in the discussion of the bills in the calendars, it dates from the earliest time. The Common Law itself had writs of waste, and writs '*quia timet*,' of a nature similar to the Chancery injunction, but the relief afforded by them was both partial and temporary, and an attempt to extend the powers of preventive relief wielded by the judges, by procuring writs of 'estrepment' returnable in the Common Pleas, was defeated by the Lord Keeper refusing to allow such writs to issue except according to the old course[1], that is to say, in a real action or action of waste pending the suit, or, after judgment (for the recovery of land) pending the execution, to prevent waste of the lands claimed or recovered[2].

Injunctions against waste were granted, not only where the Common Law remedy of writ of waste would, but for some accidental bar, have lain, as for instance, where a second life tenancy followed that vested in the offending party, and therefore no one could claim the inheritance forfeited by the wasting, but even where waste was by law allowed[3]. Thus, among the other illustrations of the restraint imposed by Chancery upon the unconscientious exercise of legal rights, in his judgment in the Earl of Oxford's case[4] Lord Ellesmere adduces this, "In Morgan and Parry's case (Pasch 27 Eliz.) a woman had an estate in a house for her life dispunishable of waste, and yet she was enjoined not to commit waste in the house, contrary to the case of Lewis Bowles." And thus the foundation of the doctrine of equitable waste was laid.

It was found necessary to adopt a rule to prevent applications for injunctions being made the means of oppression, and several orders were made for the purpose of regulating them; thus Sir N. Bacon provided that parties seeking them should give security for the truth of the allegations upon which they were obtained, and his son, Lord Bacon, made the following order on the subject[5]. "Injunctions against felling of timber,

[1] Spence, 1, 672 (Egerton, L. K. 1594).
[2] Fitz N. B. "Estrepment."
[3] Cary, p. 36 (1 Jac.), Toth. p. 188.
[4] 2 W. and T. p. 647.
[5] See Beames' notes to Bac. Ord. 21, 26, 28.

ploughing up of ancient pastures, or for the maintaining of enclosures, or the like, shall be granted according to the circumstances of the case; but not in case where the Defendant upon his answer claimeth an estate of inheritance, except it be where he claimeth the land in trust or on some other special ground."

The grant of writs of '*ne exeat*,' to prevent a debtor from escaping an action at law by absconding from the country, dates from before this period. Lord Bacon's orders provide that in civil cases *ne exeats* may be granted, according to the practice of long time used, in case of interlopers in trade, great bankrupts, in whose estates many subjects are interested, or other cases which concern multitudes of the King's subjects[1].

Discovery. Several points in regard to discovery, the characteristic process of the Court, were decided during this period. The judges, in Finch's[2] case, advised that the Chancellor ought not to retain for purposes of relief suits brought to obtain discovery, and further that, where by his answer the Defendant made title to land, the Plaintiff ought not to be allowed to proceed, but these rulings were not adopted by the Court of Chancery.

The important rule that a Defendant should not be driven by his answer to discover a forfeiture to his hurt was established, but the Court declined to extend the protection to the case where the answer might be to "his prejudice by statute laws[3]." The Court refused to compel Counsel and Solicitors to betray their client's confidence[4].

Direct answers as to the deponent's own acts, in the affirmative or negative, were required, and answers according to his belief in other cases[5]. Though the Defendant was often compelled to amend his answer against his will, he was not allowed, without special leave, to do so for his own purposes, even to state his title more fully, and never after issue joined[6].

[1] Order 89, and see Beames' note.
[2] 4 Inst. p. 85.
[3] Toth. p. 7 (32 Eliz.), p. 12 (4 Car. I.).
[4] Ch. Cas. p. 121.
[5] Toth. p. 8.
[6] Toth. p. 9 (1597), and p. 13 (9 Car. I.).

Infants and femes covertes were compelled, as other people, to answer upon oath[1].

One particular species of discovery, that sought in suits to perpetuate testimony, was the subject of several orders of the Court[2]. Commissioners to take evidence "in perpetuam rei memoriam," according to the orders of Sir N. Bacon, were to be granted to examine only aged and impotent witnesses, and the evidence was to be taken only if the person against whom it was to be used (who was made the Defendant in the writ,) did not show to the Court or *the Commissioners* good ground to the contrary. The Defendant might, if he pleased, join in the commission, and have commissioners appointed to examine upon interrogateries on his behalf. The depositions, when taken, were not to be published, until the evidence became necessary to the Plaintiff, in some trial at which the witnesses, being dead or too old or ill to travel without danger to life, could not attend, and then only the evidence of witnesses originally indicated to the Defendant was to be used, and that only as against him. The orders of Lord Bacon on this subject were to the same effect as those of his father, but they required the bill and answer to be put in before the grant of the commission. Lord Ellesmere greatly disliked suits to perpetuate testimony, regarding the concealment of the evidence given, in most cases, until after the death of the witness, as an encouragement to perjury, and he used to order the Plaintiff to file his bill upon the title and to proceed in common form to the examination of witnesses and publication forthwith[3].

The repression of outrage, which formed so prominent a feature of the Chancellors' jurisdiction in earlier days, ceased during the present period to fall under their care, except so far as it occurred in contempt of the Court itself, as where attacks were made on servers of its process, or in defiance of its injunctions. The records of outrages on process-servers under Elizabeth are extremely numerous[4], but notwithstanding this, and though allowance be made for the establishment and operation of

[1] Toth. pp. 13, 95.
[2] Toth. Appendix, p. 24.
[3] Ch. Cas. p. 9.
[4] Munro *passim*.

the Star Chamber, a comparison of the applications to Chancery in this and the preceding period bears eloquent testimony to the improvement in manners, and the development of civilised order in places where brutal barbarism had previously existed. Perjury cases too were rarely tried in Chancery after the time of Sir N. Bacon[1]. The Court became a purely civil tribunal, although the allegation of combination and confederacy survived as a mark of the more extensive character its jurisdiction once bore, and was found in every bill down to the present century.

[1] Spence, I. 690.

CHAPTER X.

THE ATTEMPTED REFORMS UNDER THE COMMONWEALTH[1].

No sketch of the history of English Equity would be complete without some account of the suggestions which were made for the reform of the procedure and practice of the Court in the time of the Commonwealth. The men who then obtained power and pre-eminence in the State were disabled by no class or caste prejudices for the discovery of the errors of its institutions, and were as determined to remove them as they were industrious in searching them out, and the machinery of government and administration for the first time passed under the scrutiny of intelligent outsiders whose detachment of mind enabled them to unveil abuses, even when their want of technical knowledge prevented the success of their attempts at reconstruction. Little improvement was actually effected at the time in the Chancery, and little of that survived the reactionary influences of the Restoration, but the diseases of the Court were diagnosed, and, to some extent, the nature of the remedies required was pointed out.

It was not now the professors of a rival system who attacked the Chancery. The need of the Court and of the relief it administered were recognised throughout all the Parliamentary proceedings for its reform. It was not the jurisdiction of the Court, but its procedure and practice, and the behaviour of its officials, and especially of those in important places, and the organisation of its offices that the reformers essayed to change.

[1] See generally on this subject Chap. VIII. of Parkes' *History of the Court of Chancery*.

The business of the Court had become very great. Lord Bacon in a letter to Parliament written in deprecation of the attacks upon him[1], estimated the number of orders he made at 2000 a year, and, in 1621, Coke stated the number of pending causes to be 35,000, and though this was probably an exaggeration, the number given by his opponent in debate, 16,000, is unlikely to have been overestimated[2]. "It was confidently affirmed by knowing gentlemen of worth that there were depending in that Court 23,000 causes," wrote a defender of "Barebones" Parliament; and Whitelocke, when objecting to his appointment as Commissioner, said that "the business of the Chancery is certainly more than of any other Court, the trouble must needs be greater, and the burden the heavier, too heavy for me to bear[3]."

Great increase of business.

This great accumulation of business was due in part to the extraordinary dilatoriness of the Court's procedure, to which reference has already been made in sketching its rules, and to the weakness of the coercion applied to a defaulting party, but much was due to the inefficiency of the judges, and more to the misbehaviour of the subordinate judges,—the masters,—and the other officials of the Court. Arrears had always existed from the time of More to that of Bacon, and though Bacon cleared them off, his successor left a new accumulation of 500 causes. Lord Coventry made an attempt to cope with the mass of work by directing that six instead of four causes should be put in the paper each day for hearing, but the frequent re-hearings, fresh arguments and references for the judges' assistance to be had, which he allowed to a greater extent even than his predecessors, had greatly magnified the evils already existing. The Court, without extending its sittings, could hardly have properly disposed of all the cases before it, had it worked its best, but when it delayed its decree till the arguments had been repeated a second and perhaps a third time, and after the decree was at last pronounced, reversed it on bill of review, and when on interlocutory applications finality was thrown to the winds and "what was

Abuses in Chancery.

---

[1] Camp. 2, p. 386.
[2] C. P. Cooper, *Proceedings in Parliament*, p. 103.
[3] Parkes, pp. 120, 130.

ordered one day was contradicted the next, so as in some cases there had been five hundred orders and faire more as some affirmed[1]," not only did causes drag on for years, but the cost and uncertainty made the offer of relief a mere mockery of the suitors. The appointment of the numerous officials who had found a home about the Court had been in some cases granted to private persons, by patent, but generally it lay with the Chancellor or the Master of the Rolls. The officials were paid by fees which had grown to be exorbitant, and were the less willingly paid because in many cases they were exacted as the price of work which was unnecessary, or could have been done by the suitor's own solicitor, and which was in fact done by underclerks who received but a small modicum of the price so paid. No reform or redress could however be obtained from the Chancellor or the Master of the Rolls, for they openly sold the appointments which conferred the right to make these exactions, and to have interfered with them would have diminished their own returns. Officials who farmed their offices for profit were little likely to be conscientious in the discharge of such duties as they had to perform, and it is not surprising that 'expedition money' for the advancement of causes referred to the masters, and other bribes were given and received, or that the underclerks increased their slender share of the nominal fees, at times, by embezzling the moneys paid to them, thus further delaying the progress of the cause. Well might a pamphleteer complain that "This Court of Chancery which was so anciently famous, and erected to so good an end, (was) like to become a mere monopolie to cozen the subjects of their monies[2]."

The Commons, in 1649, appointed Whitelocke and Keble Commissioners of the new seal, which they had made after the flight of the Lord Chancellor to the King, and the Commissioners and Lenthal, the Master of the Rolls, at once published a collection of orders for the regulation of Chancery proceedings, pending the further reforms then under their consideration. The orders are almost wholly made up of selections from Lord Bacon's and Lord Coventry's

The orders of 1649.

[1] "*An exact relation,* &c." 1654, Parkes, p. 129. [2] Parkes, p. 141.

codes, but a few additions appear, amongst them a direction that demurrers and pleas shall be put in by counsel instead of, as formerly, by the Defendant in person, thus in many cases saving the trouble and expense of a commission and answer. The orders also direct that causes should be set down in the order of their publications and so heard, and they attempt to meet the complaints of expense and of unnecessary pleadings by fixing rates of costs, and allowing costs on demurrers and pleas[1].

Next year Parliament took up the question of law reform, and after resolving, as matter which needed no enquiry, that legal proceedings and records ought to be written in English in ordinary writing, referred the consideration of fees and salaries of judges and officers, and of delays and unnecessary charges at law to a powerful committee to which the Commissioners, Law Officers and other Gentlemen of the Long Robe were directed to give constant attendance[2]. The committee's report suggested many legal improvements, amongst others the abolition of fines and recoveries, and the substitution for them of an inrolled deed, and the abolition of arrest on mesne process, but none affecting the Chancery. After the dismissal of the Rump the new Parliament (Barebones' Parliament,) which Cromwell summoned returned to the consideration of law reform, especially with reference to the Chancery. In August 1653 a great debate on the subject, lasting over two days, took place, and two papers were circulated for the information of members, which had been evidently prepared by someone who was fully acquainted with the Court and its abuses. The first[3] is entitled "Observations concerning the Court of Chancery." It dwelt on the evils occasioned by the delegation of their proper work by the Six Clerks, Register and Examiners, contrasting existing evils with the lack of them at a former, perhaps imaginary, time, when "the Labourer receiving his full wages, the business was well and soon dispatched, and the Records well kept," noting especially the delays of the Masters' office, and the 'expedition money' and unjust rewards paid to avoid them; the uselessness of the subpœna and affidavit

Proceedings in Parliament.

---

[1] These orders are printed in the appendix to Beames.
[2] Parkes, pp. 134—6.
[3] Parkes, p. 149.

offices, retained only because made monopolies in King James' time; the sale of offices by the Masters of the Rolls; the difficulty and cost of compelling an obstinate Defendant to make a sufficient answer,—"so that sometimes Defendants cannot be compelled to make perfect answers in two or three years,"—and the analogous abuse occasioned by the wilful delays of Plaintiff in vexatious suits; the inconveniences "at and after the hearing of causes, more prejudicial to the Clients than the former;" rehearings five or six deep; orders so ambiguous that the Register could draw what he pleased; needless references to the Masters; and, lastly, the difficulty after the decree was pronounced of obtaining the fruits of it.

The other paper[1] contained proposals " for the regulation or taking away of the Court of Chancery, and settling the business of Equity according to the original and primitive constitution of it; and for taking away all unnecessary fees, offices and officers and formalities now used, and for the speedy dispatch of business." The proposals comprise : " That the Court as it is now used or rather abused be wholly taken away, and some of the most able and honest men " be appointed to hear and determine all causes of equity, and be empowered to put their decrees into execution as judgments at law were, for, said the author, " as long as the Bar is more able than the Bench, as of late it hath been, the business of the Court can never be well despatched"; that, instead of the Six Clerks, Chief Register and two Examiners, "a sufficient number of godly, able, honest and experienced clerks, which be working attorneys and clerks and not overseeing officers," be appointed, and two chief clerks be elected by the attornies from their number to advise the Court on points of practice; that a certain number of godly and able men be appointed, instead of the Masters, to take oaths, and hear and determine in their order all matters of account &c. referred to them by the Court; and that bills·be perused and allowed before they be filed. It was also proposed that rules of practice be framed, and this sanguine hope is expressed, "it is not to be doubted but such rules of practice may be framed as that no cause shall depend above a year (but generally

[1] Parkes, p. 153.

not so long) before it be ready for hearing, and the whole charge of the Proceedings not to exceed ordinarily above 40 or 50s." The immediate result of the two days' debate was a resolution that "The High Court of Chancery of England shall be forthwith taken away, and that a bill be brought in for that purpose." This resolution has called down much ridicule upon the Parliament that agreed to it, but it is plain from these papers and the subsequent proceedings that merely destructive work, and certainly the total abolition of the more important part of the civil judicature of the country, was not intended. The suggestions made in this proposal, amount to little more than that the old judges and officials be removed, and new and better ones be found and put in their places, but the scheme of the bill adopted by Parliament, after the rejection of three others which were considered insufficiently drastic, was far more thorough-going.

The provisions of the bill[1] provide for the appointment of a single chief-clerk to issue process, commissions &c., with working under-clerks, and they substitute for the subpœna an open summons with the bill annexed. *The Bill touching the Chancery.* Appearance is compelled by fine and attachment, and default to file a good answer is met by the like process, committal following at once on a second insufficient answer, and, if the default be persisted in, the bill to be taken as confessed. Any justice of the peace is to have power to take answers and affidavits, and send them up, under seal, to the Chief Clerk. Demurrers and pleas in term time are to be determined on within fourteen days, and to be decided without a second hearing, and, if over-ruled, to subject the Defendant to a fine and payment of the Plaintiff's costs. Six Masters, appointed by Parliament, are to decide in turn all references, three of them sitting every day, and finishing one cause before beginning another, and causes, both before them and before the Court, are to be entered in cause books and, under heavy penalties, to be taken by the Masters and judges respectively in their turn. Commissions to take evidence are to be returned within 60 days, and, if there be none, the witnesses are to be examined in Court, and witnesses who

[1] Parkes' Appendix.

cannot be examined within the time fixed for the return are to be produced, and, if necessary compelled to attend, to give evidence at the hearing. Interlocutory stays of proceedings at law on bills of exchange between merchants, and stays of execution upon judgments (without written defeazance) are to be abolished, and no stay of proceedings at law is to go in any case except upon equity confessed in the answer, or where the party stayed is in contempt for refusal to answer.

The bill further provided that a Plaintiff, if dismissed as against any Defendant, should pay him full costs, and conversely, that a Defendant who had unsuccessfully defended a suit should also pay full costs, the unsuccessful parties being also fined. The decree of the Court was to be stringently enforced. If the Defendant did not obey it within eight days he was to be attached, and, if it were for the payment of money, execution upon his lands and goods might be levied as upon a judgment at law, all the cumbersome and expensive extravagances of "attachment with proclamations" and "commission of rebellion" being superseded.

Lastly, a table of fees much lower than the fees in use, and indeed ridiculously small, which should be paid to the officials, and (for drafting pleadings) to the parties' attorneys and counsel, was appended to the bill.

The substantive alterations proposed were, that no suit on any allegation of a trust or agreement not in writing should be entertained; that the redemption of a mortgage should be only allowed within a year from the entry of the mortgagee after condition broken, and that then double damages (interest) should be paid, and the mortgagee should be responsible only for net profits actually made by him when in possession; and that on relief against a penalty or forfeiture at Common Law, except where the default occurred without negligence, or the party relieved was an infant, double damages should be paid.

The bill never became an act, for Parliament resigned its power into Cromwell's hands, but several of its provisions were carried out in a code of ordinances which Cromwell had drawn up in 1654, and which he directed the Commissioners to put into force. The Com-

Cromwell's ordinances of 1654.

missioners, except Lisle, however, refused to obey, and stated in writing detailed objections[1] to the ordinances which had been drafted without reference to them or to the Master of the Rolls, and on their persisting in this refusal they were removed, and Lisle and Colonel Fiennes were appointed in their place, to put the ordinances into operation, and to administer equity,—of which, in the technical sense, they knew nothing.

Many of the objections of the Commissioners to the new orders are practical and just, and they make throughout a great show of care that the profits of counsel and solicitors should not be increased at the suitor's expense, but some of them are so captious as to suggest that, in their dislike to the imposition upon them of rules drawn by outside, and, probably, unprofessional hands, they were eager, rather to find the orders unworkable, than to adopt the spirit of the intended reformation.

The principle upon which the ordinances are framed is a thorough distrust of the persons who would have to enforce them, and the device adopted to prevent a recurrence of the old abuses of delay and expense is the creation of a rigid unbending rule. A plaintiff, say the orders, is to file his bill, and give security for costs before taking out the first process of the suit, which is to be an open subpœna in which he may insert the names of what defendants he pleases. If a defendant will not appear, or if, after appearing, he do not make a sufficient answer within eight days from a rule directing him to do so, he shall be attached, and, in seeking him, the bailiffs, who are to execute the attachment, may break open doors and renew the search as often as need be. Instead of commissions being necessary, Masters Extraordinary are to be appointed to take answers in the country. The granting of injunctions is restrained. Six Masters are to be appointed by the Protector, of whom three are to sit publicly every day so long as any references remain to be decided, but all differences on points of practice are to be determined by the chief clerks appointed, as in the bill of Barebones' Parliament, to superintend the procedure of suits and the formal business of the Court. Finally, and these orders are typical of the whole,

[1] Parkes, Appendix.

all causes are to be heard in the order in which they have been published, and every cause on the same day on which it is set down for hearing, and, for this purpose, the commissioners are to sit, if need be, in the afternoon, except on Saturdays. To the last orders the Commissioners objected that power to advance urgent causes was absolutely necessary, and that it would often be impossible to hear a cause on the day for which it was set down, "for causes for equity depend upon so many circumstances in cases of frauds and trusts that three or four days is not sometimes sufficient for the orderly hearing of one cause; and the sitting of the Commissioners upon the rolls' days cannot consist by reason of councel and sollicitours, who cannot do their duty at both places." The last objection has reference to the practice, already mentioned, by which the Master of the Rolls sat only when the Chancellor or Commission was not sitting, which made the two judges little more effective for the dispatch of business than either would have been alone. The practice continued to the present century, and this very objection was used by Lord Eldon as an argument against the appointment of a Vice-Chancellor. The attempt to put the Court into fetters failed, and after a couple of years the ordinance lapsed, and thereupon great confusion was occasioned by the return of the officials who had been dispossessed by them, and whose ejectment from their 'freeholds' had been another of the Commissioners' objections.

No doubt the orders were unworkable if literally followed, as it was the evident intention of their makers they should be. The means and method of a successful reform of an elaborate and complex institution must always be devised by the experience of those who are trained in its actual working and acquainted with its history, though the need for reform be usually apparent only to those who, standing outside, have not become so accustomed to its abuses as to regard them, even where their effects are plainly noxious, as the necessary incidents of its operation. The misfortune of the Commonwealth reformers was that the whole body of lawyers, whose profits were threatened, and whose calling was ignorantly and unjustly attacked by some of the reforming party, was united against them. Had the Court been once successfully reformed, and set into satisfactory working, and, as Cromwell himself said[1], had people once perceived at how cheap a rate property could be preserved, they would never have permitted themselves to be so cheated and abused again as they then were. The reactions of the Restoration would have threatened the reforms in vain.

Nothing was done. The Rump returned, and new discussions took place upon the crying evils of the Chancery, and pamphlets were published in attack and defence. But the Restoration put back the expelled officials, and restored, in the main, subject to some improvements adopted by Lord Clarendon's orders from the suggestions made in the course of the proceedings of which a sketch has just been given, the old procedure and practice. Yet the labours of the Reformers were of great value. The disorders were made public and their causes investigated: it was found they were more due to the working than to the machinery, and chiefly to the spirit in which the orders of the Court were administered, and to the license allowed in contempt of its process, and these were changed. Unjust judges presided again, and rank maladministration invaded the offices, but, for the most part, from this time onwards matters improved, until the business of the Court outgrew its powers, and the development of its jurisprudence, and of that of the rival forum, and the increasing implications of the two called for the reforms effected during the present century.

[1] Parkes, p. 165.

CHAPTER XI.

THE COURT OF CHANCERY FROM THE RESTORATION TO THE
RETIREMENT OF LORD ELDON.

THE restoration of the Stuarts put an end to the hopes of an extensive reform of the Court of Chancery which the labours and deliberations of the Commonwealth Parliaments had excited. The light which had been thrown upon the old abuses, however, made it quite impossible to set them up again without an attempt at improvement, or to start the Court exactly at the point where the outbreak of the Rebellion had found it, and the first proceeding of Lord Clarendon, who was the new Chancellor, was to publish a fresh edition of the orders of the Cromwellian Commissioners, for the regulation of the practice of the Court, of which some account has already been given[1]. Extremely little alteration was made in the original code, and the most important of the new provisions made, that no com-
<small>Clarendon's orders.</small> mission to examine witnesses in London or within 10 miles of it should be allowed without special order; that decrees should be inrolled on the first day of the Michaelmas or Easter term next after they were pronounced; and that no exceptions to a Master's report should be heard until 40s. had been deposited as security for costs, were alterations for the public benefit; while one only, forbidding Masters Extraordinary to take affidavits within 20 miles of London, was directed to the preservation of official privileges. Clarendon's orders remained the ruling orders of the Court throughout the

[1] Ante, p. (157). It will be remembered that these orders were, in a great measure, taken from those of Bacon and Coventry. Beames, p. 165.

whole of the period under consideration, for, though a few orders in particular points of practice were made from time to time, and one or two important lists of fees were issued, no fresh code was drawn up, and no fundamental alteration of the practice was introduced.

During the Commonwealth the incidents of feudal tenure had fallen into oblivion, and on the Restoration it was found impossible to restore them, and the Restoration Parliament in its first year passed an Act "for taking away the Court of Ward and Liveries, and Tenures in capite and by Knight's Service, and Purveyance, and for settling a Revenue upon his Majesty in lieu thereof[1]": the revenue, which was to replace that so vexatiously exacted from the tenants in capite, was with characteristic injustice raised by an excise of general incidence upon beer, spirits and wine.

This Act marks the introduction of the system of real property law which lasted down to the abolition of Fines and Recoveries and the associated reforms of the first half of the present century. The extremely complicated and artificial devices adopted in conveyancing and settlement, of which one main object was the strict preservation of landed property in the hands of the same families, was introduced about this time; the invention of trustees to preserve contingent remainders, upon which the security of these interests and the whole superstructure of strict settlement depended, being due to Sir Orlando Bridgman, a conveyancer of great repute during the Commonwealth, and Lord Keeper for a few years after Clarendon's fall[2]. The numerous questions raised by the new methods of conveyancing and settlement naturally found their way into that Court where alone trusts, with which they were much involved, were recognised, and where alone the redemption of mortgages and the specific performance of contracts could be enforced, and the abolition of the Court of Wards ultimately threw the guardianship of the estates of infants wholly upon the same Court.

Development of real property law.

[1] 12 Car. II. c. 24.
[2] See Lord Hardwicke's judgment in *Garth v. Cotton*, 1 W. and T. 806, and Lord Nottingham's in the *Duke of Norfolk's* case, 3 Chy. Cases, 14.

Another circumstance moreover began to operate powerfully upon the nature of the work of the Chancery. The discussions of the Commonwealth, and the liberalising of public opinion to which the Rebellion itself was chiefly due, had not been without effect upon the Courts of law, and a steady, though at first slow, amelioration of their practice and doctrines commenced, which made the necessity of the interference of the Chancellor, save in the cases where an avowed divergence between the common law and equity existed, rarer and rarer, at least this was the Chancellor's view. The introduction in the reign of Charles II. of new trials with reference to the nature of the evidence upon which verdicts had been obtained[1], for instance, enabled a remedy to be found without recourse to Equity in cases like that which brought to a crisis the great dispute between Coke and Ellesmere. "The judges who have presided in Chancery since the Revolution," wrote Lord Hardwicke in his celebrated letter to Lord Kames[2], "have for the most part endeavoured with much anxiety to preserve the boundaries of common law and equity from being confounded; and have sent forth their injunctions to stop the course of the common law with a cautious and sparing hand. But new discoveries and inventions in commerce have given birth to new species of contracts, and these have been followed by new contrivances to break and elude them, for which the ancient simplicity of the common law had adopted no remedies; and from this cause, Courts of Equity, which admit of a greater latitude, have, under the head *adjuvandi vel supplendi juris civilis*, been obliged to accommodate the wants of mankind." And he added, "Another source of the increase of business in Courts of Equity has been the multiplication and extension of trusts. New methods of settling and encumbering land property have been suggested by the necessities, extravagance or real occasions of mankind. But what is more than this, new species of property have been introduced, particularly by the establishment of the public funds, and various transferable stocks, that required to be modified and settled

Improvement in the law.

Development of Equity.

[1] Spence, 1, p. 699.   [2] Printed in the appendix to Parkes. It was written in 1759.

to answer the exigencies of families, to which the rules and methods of conveyancing provided by the common law would not ply or bend. Here the liberality of Courts of Equity has been forced to step in and lend her aid."

The result of these alterations was that the equitable jurisdiction became chiefly concerned with the adjudication and administration of proprietary rights, and while at the commencement of the present period it was fairly enough said that "the grand reason for the interference of a Court of Equity is the imperfections of the legal remedy in consequence of the universality of legislative provisions," at its close the rules of equity had become no less universal than those of common law, and the characteristic features of the Court had come to be the elaborate decree, balancing and declaring the rights *inter se* of numerous parties, the enquiry in the Master's Chambers, and the summary injunction to stay a threatened wrong. Equity when Lord Eldon retired was no longer a system corrective of the common law: it could be described only as that part of remedial justice which is administered in Chancery, while, taken generally, its work was administrative and protective, in contrast with that of the Common Law, which was remedial and retributive[1].

An innovation of great importance occurred soon after the Restoration, in the establishment of the right of appeal from the Chancellor to the House of Lords. *Appeals to the House of Lords.*

Until the reign of James I. no trace of any regular appeal to the House of Lords in suits in equity, or indeed in any suits or actions, is to be found[2], though, of course, in earlier times there were petitions to Parliament of which many instances have been given in the preceding pages[3]. In that reign a Committee of the House reported that there was no precedent for the exercise of jurisdiction by the Lords over decrees in equity except under the authority of some writ,

---

[1] Story, Chap. 1. Warren, *Law Studies*, ed. 1863, p. 582.

[2] C. P. Cooper, *Proceedings in Parliament*, &c. chap. x. Blackstone iii. p. 455.

[3] The majority of the petitions were addressed to the Lords of Parliament, and the judicial work they gave rise to was, in early time without question, and during the later middle ages with only an occasional protest, assigned to them. See Stubbs, *Const. Hist.* III. p. 485.

commission, indorsement of petition or other act proceeding from the Crown, and, in fact, several petitions by way of appeal had been made directly to Elizabeth and had been by her referred to the judges, according to whose decision the Chancellor had sustained, reversed or modified his decree[1]. Cromwell had vested an appellate jurisdiction over the Chancery in the Lord Chancellor or Lord Keeper and six of the judges, but his ordinance had not been revived. The House of Lords in the Convention Parliament, in spite of the absence of precedent and the adverse report cited above, claimed not only an appellate, but also an original jurisdiction in equity, and a hot dispute arose between the Houses in consequence, and was continued in the succeeding Parliament. Finally the Lords' claim to original jurisdiction was dropped, but during the Long Parliament of Charles II., notwithstanding a resolution of the Commons, that "any person solliciting, pleading or prosecuting any appeal against any commoner of England before the House of Lords, shall be deemed and taken a betrayer of the rights and liberties of the people of England, and shall be proceeded against accordingly," the appellate jurisdiction on simple petition was fully established[2], and Lord Nottingham, in delivering judgment in the *Duke of Norfolk's case*[3] in 1682, found comfort, among the difficulties it presented, in the reflection that, if he were wrong, the House of Lords would overrule his decision. In fact, his decision, reversed on bill of review by his successor, Lord Guilford, was restored by the House on appeal. Until the present century but few appeals were taken to the Lords, partly because of the exhaustion of the parties in the Court below, partly because all the advantage of a fresh argument could generally be obtained on a rehearing there, but chiefly, no doubt, because the Lord Chancellor himself presiding in the Lords was little likely to reverse his own previous deliberate decision.

In the century and a half which elapsed between the Restoration and the retirement of Lord Eldon, twenty-two

[1] 4 Co. *Inst.* p. 85.
[2] That is as regards final appeals: the jurisdiction to hear interlocutory appeals was not settled until 1726. C. P. Cooper, p. 161.
[3] 3 Ch. Ca. p. 1.

Lord Chancellors and Lord Keepers presided in Chancery, which gives an average tenure of office, after making allowance for the frequent occasions when the seals were in commission, of about seven years to each. The periods for which they sat were however of very various lengths, thus Lord Eldon sat twenty-five years, Lord Hardwicke twenty, Lord Thurlow fifteen, and Lords Nottingham, Cowper and Henley about ten years each, so that from time to time the changes were very rapid. Taking into consideration the political character of the appointments, for, though Lord Hardwicke and Lord Eldon alone were great ministers, and neither of them was in the first place, the Chancellorship had become a distinctly political office, one is struck by the excellence of the majority of them. A Shaftesbury might be given the seals for an immediate political purpose, a Jefferies as a reward for notorious services, or a Wright, a King, a Bathurst, or an Erskine might be appointed, in spite of his ignorance of equity, to suit party exigencies, but such appointments were rare, and in no case were they followed by a long tenure of office, and for much the greater part of this period of development and consolidation the Court of Equity was presided over by judges whose reputations have been established, not only by the writings of their biographers, but by the impartial records of their reported judgments.

_{The Chancellors.}

Lord Clarendon it is said never made an order without the assistance of some of the judges, and both he and his successor Lord Keeper Bridgman, who lost in the Chancery the greater part of the reputation he had gained at the bar and as a Common Law judge, were often assisted by the skill and learning of Hale, the Chief Baron of the Exchequer.

Lord Nottingham, who was made Lord Keeper in 1673, was of a different character, and the following extract from Blackstone embodies the traditional estimate of his work in Equity. He was, says Blackstone, "endued with a pervading genius, that enabled him to discover and pursue the true spirit of justice, notwithstanding the embarrassments, raised by the narrow and technical notions which then prevailed in the courts of law, and the imperfect

_{Lord Nottingham,1673—1682.}

ideas of redress which had possessed the courts of equity. The reason and necessities of mankind arising from the great change in property, by the extension of trade and the abolition of military tenures, co-operated in establishing his plan, and enabled him in the course of nine years to build a system of jurisprudence and jurisdiction upon wide and rational foundations"; and it is to him that the settlement of the principles of equity with regard to trusts is generally, and, it would seem from such of his decisions as remain, correctly attributed[1]. The extent and importance of his work will be more fully seen in discussing in a later chapter the growth of the leading doctrines of equity. His attitude towards the common law courts is well shown by his declaration when a case came into equity for discovery that "when this Court can determine the matter, that shall not be a handmaid to other Courts, nor beget a suit to be ended elsewhere[2]." He is described by the eulogist of his successor[3] as a formalist and a hair-splitter, but the reports of his judgments, meagre and unsatisfactory as most of them are, suffice to contradict this calumny. In the great case of the Duke of Norfolk he expressed the greatest anxiety to decide on principles which "might stand with the reason of mankind when debated abroad," and in another case he censured counsel for adopting arguments which seemed contrary to natural justice. It is clear that he understood the province of equity as Cicero and Grotius, whose writings he sometimes quoted in his judgments, did, as conversant "de hisce rebus, quas lex non exacte definit, sed arbitrio viri boni permittit," but he laid the seeds of a system of definite rules which ultimately made the discretion a fiction, and he himself declared, that with such a conscience as is only *naturalis et interna* his court had nothing to do, but only with that which is *civilis et politica*[4].

During Lord Nottingham's period of office, and partly in consequence of his advice, the Statute of Frauds[5] was passed. Its main provisions are directed against the enforcement of

[1] *Burgess v. Wheate*, 1 Eden, p. 223, Lord Mansfield.
[2] *Parker v. Dee*, 2 Cha. Ca. 200.
[3] North's Life of Guilford quoted in
Parkes, p. 212.
[4] *Cook v. Fountain*, 3 Swan, 600, Spence, 1, p. 417.
[5] 29 Car. II. c. 3.

verbal contracts, the validity of verbal conveyances of interests in land, the creation of trusts of lands without writing, and the allowance of nuncupative wills. It also made equitable interests in lands subject to the owner's debts to the same extent as legal interests were. The statute carried into legislative effect principles which had, so far back as the time of Bacon's orders[1], been approved by the Court of Chancery, and by its operation in the common law courts it must often have obviated the necessity for equitable interference. In modern times it has not infrequently been decried, especially so far as it restricts the verbal proof of contracts, but in estimating its value and operation at the time it became law it must be remembered that the evidence of the parties to an action at law could not then be received, and the Defendant might have been charged upon the uncorroborated statement of a single witness which he was not allowed to contradict, as Lord Eldon argued many years afterwards, when the action upon the case for fraud was introduced at law[2]. It was therefore a most reasonable precaution, while this unreasonable rule continued, to lay down that the Defendant should be charged only upon writing signed by him.

Lord Nottingham was succeeded by Lord Guilford, late the Chief Justice of the Common Pleas, who presided in Chancery with ability, and endeavoured to cope with the evils of its practice, of which complaints had again become loud, by restraining the numerous motions for advancing or delaying the hearing of causes, by checking the "trade in places in the cause list" which had arisen in the offices, and by setting his face against rehearings, which, in spite of Lord Bacon's orders, had become a great abuse[3]. In spite of his efforts, however, and of successive orders after this time, of which the most important was one of 1700, requiring a deposit of £50 on a petition for rehearing, judgments were frequently and repeatedly reopened in this way down to the long Chancellorship of Lord Hardwicke.

Lord Jefferies followed Lord Guilford, and then, after the

[1] O. (15).
[2] *Pasley v. Freeman*, 1 Smith L. C.
Evans v. Bicknell, 6 Ves. 173.
[3] Parkes, p. 222, Camp. III. p. 469.

Revolution, the seals were for a time in commission, and a plan was considered for leaving them permanently so, because the increase of the work of Equity was thought to be so great that no single judge, even with the assistance of the Master of the Rolls, could cope with it. The experiment was not however a success, and Lord Somers was made chancellor.

During his chancellorship a bill for the regulation of Chancery procedure was introduced into Parliament, but nothing came of it. Parliament had on several occasions since the Restoration in a rather spasmodic manner turned its attention to the Court. In 1661 an Act had been passed to regulate the fees of the Masters, but they paid no attention to it, and it was a dead letter. In 1666 the House of Commons had resolved that the interference of Equity in Common Law matters was grievous to the subject, but the Chancellors began to restrict such interferences, and no action was taken on the resolution. Now, however, in 1695, a determined attempt was made by Sir Robert Atkyns, a retired judge, to take away the supremacy which the Court of Equity had established, and to restore the old common law rules. He published[1], " An Enquiry into the Jurisdiction of the Court of Chancery in causes of Equity," in which he complained of the uncertainty of equitable decisions, and also of the expense and delay of foreclosing mortgages, and suggested that the common law courts should restrain equitable interferences with their jurisdictions by writ of prohibition. In 1699 he presented to the House of Commons a petition against the increasing jurisdiction of the Court of Equity, which, he says, he had observed, in the several public employments he had held, was every day more and more invading the common law, 'the birthright of every Englishman.' Nothing, however, came of his efforts, and the Court of Chancery remained untrammelled by any effective restriction upon its equitable jurisdiction. The incident is important on account of the high reputation of the petitioner and his late judicial dignity, and, moreover, it serves to show how thoroughly the supremacy of Equity was established, and how apparent the growth of its jurisdiction was.

[1] Parkes, p. 260.

After he had been dismissed from the Chancellorship Lord Somers, in 1706, introduced a bill into Parliament, which, as the statute 4 and 5 Anne, c. 16, became the most important act of law reform which the 18th century produced, or which had been passed since the great statute of Jeofails of Elizabeth.

Most of the provisions of the Act relate to improvements of the Common Law, and by some of these the need for equitable interference was removed. Thus it was provided, that performance of the condition after the day, or otherwise not strictly according to the condition, might be pleaded to an action on a money bond, or the sum due with interest and costs might be brought into Court in satisfaction, and that an action of account might be brought against the executor or administrator of a guardian, bailiff or receiver, or by one joint tenant or tenant in common, or his executor or administrator against another, or his executor or administrator. The Act provided also that no subpœna should be issued in Equity until the bill was filed, except for an injunction to stay waste or to stay an action already commenced at law,—a point upon which there had been many variations of practice,—and that a plaintiff in Equity should no longer be at liberty to dismiss his bill on payment of nominal costs, but should pay full costs,—a rule which had already been introduced by Lord Chancellor Jefferies.

Law reform, 4 and 5 Anne, c. 16.

Lord Somers had proposed[1] to provide further that the common law courts should have power to admit evidence taken *de bene esse* before the trial where the witness, from absence beyond the seas, or illness, could not appear, but this the Commons refused to agree to. They pointed out the great superiority of *viva voce* evidence given at the hearing over that given on depositions, and, while admitting that evidence of the latter kind was already received in the cases suggested by the bill, they urged that the admission of such evidence should be as little encouraged as might be:—that is, they insisted that the costs of a suit for discovery in Equity should be a condition precedent to its use. Other suggestions, that bills should be taken *pro confesso* for want of appearance; to shorten decrees

[1] Parkes, p. 271. Camp. IV. p. 197.

by the omission of recitals; and to make debts and similar property available for judgment creditors: reforms of the utmost utility, the Commons rejected in an even more summary manner. Numerous petitions from officials of the Courts had been presented against the bill, and it is impossible to doubt that the true reason of the Commons' alterations was that suggested by Bishop Burnet[1]. "Several clauses, however beneficial to the subject, which touched on their (i.e. the under officials, clerks and attornies') profit were left out by the Commons."

Some of the credit of this statute must probably be given to Lord Cowper, who was Chancellor when the House of Lords approved and supported it. He was an upright and conscientious judge, and for the first time he, as Chancellor, refused to receive the new year's gifts, which it had become customary for the officials, and even the counsel of his Court, to present. His delicacy in this respect contrasted strongly with the conduct of his successor Lord Macclesfield, who, after being Chancellor for seven years, was impeached and convicted, in 1725, of trafficking, and conniving at trafficking by the Masters and others, with the suitors' money, and of making irregular orders[2]. Lord Macclesfield undoubtedly fell a victim to the improvement of public morality which no longer suffered the open sale of high offices, such as the Masterships.

Lord Macclesfield, 1718—1725.

The growth of the business of the Court is shown by the statement, made in the discussion on the impeachment, that every estate in England passed through Chancery, on an average, once every thirty years, and by the evidence given that the price of a Mastership had increased since the Revolution from £1000 to £6000, a chief part of the emolument of the office down to this time arising from the employment of the suitors' funds deposited with the Master.

The immediate results of this scandal were the promulgation of an order, endorsed by Act of Parliament, directing that all suitors' money in Court should be paid into the Bank of England instead of remaining in the hands of the usher or the Masters as hitherto, and the creation of the Accountant-General's office.

[1] Quoted in Parkes, p. 279.   [2] Parkes, p. 294. Camp. IV. p. 539.

Lord Macclesfield in spite of his faults had been a wise and careful judge, and in his short Chancellorship of seven years several cases of great importance were decided with regard to the doctrines of fraud, specific performance, relief against penalties, and the guardianship of infants[1].

The seals were next successively in the hands of King, a common law lawyer, who knew no equity and before whom, it is said, causes were equitably arranged by the candour of the leaders of the Chancery Bar, the future Chancellors Yorke and Talbot, and Talbot, who died of overwork, as his biographer alleges, in his anxiety to cope with the business of the Court. And in 1736, Lord Hardwicke (Phillip Yorke), who bears of all the judges who have ever sat in the Court the greatest reputation for learning and ability, was made Lord Chancellor.

It was under Hardwicke that the full development of the jurisdiction of Equity was attained, not, of course, by the full working out of its principles, nor even by the limitation and definition of its doctrines, for in both of these directions much work was done by his successors, and especially by Lord Thurlow and Lord Eldon, but during the twenty years he presided in the Court most of the great branches of the jurisdiction were fairly mapped out, and not only is authority on most of the important questions of equity to be found in the pages of his reporters, Atkyns and Vesey (Senior), but this authority was that chiefly relied on and regularly cited until after Lord Eldon's time. *Lord Hardwicke, 1736—1756.*

His letter to Lord Kames, referred to on a preceding page[2], which he wrote after he had resigned the Chancellorship, gives us his view of the important question how far equity remained discretionary in his time. "Some general rules there ought to be, for otherwise the great inconvenience of *Jus vagum et incertum* will follow; but yet the Prætor must not be so absolutely and invariably bound by them, as the judges are by the rules of the common law; for if he were so bound...he must sometimes pronounce decrees which *Discretion and rule in equity.*

---

[1] *Savage v. Foster, Cuddee v. Ruddee, Peachy v. Somerset,* and *Eyre v. Duchess of Shaftesbury.* (See Chap. XII. post.)

[2] It is printed in the Appendix to Parkes, p. 506. Ante, p. 166.

would be materially unjust, since no rule can be equally just in the application to a whole class of cases, that are far from being the same in every circumstance. This might lay a foundation for an equitable relief even against decrees in equity, and create a kind of superfœtation of courts of equity." His own decisions did much to limit the discretion of his successors, though, as will be seen later on, even Lord Eldon thought that rules of equity should be as certain almost,—not entirely,—as rules of law. The current towards definition became in Lord Hardwicke's time extremely strong. Though he again and again laid down general rules after the greatest deliberation, and sometimes expressly proclaimed his intention of doing so, he nevertheless 'utterly repudiated' the power of legislation, and the distinction between a real discretion and the fiction known as a judicial discretion could hardly be put more strongly than in the following passage from a judgment of his contemporary Sir Joseph Jekyll, M.R.[1]: "I own and cannot forbear declaring, that were I to consider the matter, not as sitting in judicature, but taking into consideration all manner of considerations, such as honour, gratitude, private conscience, &c., I must think this claim should never have been made." But "the law is clear, and Courts of equity ought to follow it in their judgments concerning titles to equitable estates; otherwise confusion would ensue; and though proceedings in Equity are said to be *secundum discretionem boni viri*, yet when it is asked *Vir bonus est quis?* the answer is *Qui consulta patrum, qui leges juraque servat;* and it is said in *Rook's* case, that discretion is a science, not to act arbitrarily according to men's wills and private affections: so the discretion which is exercised here is to be governed by the rules of law and equity, which are not to oppose, but each in its turn to be subservient to the other; this discretion in some cases follows the law implicitly, in others, assists it, and advances the remedy; in others again, it relieves against the abuse, or allays the rigour of it; but in no case does it contradict or overturn the grounds or principles thereof as has been sometimes ignorantly imputed to this Court. That is a discretionary power which neither this nor

[1] *Cowper v. Cowper*, 2 P. W. pp. 735, 753 (1734).

any other Court, not even the highest, acting in a judicial capacity, is by the constitution entrusted with."

The contradictory statements of Blackstone, who was also Hardwicke's contemporary, that "there can be no established rules and fixed precepts of equity laid down without destroying its very essence and reducing it to positive law[1]," and that "the system of our courts of equity is a laboured connected system, governed by established rules, and bound down by precedents, from which they do not depart, although the reason of some of them may be liable to objection[2]," point, on the one hand, to the (partial) inauguration of such a system as is described in the second passage, and, on the other, to a vivid recollection of a time when the first description was—in a much greater degree than at the time when the passages were written—a true one, and to an unchanged tradition in its favour.

Lord Hardwicke's judgments are remarkable for the clearness and the generality of the principles enunciated in them, as well as for the extensive knowledge of the common law which many of them display; they afford excellent instances of judicial legislation. One of them, that in *Chesterfield v. Janssen*, has acquired great celebrity for the analytical discussion of the kinds of fraud against which Equity would relieve, and another is worthy of particular mention, that in *Penn v. Baltimore*, for the example,—an extreme one,—which it affords of the magnitude of the interests Equity sometimes had to deal with; for it was decided in that case that it was within the jurisdiction of the Court to grant specific performance of an agreement as to real property situate in America, comprising two provincial governments and three counties, a matter which the Chancellor described as "worthy the judicature of a Roman Senate rather than of a single judge." The jurisdiction existed, he said, because the Court acted by a decree *in personam*, "the strict primary decree in this Court as a Court of Equity."

One great disservice Lord Hardwicke did to his Court: he carried the practice of requiring fresh arguments to great extremes, and delayed his important judgments for months and sometimes for years. A great arrear of causes ready for hearing

[1] Introduction, s. 2.   [2] Vol. III. p. 432.

was accumulated in his time, and no subsequent judge ever succeeded in overtaking it. His dilatory practice was, moreover, imitated by several of his successors, and surpassed by one of them, Lord Eldon.

He published two important orders in 1741 and 1747 respectively, the first extending the requirements of leave and a deposit of £50, previously required in cases of bills of review, to supplementary bills filed, before the decree complained of was inrolled, to attain the same object, the rehearing of the cause; the second extending a section of 4 Anne, c. 16, allowing full costs, instead of 40s. only, to be given where a plaintiff brought his suit to a hearing on the bill and answer only and it was dismissed.

As Phillip Yorke, Lord Hardwicke had sat on a Committee of the House of Commons to enquire into the fees of the officers of the Court. The Committee reported[1] that no enquiry into the conduct of these officers had been held since the time of Charles I., and that they had exceedingly increased since that time by patents and grants, and that many 'honorary attendants' had found a place within the offices of the Court, who at the time of the report, claimed large fees; that the prodigious length to which the documentary proceedings had grown, extending often to several thousand sheets in a cause, was a great abuse; and that in many cases the officials did not know what the authorised fees were. The Committee resolved "that the interest which a great number of officers and clerks have in the proceedings of the Court of Chancery, has been a principal cause of extending bills, answers, pleadings, examinations and other forms and copies of them, to an unnecessary length, to the great delay of justice and the oppression of the subject," and amongst their recommendations were that a list of permissible fees be published, and a summary remedy for the demand of greater be provided, and that no expedition money be paid in any case, or any office for the future be sold.

As Chancellor, Lord Hardwicke did not act very fully upon the report and recommendations in which he had concurred, but he published in 1743 a list of permissible fees,

[1] Parkes, p. 307.

which, no doubt, effected a reform at the time, and he made the important order that no one should be compelled to take office-copies which he did not require. The list of fees, extending over 76 pages in Beames, and comprising more than 1000 items, is an appalling example of the abuses which the unrestrained farming of the Offices of the Court, and the payment of all officials by fees had developed.

Two judges of considerable reputation followed Lord Hardwicke in the 18th century. Henley, made Lord Northington, who was appointed Lord Keeper in 1757, and who is chiefly remembered for his connection with the great case of *Burgess v. Wheate*[1], in which he held, in opposition to Lord Mansfield, that there could be no escheat through failure of the heirs of the cestui que trust, and practically settled the length to which the analogies between legal and equitable estates were to be pressed, and Lord Thurlow who was made Chancellor in 1778. Lord Thurlow sat for fourteen years, and in that time decided many cases which became leading authorities in Equity. By his judgment in *Fox v. Mackreth*[2], he assisted to lay the foundation of the wide reaching doctrines which have in modern times been applied to restrain every person in a fiduciary position from dealing for his own advantage with the subject of his trust; by his judgment in *Ackroyd v. Smithson* he opened the way for an extensive development of the gratuitous and vexatious complexities of 'conversion'; and both by decisions and suggestions he identified his name with the growth of the latest born of all the great principles of equity, those governing the separate estate of married women, the idea of a 'restraint upon anticipation' originating in a suggestion made by him on being appointed trustee of a marriage settlement.

Lord Thurlow 1778—1792.

The improvement of the common law to which reference has already been made is closely connected with the history of equity, though the time had now passed when branches of equitable jurisdiction could be dropped because the relief they were constructed to afford, or some other as adequate, was at length offered by the common law courts. Lord Eldon over

[1] Eden, 177.   [2] For these cases see post Chap. 12.

and over again affirmed that cases once dealt with in Equity, upon which authorities were to be found in the Chancery reports, would not on any such ground be abandoned, and it cannot be wondered that he refused to subject himself to the labour, and parties to the cost and danger, of determining whether the judicial legislation of another Court had ousted the settled jurisdiction of his own, well as such a course would have corresponded with the declaration, that it was better parties to any litigation should be inconvenienced or delayed than that the public interest should be impeded, a declaration often made to excuse the apparent evils which the separation of equity and law entailed[1], strangely contradictory, though it was, of the very purpose of the original establishment of the extraordinary jurisdiction of the Court of Chancery.

Improvement of the common law.

The amelioration of the common law was to a great extent effected by the introduction into the working of the elder system of principles developed by its rival. Lord Mansfield, with whose name so much of the substantial improvement is associated, said that he never liked the law so much as when it was most like equity. The chief means of this improvement were the actions on the 'common courts' for money had and received and money paid. Speaking of this class of actions, Lord Mansfield said[2] "it lies for money paid by mistake, or upon a consideration which happens to fail; or for money got through imposition (express, or implied) or extortion; or oppression, or an undue advantage taken of the Plaintiff's situation, contrary to laws made for the protection of persons under those circumstances. In a word, the gist of this action is, that the Defendant upon the circumstances of the case is obliged by the ties of natural justice and equity to refund the money." It is obvious that when such a statement as this could be made from the Bench, the judges had got far towards adopting the fundamental principles of equity. Some years later Buller, J.

---

[1] See for instance Lord Hardwicke's letter to Lord Kames.

[2] *Moses v. Macferlane*, 2 Burr 1012 (1760). The action was brought to recover money paid to the Defendant by the Plaintiff under the judgment of an inferior Court, obtained *mala fide*.

(who often sat in Equity for Lord Thurlow) expressly compared[1] the action just referred to, to a bill in Equity, and therefore, he said, the Plaintiff must show he had equity and conscience on his side. The introduction of the action for deceit in the case of *Pasley v. Freeman*[2] has already been referred to; it became the starting point of a series of decisions which practically assimilated the doctrines of common law, in regard to fraud, with those of equity. The process, in fact, which Blackstone[3] described as working around him, was continued long after his day, until in many of the cases, where it granted a relief rather than conducted an administration, and chiefly by the development of the common law in the manner described, the extraordinary jurisdiction of the Court of Chancery came to be concurrent with that of the courts of common law. Besides developing the principles of the Common Law along equitable lines the judges introduced a practice of preventing abuses of their judicature by exercising a summary control over the procedure of their Courts. Thus by dispensing with the profert, they enabled a Plaintiff to sue upon a lost bond[4]; by striking out unconscientious pleas, they prevented an unrighteous advantage being taken of a technical defence[5]; and by withholding the postea, by the aid of which alone advantage could be taken of the judgment, in cases where it was patently unjust to allow the Plaintiff to succeed unconditionally in his action, they forced an unconscientious Plaintiff to come to terms.

It was, therefore, to administer a system which could no longer claim to be the only judicature animated by a progressive spirit, and anxious to cope with new evils as they arose, that Lord Eldon came when he was appointed Chancellor in 1801. He definitely brought to a conclusion the work of binding down the Chancellor's discretion to which reference has been so frequently made in these pages. Lord Eldon, wrote his contemporary Kent[6], "has secured to himself

Lord Eldon 1801—1827.

[1] *Straton v. Rastall*, 2 T. R. 366 (1788). (Both these cases are cited in Warren's L. S.)
[2] Smith, L. C.
[3] Vol. iv. p. 442.
[4] The statutes 14 Geo. II. c. 20 and 9 and 10 Will. III. c. 17, granted relief in the cases of a lost recovery deed, and of a lost bond respectively.
[5] Warren, *Law Studies*.
[6] Commentaries, Vol. i. p. 490.

a title to the reverence of his countrymen by resisting the temptation, so often pressed upon him, to make principles and precedents bend to the hardship of a particular case." "The doctrines of this Court," he said himself[1], "ought to be as well settled and as uniform, almost, as those of the common law, laying down fixed principles, but taking care that they are to be applied according to the circumstances of each case. I cannot agree that the doctrines of this Court are to be changed by every succeeding judge. Nothing would inflict on me greater pain than the recollection that I had done anything to justify the reproach that the Equity of this Court varies like the Chancellor's foot." Certainly the reproach he dreaded cannot justly be inflicted upon his memory. Had the guiding principles of his judgments been as clearly enunciated, and in as general terms as those of Lord Hardwicke, the number of his reported decisions (which fill thirty-two volumes), the care with which he considered them, the weight of his authority, and the force of his example and precept would have gone far to remove the blight of uncertainty which magnified the evils of the complexity and irrationality of much of the law of his day. From his time onward the development of equity was effected ostensibly, and, in the great majority of cases, actually, by strict deduction from the principles to be discovered in decided cases, and the work of subsequent Chancery judges has been, for the most part, confined, as Lord Eldon's was, to tracing out these principles into detail, and to rationalising them by repeated review and definition. So long, however, as a single judge presided in Equity and formed an unassisted conclusion on law and fact, it was inevitable that the individual bent of his mind should gravely influence the character of his decisions, and it was therefore with no reflection upon the adherence of Lord Eldon to the principles he professed, that Sir Samuel Romilly, who, as leading counsel in the Court of Chancery and a man of unusual clearness of view, was peculiarly qualified to form an opinion on the subject, based his objection to the appointment of a Vice-Chancellor in 1813 upon the frequency with which his decisions would be reversed on appeal

[1] *Gee v. Pritchard,* 2 Swan 414.

to the Chancellor. The anticipation was in some degree fulfilled, partly no doubt from the cause suggested, but partly also by reason of the want of consideration by which the decisions of the second Vice-Chancellor under Lord Eldon, Sir John Leach, were sometimes marked. His practice, it was satirically said, was "terminer sans oyer," while that of the Chancellor was "oyer sans terminer."

The terrible delays and the accumulation of arrears, which the most energetic Chancellors had been unable to prevent or dispose of, were intolerably increased by the dilatoriness of Lord Eldon and the constitutional indecision of his mind, but these and the other abuses of the Court will be considered in a later chapter in dealing with the reforms introduced during the present century.

CHAPTER XII.

GROWTH OF MODERN EQUITY. SECTION I.

The general characteristics of the leading cases.

MANY of the principles of modern equity had been already adopted by the Chancellors, and, as we have seen, most of its great heads had already appeared as more or less distinct divisions, before the Great Rebellion. There is, however, a marked difference between the earlier and the later equity. Before Lord Nottingham's time there was little system or definition to be found in the relief administered by the Court. No volumes of reports existed, and, though precedents could be extracted from the Registrar's Books, and were recorded in the note-books of Counsel, these must have been few, vague and unreliable. All that practically existed to control or assist the individual inclination of the judge was the tradition of the Court, on some points, that is, those which most frequently occurred, no doubt strong and clear, on some uncertain and shifting, but on most entirely silent. A general idea existed as to the kind of case in which Chancery would or would not relieve, but that was all. It is not suggested that there was any sudden alteration, or that, as soon as Lord Nottingham,—for his immediate predecessors belong rather to the earlier period than to his own,—was placed upon the Woolsack, a developed system of equity forthwith began to be administered, the case is entirely different, for, so far from there being then any such system ready to hand, almost every Chancellor who followed Lord Nottingham down to Lord Eldon, added important doctrines to those accepted by his predecessors. But from that time the modern spirit pervaded the Court, the Chancellor, for the most part, appeared as a judge administering rights and not, at least not intentionally, as a legislator creating them, or as a moralist dispensing justice according to ethical standards distinct from those of positive law. The earlier cases influenced the decision of those now to be considered, but they rarely determined it, the decisions after Lord Nottingham, on the other hand, were generally regarded as, and intended to be, deductions from those that preceded, and were designed to supply rules for those that followed them.

I have found it impracticable to divide the growth of equity during the last two centuries in any satisfactory manner, for though there have been great Chancellors who have sat for long periods, and deeply impressed the stamp of their individual characters upon the system, its development has been so irregular, and the important additions to each head of jurisdiction so little connected, that it is hopeless to seek for standpoints from which, with advantage, to review the work done in the intervening periods. The space at my disposal would not allow me to attempt, even if I possessed the necessary knowledge to do so, to sketch the history of the doctrines of equity during this long and important period as a whole, and I do not propose to do more than to give a short account of the introduction of some of the principal doctrines adopted under the chief heads of jurisdiction. To search out the very first reported decision in a Court of Equity of each, even of the doctrines selected, would entail an expenditure of labour that the result would ill repay. In early days many a decision was pronounced and forgotten, and years later, after, it may be, much consideration, was pronounced again to be reported and adopted as the rule of the Court. It is the second judgment, not the first, which in such a case is of interest. The first if it be reported and discovered is a curiosity, but is of no more importance to legal history than the Aztec buildings of Central America are to the history of architecture.

Until the retirement of Lord Eldon equity was developed wholly by judicial legislation, it was entirely constructed upon precedent. In such a system, at least until the publishing and citation of contemporary reports becomes an established practice, it must often happen that conflicting decisions will occur and create uncertainty, and questions will arise from time to time for the determination of which no precedent exists. In each of these cases sooner or later the judge has to make up his mind what the rule of the Court shall be, and if the point be important the decision he arrives at, if known and accepted, becomes a leading case. The process here described is illustrated over and over again in the Chancery Reports from the time of Nottingham to that of Eldon. A great Chancellor gathers up a more or less numerous, but usually small collection of earlier cases, extracts from them a general rule, which perhaps has previously been stated, but as often departed from as followed, and lays it down as a guide for future decisions, secured against reversal by the weight of its author's reputation, and the care by which its enunciation was marked, but offering an admitted foundation for the refinements and distinctions suggested by the circumstances of subsequent cases. A typical example of this is furnished by Lord Eldon's judgment in *Mackreth v. Symmons*[1]. Such cases have naturally grown rarer with the increasing volume of reports, and this is still more so with the leading case of the other kind, in which a rule has had to be devised to meet circumstances hitherto unprovided for by the aid of analogies drawn from accepted principles, and arguments '*ab inconvenienti*'; of such cases *Garth v. Cotton*[2] is a famous instance.

The continuity of the growth of equity is well shown by the dates of the decisions of the leading cases in the collection of Messieurs White and Tudor. There are 64 cases, or, putting aside one decided by Lord Ellesmere, and two decided under Lord Coventry[3], 61 cases, of which the first was decided by Lord Keeper Bridgman, and Hale, C. B., in 1670, and the last by Plumer V. C. in 1816; 32 fall before and 29 after the year 1750, 5 were decided under Lord Macclesfield, 3 under Lord King, 6 during Lord Talbot's short Chancellorship of 3 years, 11 during Lord Hardwicke's Chancellorship of 20 years, 14

[1] 1 W. and T. 355.
[2] 1 W. and T. 806.
[3] *Earl of Oxford's case* (Injunction), *Warmsley v. Tanfield* (Assignment of Possibility), *Townley v. Sherborne* (liability of trustee for co-trustee).

during the alternating Chancellorships of Lord Thurlow and Lord Loughborough between 1778 and 1801, and 11 during the remaining 16 years under Lord Eldon. It would be surprising that so many important questions should have remained to be decided by the later Chancellors after the regular administration of the Court, with strict respect to precedent, wherever it was clear and in point, for so many years, by judges of the ability and reputation of Nottingham, Cowper and Hardwicke, if the scarceness and unreliability of the reports until the end of the last century were forgotten. The earlier reports, such as those "Tempore Finch," and the "Equity Cases Abridged" are often mere notes of the decisions without the facts of the cases, or the reasons of the judgments, and, though Lord Hardwicke is moderately well reported by Atkyns, yet Lord Redesdale writing at the end of the 18th century, could still complain of the extreme scarcity of authority, and Lord Eldon, some years later, could describe Lord Redesdale's book as "a wonderful effort to collect what is to be deduced from authorities speaking so little that is clear," so that "the surprise is not from the difficulty of understanding all he has said, but that so much can be understood[1]." "It is a misfortune," said Counsel in a case argued before Lord Hardwicke[2], "that accounts of Courts of Equity are conveyed to the public in loose notes by persons not concerned in the cause, and mistaken, and that general rules are drawn from particular premises." But perhaps the most striking illustration of the insufficiency of the earlier reports is the discovery of important cases long after their decision, as occurred when *Robinson v. Longe* was published from a private note by Mr Cox half a century after it was decided by Lord Hardwicke, and then, being found to be utterly opposed to the practice of the Court, was solemnly over-ruled by Lord Eldon in *Aldrich v. Cooper*[3].

The arguments in these leading cases are almost wholly based on precedents supposed either to be directly in point, or

---

[1] *Lloyd v. Jones*, 9 Ves. p. 54.
[2] *Chesterfield v. Janssen* (1750), 1 W. and T. 624.
[3] 2 W. and T. 82. Most of the books of equity reports of the last century were published many years after the decision of the cases they contain.

to furnish guiding analogies in the discussion upon which they were cited. The importance of precedents for the guidance of the Court was well recognised, as already shown, so early as Elizabeth at least, but their binding force was hardly established till Lord Hardwicke's time. He "utterly disclaimed" the power to legislate, and both he and his successors repeatedly followed rules which they personally disapproved of, and they would have entirely repudiated the apology put forward for the frequent reversals of the decrees of Chancellors upon rehearings by their successors, of a learned writer in 1735[1]. The Chancellors, the writer urged, are individually responsible in conscience for their judgments, and therefore each must decide according to his own reason and judgment, and he cites Lord Nottingham's dictum to that effect in the *Duke of Norfolk's* case. Besides, he adds, with the courage of his opinion[2], "non est inconveniens judicium esse uno tempore justum, et postea ejus contrarium justius." During the 18th century the apology ceased to be needed. Surprisingly little of the argument in these cases was based upon public policy, even where the cases were admittedly new, but occasionally the probable consequences of giving or refusing a particular decision were urged with effect, as in the important case of *Chesterfield v. Janssen*[3], where the question of setting aside a purchase from a reversioner was discussed, and in *Hugenin v. Basely*[4], where Romilly's celebrated argument was largely based on the danger of allowing a gift obtained by misemployment of religious influence to stand. On the whole, however, making allowance for many striking exceptions, both arguments and judgments, forcibly illustrate one of Austin's objections to judicial legislation: that it is, as it were, accidental law making, the decision of the case, and not the promulgation of a rule, being the direct object of the judge, who consequently pays small, if any, attention to the consequences or tendencies of the law he is creating.

[1] Preface to "Reports in Chy." 3rd ed.
[2] Citing "Gomez."
[3] 1 W. and T. 624.
[4] 2 W. and T. 597.

The influence of Roman Law upon equity has several times been adverted to in this essay, and a fresh perusal of these leading cases has confirmed the opinion I have already expressed, that the earlier has directly contributed very little to the later system. In cases relating to the descent of personalty on an intestacy, or under a will, the Civil Law rules were, of course, more or less adhered to, for they had been originally adopted in such matters by the Ecclesiastical Courts. Thus the House of Lords in the case of the half-blood next-of-kin heard civil as well as common lawyers, and in cases like *Ashburner v. Macguire*[1], and *Scott v. Tyler*[2] there was much discussion of Roman Law. The sources from which the passages from the Institutes and the Digest which were cited in Equity were almost invariably taken,—the text books of Ecclesiastical law, Godolphin and Swinburne,—indicate clearly the uses to which they were applied. References to the Digest and the later Civilians occasionally occurred in the arguments and judgments in cases of a different character, but they were rare, and were used merely as illustrations, or in support of arguments of a general nature, as a modern lawyer might employ references' to the Code Napoléon. The definitions of fraud and negligence propounded and discussed by the Roman jurists, for example, were employed in this way, and it was no doubt for the sake of these that, at a time when the authorities of equity were certainly to be found solely in the English reports, Lord Westbury[3] advised his pupils to make a constant study of the Digest. Certainly the general opinion has long been that the debt of equity to Roman Law was much greater than that here suggested, and comparisons between the two systems were common in the text books of the last century. The editor of the Reports of Lord Nottingham's time, for instance, annotated them with reference to Roman Law rules, for the assistance of practitioners. It was the fashion to trace prominent doctrines to the older law: thus Lord Eldon in *Mackreth v. Symmons*[4] traces the vendor's lien for unpaid

Roman Law.

[1] 2 W. and T. 246. (1786) (ademption of legacy).
[2] 2 W. and T. 120. (1787) (legacy giving subject to a condition in restraint of marriage).
[3] Life of Lord Westbury. Nash.
[4] 1 W. and T. 355.

purchase money to the rule "quod vendidi non aliter fit accipientis quam si aut pretium nobis solutum sit, aut satis eo nomine factum, vel etiam fidem habuerimus emptore sine ulla satisfactione[1]," but on turning to the earliest case where the lien was allowed, it is found to have been grounded "on natural equity, that the lands should stand charged with so much of the purchase money as was not paid, and that without any special agreement for the purpose[2]."

The arguments indeed, in the leading cases, closely resemble those with which our present Courts are familiar, though one suggestion frequently made during the last century, that a case against the pleader lacked authority because decided by a Chancellor newly come to the Court, Counsel would now hardly venture to employ.

In many of these cases the deciding judges were well aware that their decisions would be of great importance to the future course of the Court, and they brought to them the ability and care which the occasions demanded. The deliberate intention to settle the law by the enunciation of general principles is often apparent and is sometimes expressed. Thus Lord Hardwicke, whose judgments are especially conspicuous for this, in *Ryall v. Rolles*[3], after stating his concurrence with the elaborate opinions which had been delivered by the judges, added "as this is a case of great expectation and consequence I will reduce the grounds to some general principle." These were leisurely times in the Court. An argument by half-a-dozen Counsel on each side, repeated at the Chancellor's request some months later, and then consideration for a year or two frequently preceded an important judgment. The following list is taken almost at random from the reports.

CASE.	HEARING.	JUDGMENT.	JUDGES.
Ryall v. Rolles.	Nov. 1747. Feb. 1748.	Jan. 1750.	Hardwicke and Judges.
Garth v. Cotton.	Twice in 1750.	Feb. 1753.	Hardwicke.
Fox v. Mackreth.	— —	July, 1786.	Kenyon M. R.
,,	May, 1787. Nov. 1787.	Dec. 1788.	Thurlow.

[1] Dig. 18. 1, 50. 11. [2] *Chapman v. Tanner*, 1 Vern. 267 (1684).
[3] 2 W. and T. 799.

CASE.	HEARING.	JUDGMENT.	JUDGES.
Scott v. Tyler.	Easter, 1787.	Dec. 1788.	Thurlow.
Ashburner v. Macguire.	1784.	1786.	Thurlow.
Dearle v. Hall.	—	1823.	Plumer M. R.
,,	—	1828.	Eldon.

Certainly in some cases when the Chancellors made law they made it with deliberation.

SECTION 2.

The doctrines of the leading cases.

I propose to arrange the subjects I have now to consider in the order stated below, roughly following that already adopted in a previous chapter. No doubt a more satisfactory arrangement might be drawn up if time permitted, but where the several heads of jurisdiction conform so little to general principles, and have been adopted or elaborated upon grounds so various, and at periods so far apart, as is here the case, it is hopeless to attempt to represent them in anything like a connected and logical order.

1. Trusts and subjects connected with Trusts.
    Conversion.
    Joint ownership.
    Assignments of choses in action.
    Powers.
2. Subjects connected with Administration.
    The liability of personalty.
    Legacies.
    Marshalling.
    Election.
    Restraints on marriage.
3. Subjects connected with Married Women's property.
    Separate estate.
    Equity to a settlement.
    Assignment of wife's reversion.
4. Guardianship of Infants.

5. Mortgages.
   Tacking.
   Consolidation.
   Vendor's lien.
   Equitable mortgage.
   Notice.
6. Subjects connected with fraud.
   Catching bargains.
   Undue influence.
7. Mistake.
   Compromise.
8. Penalties.
9. Sureties.
10. Specific Performance.
    Delivery of chattels.
    Separation deeds.
11. Injunctions.
    Equitable waste.
12. Discovery.
    Purchase for valuable consideration.

I. *Trusts.*

"In my opinion," said Lord Mansfield in *Burgess v. Wheate*[1], "trusts were not on a true foundation till Lord Nottingham held the Great Seal. By steadily pursuing, from plain principles, trusts in all their consequences, and by some assistance from the Legislature, a noble, rational, and uniform system of law has been raised. Trusts are made to answer the exigencies of families, and all purposes, without producing one inconvenience, fraud or private mischief which the statute of Henry VIII. was meant to avoid." The help from the Legislature here referred to was that given by the *Statute of Frauds* which, reversing the rulings of Lord Nottingham's immediate predecessors, enacted that lands held on trust should be liable to execution on judgments against the cestui que trust, and be

[1] 1 Eden, p. 223.

bound by his obligations in the hands of his heir to the same extent as lands of which he was seised at law. The statute further declared that declarations and creations of trusts in lands, unless evidenced by writing, and assignments of such trusts, unless made in writing, should be void.

Many important questions relating to trusts came before Lord Nottingham, and the spirit in which he dealt with them is well illustrated by his exclamation in the Duke of Norfolk's case[1], "Pray let us resolve cases here," said he, "that they may stand with the reason of mankind when they are debated abroad. Shall that be reason here that is not reason in any part of the world besides? I would fain know the difference why I may not raise a new springing trust upon the same term, as well as a new springing term upon the same trust; that is such a chicanery of law as will be laughed at all over the Christian world." In that case he held, contrary to the advice of the Judges, that a trust of a term might be limited in tail with remainder over, to attend the inheritance, provided such remainder must necessarily take effect, if at all, during a life or lives in being at the time of the creation of the trust. How far a fee could be limited on a fee was, he said, not then determined, but it soon would be, if parties continually tried to do what the law forbad. It was not, however, till nearly a century later, that the rule applying precisely the same rules of limitation to trust as to legal limitations was settled[2].

The construction of equitable limitations might still, in the time of Lord Nottingham, be affected by considerations other than those admitted in Courts of Law, 'in cases of extremity[3],' but Lord Hardwicke stated the principles of interpretation to be identical in Chancery and at law, with the exception that words of regulation or modification, as 'equally to be divided,' might be read by the light of equitable considerations, a practice soon after adopted by the Judges themselves, and from Lord Thurlow's time there has been no exception to the rule[4].

[1] 3 Ch. Cas. p. 33.
[2] By Lord Northington in *Duke of Marlborough v. Earl of Godolphin*, 1 Eden 404 (1759).
[3] *Nourse v. Yarmouth*, Cas. temp. Finch, 159.
[4] 1 Spence, 520, *Jones v. Morgan*, 1 Bro. C. C. 206.

K.

The husband was held to be entitled to curtesy out of his wife's trust estate, and this was clearly settled before Lord Cowper's time[1], but, by a singular anomaly, the wife was not allowed her dower out of her husband's trust estate, no doubt because of the difficulty which the right of a dower out of lands acquired by the husband, relinquishable, as it was, only by the formality of a fine, imposed on sales and purchases. Jekyll, M. R., attempted to remove the anomaly[2], but his decision was over-ruled as disturbing too many settlements. Lord Hardwicke extended the right of curtesy to the equity of redemption of the wife's mortgaged lands[3].

In the great case of *Burgess v. Wheate* in 1759, already referred to, Lord Mansfield described equitable interests as, in all respects, governed by the same rules as legal estates, and advised that on the death without heirs of a cestui que trust his interest ought to escheat to the Crown. This, however, was not approved by the Lord Keeper Northington, who declined to hold that, as regards third persons, the trust could be treated as a nullity, but agreed that "where there is a trust it should be considered in this Court as the real estate between the cestui que trust and the trustee and all claiming by or under them," and this represents the modern rule, though the escheat of trust estates on failure of heirs of the cestui que trust has been introduced by statute[4]. A purchaser without notice from the trustee has never been held to be bound by the trust, as Lord Mansfield's dicta, if fully pressed, would require.

Following the principles indicated in the passage quoted from his judgment above, Lord Nottingham held that a merger at law was of no avail to oust a cestui que trust, and he severed an attendant term in order to protect an interest which was recognised in equity, though not at law[5].

The presumption of a resulting trust where a purchase is made in the name of another, or a conveyance made without consideration, Lord Nottingham held to be rebutted if the grantee were a child of the actual purchaser or

Resulting trust.

[1] *Watts v. Ball*, 1. P. W. 108 (1708).
[2] Per Lord Mansfield *Burgess v. Wheate*, Eden 195.
[3] *Casborne v. Scarfe*, 2 W. and T. 1171.
[4] 47 and 48 Vic. c. 71.
[5] *Nourse v. Yarmouth*, Ca. temp. Finch 155.

grantor. In other cases he held that evidence of acts of ownership on the part of the latter would strongly support the presumption[1], but in this case, it was not reasonable that the father's perception of profits, he said[2], "or doing such acts as these, which the son, in good manners, does not contradict, should turn a presumptive advancement into a trust." And the same rule was adopted in the leading case of *Dyer v. Dyer*[3] in 1788, where, however, a suggestion of Lord Nottingham, that the fact that the son was already advanced, or not advanced, would be material upon the question whether the presumption or the counter presumption should prevail, was disapproved, for the father ought to be sole judge of the sufficiency of the advancement. Many distinctions as to what is, and what is not sufficient to rebut the presumption of advancement were suggested by intermediate and later cases, but these are now disregarded, and the modern rule seems to be that, where the grantee is a near relation of the purchaser or grantor, naturally or by adoption, no presumption of a trust exists, but a trust may be established by evidence of the latter's intention[4].

Voluntary trusts and settlements, except where they fall within the statute 13 Eliz. c. 5, or, as against subsequent purchasers, are avoided by the statute 27 Eliz. c. 4, are not regarded as revocable in equity. "If a man will improvidently bind himself up by a voluntary deed, and not reserve a liberty by power of revocation, this Court will not loose the fetters he hath put upon himself, but he must lie down under his own folly," said Lord Nottingham in an early case[5], and when it was argued before him that voluntary trusts (in the case in question in favour of the settlor's children) must be taken as fraudulent, he decreed the contrary "with great earnestness and not without some reflection on the Defendant's Counsel, as if the fee was more regarded than the justice of the cause[6]." On the other hand, Lord Eldon settled the rule that an imperfect declaration of

Voluntary trusts.

[1] *Cook v. Fountain*, 3 Swan 592 (1676).
[2] *Grey v. Grey*, 2 Swan 599 (1677).
[3] 1 W. and T. 236.
[4] *Fowkes v. Pascoe* 10 Ch. 343. *Bennet v. Bennet* 10 C. D. 474.
[5] *Villars v. Beaumout*, 1 Vern. 101.
[6] *Bisco v. Banbury*, 1 Ch. Ca. 289.

trust will not be assisted in Equity, where there is no consideration given[1], and an imperfect gift will not be supported as a declaration of trust[2], although if a donor has completely transferred his interest, then the rights of the donee are as fully protected as those of any other cestuis que trust. 'Good consideration,' that is the claims of natural affection in favour of near relations, was frequently allowed in Equity to distinguish settlements made in favour of children and others from other voluntary settlements, until the distinction was finally exploded in *Jefferies v. Jeffries*[3] about the year 1840. The principles of the rules just stated have been departed from to some extent by the assistance given to the defective execution of *powers* in favour of the donee's near relatives, and on the other hand, by the readiness of the Court to regard voluntary settlements as tainted by fraud or 'undue influence,' the mere absence of a power of revocation, if unexplained, being often allowed as sufficient indication of the latter[4].

Trusts for payment of creditors, though completely declared, so long as they are not communicated to the creditors, are looked upon as mere dispositions for the settlor's own convenience, and are therefore revocable by him. This exception was introduced in the case of *Walwyn v. Coutts*[5] by Lord Eldon, and was settled in *Garrard v. Lord Lauderdale*[6].

Past immoral consideration, according to modern views, is treated simply as no consideration at all, and a settlement for which it forms the sole motive is regarded as voluntary, and this view was taken by Lord King[7], but the rule was not then settled, thus Lord Talbot postponed payment of a bond given to the obligor's mistress until after payment of his simple contract debts[8], and Lord Hardwicke set such a bond aside

[1] *Ellison v. Ellison*, 1 W. and T. 291 (1806).
[2] *Antrobus v. Smith*, 12 Ves. 39 (1806). Richards v. Delbridge, L. R. 18 Eq. 11. Henry v. Armstrong, 18 C. D. 668.
[3] Cr. and Ph. 138. (Lord Mansfield had suggested that the fulfilment of a moral obligation would afford consideration to support a contract, and the definite limitation of 'valuable consideration' to the grantee's or promisee's loss was not arrived at until the present century.)
[4] (See *fraud*, &c. post.)
[5] 3 Mer. 707.
[6] 3 Sim. 14 (1830).
[7] *Marchioness of Annandale v. Harris*, 2 P. W. 434 (1727).
[8] *Cray v. Rooke*, Cas. Talbot 155.

expressly on moral grounds[1]. Had the Plaintiff not known that the obligor was married, he said, she might have been entitled to relief. But "she entered into the family, knowing it, and continued so as to occasion a separation; and this court ought to endeavour to preserve virtue in families."

From the middle of the last century much difficulty was caused by the inability of a trustee for sale to give a receipt for the purchase money which would exonerate the purchaser from liability upon its wrongful application by the trustee. In the leading case of *Elliot v. Merryman*[2] the clear rule was laid down that, where there is a trust for sale to pay debts, and in the will or deed creating the trust particular debts are referred to, the purchaser is bound to see to the payment of such debts, but of no others. This, however, proved to be insufficient, and many refinements were introduced by subsequent decisions, and these have now been cleared away by successive statutes of the last fifty years, by which the receipt of the trustee has been made practically sufficient in every case, except, of course, where the purchaser has notice that he intends to misapply the money[3].

Receipt on sale by trustee.

Chancery in early days had undertaken to interpret limitations of trusts according to the presumed intention of the settlor, and to rectify deeds and documents which were drawn up by mistake so as not to carry out the wishes of the parties. When the stricter interpretation of trust limitations, as already described, became the rule, a beneficial distinction between executed and executory trusts was introduced. In the leading case of *Glenorchy v. Bosville*[4] this distinction was stated by Lord Talbot, who held that directions in a will to settle an estate, which, if repeated in the settlement, would have given the first taker a tenancy-in-tail, should be construed to give a tenancy for life only, that being the clear intention of the testator. And in another case[5] the same Chancellor applied the rule to executory limitations in

Executory trusts.

---

[1] *Priest v. Parrot*, 2 Ves. Snr. 160.
[2] 1 W. and T. 72 (Verney, M. R. 1740).
[3] Conveyancing Act 1881, § 36.
[4] 1 W. and T. 1 (1733).
[5] *Legg v. Goldwire* (1736) 1 W. and T. p. 17.

marriage articles, holding that a subsequent settlement, made after marriage, might be corrected by the articles construed according to the real intention of the parties. Lord Hardwicke at one time disputed the rule, but afterwards fully admitted it, and it has ever since remained an accepted principle of the Court[1].

No formalities, other than the writing required in some cases by the Statute of Frauds, have ever been necessary for the creation of trusts, and the Court has carried its determination to respect indications of a desire on the part of a donor to place the donee in a fiduciary position so far that it has undoubtedly on many occasions overshot the mark and deprived donees of interests and discretions which were intended by the donors to be theirs. The earliest important case on this point is *Eales v. England*[2], in which Lord Somers held the words "my will is that he give...to C, at his death..." following a legacy in a will, imposed on the legatee a trust for C, who therefore, since no trust may fail for lack of a trustee, on the legatee's death during the testator's life, became entitled to the property. This was well enough, but it may be questioned whether the interpretation as obligatory of a request to a legatee at her death to divide among such of the relations of the testator, her husband, as she should think fit, in *Harding v. Glynn*[3] some forty years later, did not go too far. At the beginning of the present century the rule was settled that to create a precatory trust the object and the subject of it must be certain, except that where the object was a charity it was not essential that the particular charity intended should be determinable, and that the words used must be imperative[4].

In *Shaw v. Lawless*[5] in 1838 the House of Lords, reversing Lord St Leonards, refused to construe a recommendation in a will as obligatory on a devisee, although urged to do so on the ground that the testator, being in a position to command, and expressing a wish, ought to be taken to command, an argument

[1] Sackville West v. Viscount Holmesdale, L. R. 4 H. L. 543.
[2] Prec. Chancery, 200 (1702).
[3] 2 W. and T. 1077 (Verney, M. R. 1739).
[4] *Morrice v. Durham*, 10 Ves. 536 (Eldon). *Cary v. Cary*, 2 Sch. and Lef. 189 (Redesdale).
[5] 5 Cl. and F. 129.

that had prevailed in some of the earlier cases, and since that time the inclination of the Court has been against constructions of this description, which have been described as 'making a will for the testator,' and which the Judges admit have often disappointed his intention[1]. Where directions to divide among a class have been held to impose a trust the Court has never allowed the non-execution of his duty by the trustee to prejudice the cestuis que trust, and, from the time of Jekyll, M.R.[2], it has acted on the maxim that 'equality is equity,' and divided equally, unless some principle of selection has been indicated by the settlor, as where the division is to be 'according to the necessities' of the cestuis que trust, in which case the Court will enquire and apportion, following an example set by Lord Hardwicke[3].

The position of the trustee has been settled by a series of decisions extending down to the present time, modified by statutes passed to relieve him from the intolerable responsibilities cast upon him by the Court, which has not always borne in mind the caution of Lord Coventry, "that parties trusted be not too much punished lest it should dishearten men to take any trust."

The trustee.

In the reports of Lord Nottingham's time are two cases[4] in which it was sought to compel trustees to accept trusts: in *Clifton v. Sacheverell* the trustee was ordered to accept on having a full indemnity from the cestui que trust, and in *Hussey v. Markham* a similar decree was made on the following conditions, suggested by the trustee, that the Master be directed to take accounts every year and to allow costs and charges, and that the trustee be not chargeable with any money but what he, or others by his orders, should actually receive, and be not obliged to pay for any loss unless it were occasioned by his wilful negligence or default. A trustee would not now be compelled to accept a trust unless he had agreed to do so.

The same Chancellor[5] held that where a trustee was robbed

---

[1] Re Adams and the Kensington Vestry, 27 C. D. 394.
[2] *Doyley v. Attorney-General*, 2 Eq. Ca. Ab. 195.
[3] *Gower v. Mainwaring*, 2 Ves. 87.
[4] Cas. temp. Finch, pp. 32, 258.
[5] *Morley v. Morley*, 2 Ch. Cas. 2 (1678).

by his servant of the trust money he might be allowed the amount lost in his account, and it would seem that, so far, the liability of the trustee for losses was placed upon the ground of negligence. A case[1] occurred, however, in 1685 in which the trustee, who had released the security on which the trust money was lent, pleaded that he had received no consideration for being trustee, and that therefore the Plaintiff, in order to recover, must establish fraud on his part, or that he had had the money and applied it to his own use, but these pleas were over-ruled, and the modern doctrine that the trustee must show that he has lawfully discharged himself of the trust property, was distinctly stated. It was also held that an infant might incur liabilities as a trustee, and the Defendant was ordered to replace the capital with interest.

At this time the common mode of investment of small sums of money, was by loan upon the joint bond of a borrower and his sureties, and this mode was adopted by trustees without their being held responsible for the failure of the obligors. Early in the last century this practice began to be questioned, and it was held that, at any rate, if the loan were upon a single bond only and the borrower failed to repay it, the trustee would be liable[2]. Lord Hardwicke[3] decided that, where the will or settlement contained directions as to investment, the trustee was bound by their terms, and towards the end of the century it was finally settled that trust money ought not to be lent on personal security except by the express licence or direction of the testator or settlor[4].

By Lord Eldon's time, the range of permissible investment was restricted, in the absence of directions in the terms of the trust, to permanent Government securities only[5].

The onerousness of the trustee's position was during the same period increased in another way. His liability was ex-

[1] *Jevons v. Burk*, 1 Vern. 342.
[2] *Terry v. Terry*, 1 Gilb. 10 (1709). *Brown v. Litton*, 1 P. W. 140 (1711).
[3] *Trafford v. Boehm*, 3 Atk. 444.
[4] *Adye v. Feuilleteau*, 1 Cox 24. *Holmes v. Dring*, 2 Cox 1 (1788). Lewin 8 Ed. p. 306.
[5] *Howe v. Lord Dartmouth*, 2 W. and T. 330. The range of permissible investment has been gradually extended by Lord St Leonards' Act, 1859, and subsequent Acts. See Hood and Challis, *Conveyancing Acts*, 3rd ed. p. 223.

tended beyond what he actually received, to what he ought to have received, and in *Lowson v. Copeland*[1], in 1787, a trustee was condemned to pay the amount of a bond debt which he had neglected to call in. It had been decided in the time of Charles I.[2] that, without his own default, his 'dolus malus' or 'any evil practice, fraud or ill intent' in permitting the receipt, a trustee was not liable for what his co-trustee received and lost or embezzled, but Lord Eldon added this to the rule, that "as soon as a trustee is fixed with knowledge that his co-trustee is misapplying the money, a duty is imposed upon him to bring it back into the joint custody of those who ought to take better care of it[3]," and if he neglect this duty he will be liable for the whole subsequent loss.

The rule governing the trustee's liability determined by these and subsequent cases is practically this. He may deal with the trust property only within narrow limits marked out by the terms of his trust and by law, if he transgress these limits, though he take the utmost care, and loss follows, he will be liable, for he cannot discharge himself by alleging the unauthorised transaction; if he keep within the limits he is not liable provided he takes the care that a reasonable man would take of his own property. It is upon the last proviso that most of the recent discussions on the subject have turned, and particularly with regard to the employment of agents in the course of making proper investments[4].

The restriction of the range of permissible investment involved, not only an extension of the trustee's liabilities, but, in the case of property given or bequeathed in succession, the right also of the cestui que trust in remainder to demand that existing but improper investments be changed for others within the authorised class although these might produce a smaller income for the tenant for life. This rule was established by Lord Eldon in *Howe v. Lord Dartmouth*[5] and it applies wherever property is so bequeathed, or given, unless

[1] 2 Bro. C. C. 156.
[2] *Townley v. Sherborne*, 2 W. and T. 960.
[3] *Brice v. Stokes*, 2 W. and T. p. 974
(1805).
[4] **Speight v. Gaunt**, 9 App. Cases 1. Trustee Act 1888.
[5] 2 W. and T. 330 (1802).

it be bequeathed or given specifically, or with directions to allow the existing investments to continue.

In return for his trouble and danger the trustee is entitled to no remuneration, although he is secured his proper costs and expenses in full. This was decided by Lord Nottingham[1], and the rule was re-affirmed in *Robinson v. Pett*[2] by Lord Talbot, for, he said, "on these pretences, if allowed, the trust estate might be loaded and rendered of little value."

The trustee had, however, the remote possibility of retaining the property freed from the trust on the death intestate and without heirs of the cestui que trust, as we have seen, until the Intestates Estates Act of 1884 removed this also. But this strict rule was not extended to a constructive trustee, for he does not stand in a fiduciary position, and from the time of Lord Harcourt he has been held entitled to adequate remuneration for work done in respect of the trust estate[3].

Conversion.

The doctrine of conversion rests upon the distinction which our law has unfortunately allowed between the successions upon intestacy to real and to personal property. Equity adopted the maxim that what ought to be done must be taken as done, and, so early as the reign of Charles I., a case occurs in which the heir sued his ancestor's executors for the performance of the ancestor's covenant to invest money in land, claiming the money as, in the view of Equity, real estate. The principle of the claim was not disputed, but the Plaintiff failed because the ancestor had become solely entitled to the lands covenanted to be purchased, and was placed therefore in a position to sell the land again, had he bought it according to the covenant[4], that is because, in the language afterwards employed, the money had been 'at home.'

The right of the heir to enforce his ancestor's contract to purchase lands against the intended vendor, and to compel the ancestor's executor to provide the purchase money was estab-

---

[1] *How v. Godfrey*, cas. Finch 361. (1712).
[2] 2 W. and T. 230 (1734).   [4] *Ferrers v. Ferrers*, Rep. in Chy. 17.
[3] *Brown v. Litton*, 1 P. W. 140

lished soon after the Revolution[1], and the doctrine that money agreed to be invested in land descends, as land, to the heir, and land agreed to be sold, as money, to the next of kin, was by that time fully recognised, and, twenty years later, Lord Macclesfield declared it to be a settled rule of the Court[2]. The qualifications that the conversion is at an end if the money or land comes into the actual possession of one who is absolutely entitled to the benefit of the covenant, and that if, while it remains in the hands of trustees, one who has an absolute right to demand the payment or surrender of it to him, or its reconversion if the notional conversion were actually carried into effect, gives any indication of an intention to keep it in its actual state, were also recognised[3], but the nice distinctions upon these heads, and especially as to what should be taken as a sufficient indication of intention to elect against the conversion, which afterwards confused the Court, were, for the most part, evolved about Lord Eldon's time.

It was settled by the leading case of *Fletcher v. Ashburner*[4] that the partial failure of the purposes for which a conversion is directed will not put an end to it.

In the celebrated case of *Ackroyd v. Smithson*[5], where lands were devised on trust for sale and division among certain legatees, Lord Thurlow held, contrary to the then received opinion, that the testator's heir, and not his next of kin, was entitled to the shares that lapsed by the deaths of some of the legatees in the testator's lifetime, for he takes whatever of the real property of his ancestor is not disposed of by his ancestor's will, even though, according to a subsequent decision, the will expressly forbid it[6]. In such a case the heir takes the property as personalty in accordance with the rules formerly stated, so if he die intestate fresh disputes may arise between his heir and next of kin.

---

[1] *Holt v. Holt*, 2 Vern. 322 (1694).
[2] *Scudamore v. Scudamore*, Prec. Chy. p. 543 (1720). *Lingen v. Sondray*, 1 P. W. 172 (1711).
[3] *Chichester v. Bickerstaff*, 2 Vern. 295 (1693). *Seeley v. Jago*, 1. P. W. 389 (1711).
[4] 1 W. and T. 968 (Sewell, M. R. 1779).
[5] 1 W. and T. 1027 (1780).
[6] *Fitch v. Weber*, 6 Hare 145 (1848).

Further questions as to conversion have arisen, where trustees, the Court, or some other authority, have altered the nature of land or personalty without the owner's direction, between his heir and next of kin or claimants under them. These have at length been to some extent settled by the rule laid down by Jessel, M. R., that wherever a conversion is actually and rightfully made by trustees or the Court all the normal consequences of the change must follow[1].

Happily, the rareness of intestacy at the present time has greatly diminished the importance of these gratuitous and artificial difficulties. When they came most frequently before the Court it was not at all uncommon for a man with property to dispose of, to allow the realty to descend as the law happened to direct, even if he made a will as to his personalty, and the rule which prevailed down to 1837, that a will of realty spoke, not from the death of the testator, but from the time of its execution, assisted to increase the amount of descended land, but at the present time that amount is extremely small, not exceeding, on the average, it is said, two per cent. of the whole quantity of land which is annually transferred on death.

The doctrines of conversion are the most flagrant instance of the needless complexity introduced into our law during the last century by the equity judges. They were wholly mischievous, for they encouraged litigation between two classes of persons who, before the death of their relative, were taken to be absolutely without interest in his property. The neglect of trustees to perform their duty, to buy or to sell as the case might be, could not, it was argued, be allowed to affect the devolution of the property, but the supposed wrong done by the trustees to the heir or next of kin is illusory, for at the time when, if at all, they ought to have effected the conversion, neither of the rival claimants was entitled to complain of their inaction. Perhaps had the occasion arisen when testamentary privileges were, not better established, but more generally exercised, the Court would have refused to interfere, or to consider the circumstances of the chain of accidents which brought property to one or the other of the claimants.

[1] Steed v. Preece, 18 L. R. Eq. 92.

Joint ownership.

Equity from an early period has been little inclined to favour the right of survivorship which the law regards as an incident of joint tenancy, and a case[1] occurred at the beginning of the reign of Charles I. where the share of money lent upon mortgage by one of two mortgagees was decreed to be subject to his will, and not the property of the other who survived him. This case was decided to some extent on its special circumstances, but the rule against survivorship was clearly enunciated in 1677 in the case[2] of property purchased by partners in trade, and 50 years later King, L. C., affirming the decision of the Master of the Rolls, in the leading case of *Lake v. Craddock*[3], settled the rule, that in all cases where purchasers contribute their money in unequal proportions, though they be joint tenants at law, in equity they will be looked upon as tenants in common, among whom no right of survivorship obtains, subject to the condition that the inequality appears on the face of the purchase deeds[4]. Lord Hardwicke extended the rule, and placed it on its modern basis by omitting this condition[5]. The rule so determined and the difficulty as to the efficiency of trustees' receipts, already mentioned, occasioned considerable difficulty, where trust money was invested in the names of several trustees, in conveyancing for it was desirable in such cases that the trustees should hold the property as joint tenants, and to effect this it was found necessary to introduce cumbersome 'joint account' and receipt clauses in the purchase deeds. The difficulty has now been removed by a recent statute[6] which makes a simple statement that the money is advanced on a joint account sufficient to constitute grantees joint tenants both at law and in equity.

[1] *Petty v. Styward*, 1 Ch. Rep. p. 31.
[2] *York v. Eaton*, 2 Free. 23. This was an adoption from the *lex mercatoria*. Smith's *Mercantile Law*, 10th Ed. p. lxxviii.
[3] 1 W. and T. 217 (1732).
[4] *Lake v. Gibson*, 1 W. and T. 215.
[5] *Rigden v. Vallier*, 3 Atk. 735.
[6] Conveyancing Act, 1881, § 61.

Assignments of choses in action.

These assignments, as we have already seen, were always permitted in equity, though they were void at law until the passing of the Judicature Act, which now enables an assignor to pass a legal interest to his assignee, provided the assignment is absolute and made in writing and written notice of it is given to the debtor. Equity allowed assignments of every kind and by the most informal expression of intention, except where, in the case of equitable interests in land, the Statute of Frauds required a writing. Lord Keeper Bridgman, however, who was by no means inclined to favour equitable doctrines which conflicted with rules of law, refused to assist an assignee unless the consideration for the assignment was a pre-existing debt[1], and it seems that the conditions upon which the assignment would be supported were not ascertained until some years after his time. The rules upon this subject were considered and settled by Lord Hardwicke and the Judges in *Row v. Dawson*[2], where a direction to the Exchequer authorities to pay to the assignee a sum out of moneys due to the assignor, was held good against the assignees in bankruptcy of the latter, and in the great case of *Ryall v. Rowles*[3], which was elaborately debated by Lord Hardwicke and the Judges about the same time. In the second case the Court held, upon the analogy of the Common Law, that an assignment, by way of mortgage, of debts and chattels belonging to a trader was void under the Bankruptcy Act of 21 James I., because the assignor had not done all that the nature of the property permitted towards its delivery to the assignee. It is noteworthy that in advising on this case the Judges referred to Roman Law only to distinguish its provisions from the rules of Equity, for, they said, the latter know nothing of a 'hypotheca' which passes a lien to the hypothecarius without delivery and without conveyance of the legal estate. Following out the condition here imported, it was decided[4] in 1823 that, to make the assignee of a chose in action secure, notice must be given to the

[1] 2 Free. p. 144.
[2] 2 W. and T. 797.
[3] 2 W. and T. 799.
[4] *Dearle v. Hall*, 3 Russ. 1.

debtor or trustee, or in default thereof a subsequent assignee giving notice will obtain a better title. But the condition as to notice has never been extended to interests in realty. Subject to this condition as to notice, an equitable assignment is an 'innocent conveyance,' and, according to a rule recognised from the time of Lord Hardwicke, the assignee takes subject to all equities affecting the property at the date of the assignment[1].

A covenant to assign future personalty was decided by Lord Eldon to bind the property so soon as the covenantor acquired it, and this was approved by the House of Lords in *Holroyd v. Marshall*[2] under Lord Westbury's guidance, with the proviso that the property to be assigned must be sufficiently identified by the covenant. The proviso was expressly founded upon the equitable doctrine of specific performance, upon which the support of assignments of choses in action has always rested, but the rule laid down was not at once understood, and the difficulties created by subsequent decisions on the subject have only recently been, to some extent, cleared up by another decision of the House of Lords[3].

The rules governing the assignment of chattels without delivery, which has always been greatly discountenanced by our law, were the subject of much debate in the case of *Ryall v. Rowles*[4], and have, during the present century, been the occasion of repeated Bills of Sale Acts, but it cannot be said that these Acts have settled the law in regard to them[5].

Powers.

A 'power' is an authority given, usually by a will or a settlement, to one who is not the owner to dispose of a legal or an equitable interest in property either generally, or in favour of some of a specified class. It frequently happens that in the creation of the power conditions are provided as to the mode of its exercise, and in exercise of its characteristic juris-

[1] Gilbert, p. 286.
[2] 10 Ho. Lo. Ca. 191 (1862).
[3] Official Receiver v. Tailby, 13 App. Ca. 523.
[4] Ante, p. 207.
[5] "There is no darker page in the annals of English jurisprudence than the law of bills of sale." Cave, J., *Exp. Collins*, 59 L. J. Q. B. 20.

diction to relieve against accident and mistake, equity has offered its assistance where exact compliance with such conditions has not been rendered. Lord Nottingham in *Bisco v. Banbury*[1] went a great way in this direction. A term had been created in a marriage settlement for raising portions for children, and on the settlor's re-marriage another term, for the same period and issuing out of the same property, was created by a second settlement, and subsequently portions were declared upon the second term. These it was argued were of no avail, for the second term being for the same period as the first was void, and to suppose the portions to exist without the terms on which they were declared was to suppose " accidens subsistere sine substantivo in quo existat." Lord Nottingham admitted the argument, but defeated its premises by removing the portions to the first term, for, he said, "the intent was to raise the money, though (the settlor) pitched not on proper means." The case is of no importance as a precedent, but it illustrates the manner in which the execution of powers was regarded. In 1702 the rule and its reason were stated in a judgment of the Court reported in the following terms[2], " wherever a conveyance is made upon good consideration, if there be any defect in the execution of it...this Court has always supplied the defect; as in the case of feoffment, to supply the defect of livery, in devise of a copyhold, to supply the defect of a surrender; and much more in the case of a power, as where any circumstances are omitted in the execution of it; and one reason given was because the circumstances are imposed only that the party may not be surprised in the execution of it. And it was further held, that payment of debts, provision for a wife and children, marriage or purchases were considerations for which this Court had supplied such defects: and though provisions for a wife or children after marriage are not valuable considerations, yet they are good considerations, and were always helped in this Court." An instance of the kind of assistance rendered by the Court is afforded by *Tollet v. Tollet*[3] where a power to

[1] 1 Ca. Ch. 287. [2] *Fothergill v. Fothergill*, 2 Free. 256.
[3] W. and T. p. 269 (1728).

jointure by deed was held to be well exercised by will. But, as the assistance given is only to remedy the non-observance of unessential forms, there must be shown a clear intention to execute the power, and no form which imposes a substantial condition on its exercise must be omitted. Thus Lord Eldon decided in *Reid v. Shergold*[1] that an execution by deed would not do where it ought to have been by will, for the important power of revocation intended to be reserved to the donee would otherwise have been lost. The uniform rule of the Court, it was declared in Lord Northington's time, is to aid defective executions in favour of purchasers for value, creditors and charities, and to these must be added, as in the cases cited, the wife and children of the donee.

Non-execution of powers, unless prevented by fraud, has not been relieved against in modern times[2], for the Court will not take away from the party entitled in default what, on the default occurring, has become his property. The Legislature has adopted, but to some extent has limited, the principles of Equity on this head. It has enacted that every execution of a power by a will executed as required by the Wills Act, and none other, shall be a sufficient execution by will, and that every execution by a deed with two attesting witnesses shall be a good execution by deed[3].

Where a power was created to divide a fund amongst a class, something, it was held, in the absence of special direction, must be given to every member of it, and Equity intervened to extend this principle by refusing to allow small or 'illusory' appointments to any of the class. The Court went so far, it is said, in an early case[4] as to require an equal division; and in *Gibson v. Kinven*[5], in 1682, where five shillings only had been given to one child, the Chancellor upset the appointment, "for that the distribution was so very unequal, and that without any good reason shown to warrant it, and therefore

Illusory appointments.

[1] 10 Ves. 370.
[2] Non-execution is clearly distinguished from imperfect execution in *Tollet v. Tollet.*
[3] Wills Act, 1837, and 22 and 23 Vict. c. 35, § 12.
[4] In *Wall v. Thurborne*, 1 Ver. 416 (1686), so stated in *Asty v. Asty*, Prec. Ch. 256, but apparently no decision was given.
[5] 1 Vern. 66.

K.   14

he thought fit to rectify it in this case, and could not do so otherwise than by an equal distribution." Later Chancellors refused to play the part of the Roman Prætor by investigating the reasons for 'illusory' appointments, but they set the appointments aside if they thought the disproportion too great, until the statute 1 Will. IV. c. 46, abolished the doctrine. Subsequently, 37 and 38 Vic. c. 37 removed the necessity to give something to every member of the class altogether.

The doctrine just mentioned leads to a more important one. In Lord Hardwicke's time a case came before the Court where the donee of a power to jointure, being in debt, married, and jointured his wife on an agreement by her to apply all but £20 a year of the jointure in payment of his creditors[1]. This the Chancellor regarded as a 'fraud upon the power,' and he set aside the appointment except as to the £20 a year. The rule, that an appointment under a power, if made for sinister purposes, is void, was from that time well established[2]. But where the sinister motive only partially affected the appointment the practice subsequently adopted was to set aside the appointment *in toto*, unless, according to a rule laid down by Grant, M. R.[3], that portion of the property which was appointed to a proper object had been so appointed upon a consideration, such as marriage, which could not be restored, or unless, according to the rule in *Topham v. Duke of Portland*[4], the Court could distinguish what of the appointment was due to an authorised, and what to an unauthorised purpose[5].

Fraud on power.

2. *Administration.*

It is a fundamental rule that, apart from the testator's directions to the contrary[6], his personal estate is the primary, as it was originally the sole fund out of which his debts must be paid. The real estate was, before the reign of William IV.[7],

[1] *Lane v. Page*, Ambler, 233.
[2] *Aleyn v. Belchier*, 1 W. and T. 445 (1758).
[3] *Daubney v. Cockburn*, 1 Mer. 626 (1816).
[4] 1 D. G. J. and S. 517 (1860).
[5] *Henty v. Wrey*, 21 C. D. 332.
[6] The Court was always very ready to discover a direction in the will charging the debts upon the realty or part of it.
[7] 3 and 4 Will. IV. c. 104 (47 Geo. III. c. 74, bound the lands of a trader).

not subject to simple contract debts at all unless devised or charged for their payment, but it had always been bound in the hands of the heir by the ancestor's covenant for himself and his heirs, and after the first statute of 'Fraudulent Devises'[1] it was bound by such a covenant in the hands of the devisee also. The question then arose whether, when the realty was charged with his debts by a testator it was to be primarily liable in exoneration of the personalty, or to be charged after the exhaustion of the latter only. This was always regarded as a matter of intention; Lord Somers, for instance, holding that, where the debts exceeded the personalty it must be inferred that the testator intended in charging his realty to relieve the personalty altogether[2]. At the end of the 18th century the question came before Lord Thurlow in *Ancaster v. Mayer*[3], and he stated that the rules on the subject were then in a most uncertain condition, and laid down the rule which has ever since been adhered to, that a mere charge would not suffice to remove the primary liability of the personal estate, but, to effect this, a clear indication of the testator's intention must appear upon the will, or deed creating the charge[4]. The rule first stated above involved the payment out of the personalty, not specifically bequeathed, of mortgages and charges for which the testator or intestate was liable, and, since heritable debts are unknown in England, the heir or devisee on whom the charged estate devolved could require the executor to remove the burdens upon it. An exception to this rule was introduced where the charged estate had come to the testator '*cum onere*' even though he had covenanted to pay the debt. This was recognised so early as 1696[5], and was settled as a rule of the Court by Lord King. Successive statutes of the present century have been passed to abolish the principal rule itself, and now, in default of directions by the testator, charged realty passes to the heir or devisee subject to the charge[6].

Payment of debts out of real estate.

[1] 3 and 4 W. and M. c. 14.
[2] *Bamfield v. Wyndham*, Prec. Chy. 101 (1699).
[3] 1 W. and T. 723.
[4] *Trott v. Buchanan*, 28 C. D. 446.
[5] *Magnell v. Howard*, Prec. Chy. 61. *Evelyn v. Evelyn*, 2 P. W. 659 (1728).
[6] Locke King's Acts, 17 and 18 V. c. 113, 30 and 31 V. c. 69, 40 and 41 V. c. 34.

In the distribution of 'equitable assets,' that is real property charged or devised for the payment of debts, Equity, from the beginning of the present period, followed the rule of equality, and distributed *pari passu* among all the unsecured creditors[1], but it preserved the legal priorities of the different classes of creditors against all other assets. Hinde Palmer's Act of 1870, however, abolished these priorities both at law and in equity.

The Statute of Frauds introduced important alterations with regard to wills, abolishing nuncupative wills of realty, and requiring those of personalty, exceeding £30, to be proved by three witnesses present at the time of the declaration of the will, and to be made at the testator's own home, unless made by him '*in extremis.*' From this time such wills, against which the Chancellors had long set their faces, became rare, but the interpretation of written wills continued to supply the Court of Chancery, and still supplies the Chancery Division with much of its work.

<small>Interpretation of wills.</small>

Two important points in regard to the revocation of wills were decided soon after the statute. A decision of Trevor, M. R. in 1701, that marriage and the birth of issue revoked a will of lands,—a decision previously arrived at by the Ecclesiastical Courts in regard to wills of personalty[2],—though it was dissented from by Lord Hardwicke, and was contrary to the express words of the Statute of Frauds, that nothing but what was there specified should operate to effect a revocation, let in the numerous discussions that afterwards perplexed the Courts of Law and Equity as to what alteration of the testator's circumstances would revoke a will. These questions were settled by the Wills Act, which restricted revocation, by reason of such alteration, to the case of marriage only. Lord Cowper decided that, as the revocation of a will is based upon intention, the revocation of a duplicate will revoke the original also[3]. In *Roach v. Hammond* Wright, L. K., decided that a will of personalty speaks from the death of the testator, and this rule was extended by the Wills Act to all wills[4].

[1] *Foly's* case, 2 Free. 49 (Nottingham).
[2] Williams on Executors, 8th Ed., p. 190.
[3] *Onions v. Fyrer*, 2 Vern. 741 (1716).
[4] Prec. Chy. 401 (1714). The actual

Legacies.

In the course of administration many questions upon the construction and effect of legacies came before the Court, of which the following are the more important.

A legacy to a creditor, provided it be as great as, or greater than the debt, and be not subject to any condition, is presumed, according to a rule settled by the case of *Talbot v. Shrewsbury*[1], in 1714, to be intended as a satisfaction of the debt, for the testator is taken to be just before he is generous, although, as Lord Cowper said in an earlier case, "it might be good equity to construe him to be both just and kind, if he intended to be both[2]." The presumption, though accepted, has often been disapproved, and slight evidence will suffice to oust it[3]. Even extrinsic evidence of the testator's intention is admitted against the presumption, although in modern times such evidence is generally rejected as an aid to the construction of wills[4].

Satisfaction of debts.

A corresponding rule had been applied so early as 10 Charles I.[5], where a portion had been agreed to be given to a child, and a subsequent legacy was left him.

The converse rule, that a legacy to a legatee to whom the testator stands *in loco parentis*, in the absence of evidence of the contrary intention of the testator, is adeemed by an advancement made to the legatee by the testator after the date of the will is traced by Lord Eldon to the time of Lord Hardwicke[6]. Lord Eldon disapproved of the rule, for the father, he thought, should be sole judge of the necessities of his children, and, since his wishes or his circumstances might have changed after he made his will, it ought not to be inferred that the legacy was intended by him as his child's whole provision. Lord Thurlow had

Ademption of legacies by advancements.

decision was that, where there is a legacy to 'relations,' the next of kin at the death take.
[1] 2 W. and T. 378.
[2] *Cuthbert v. Peacock*, Salk. 155.
[3] *Chauncey's Case.* 2 W. and T. 379. King, L. C. **Atkinson v. Littlewood**,

L. R. 18 Eq. 595.
[4] See *Kirk v. Eddowes*, 3 Ha. 509. Wigram, V. C.
[5] *Lake v. Lake*, Rep. Chy. 42. Taussaud v. Taussaud, 9 C. D. 363.
[6] *Exp. Pye*, 2 W. and T. 364.

previously refused to extend the rule to the case of illegitimate children. In *Pym v. Lockyer*[1] Lord Cottenham, contrary to the opinion previously current, decided that where a legacy is in this way adeemed, it is adeemed *pro tanto* only, and not altogether.

On similar principles a second legacy given in a codicil has been presumed to be a substitution for a legacy previously given, and in *Jones v. Selby*[2] in 1710 a legacy was taken to be in place of a *donatio mortis causa*, but in *Hooley v. Hatton*[3] in 1772, this presumption was much restricted, and was placed on a more rational basis. Where a second legacy is given *totidem verbis*, or in slightly altered terms, of the same amount, and in the same instrument, it is *primâ facie* a repetition, but if it is given by a different instrument, it is *primâ facie* cumulative[4].

Substitution of legacies.

The distinction between demonstrative, specific and general legacies was taken over by Equity from the Ecclesiastical Courts.

General legacies have this disadvantage, that they abate if necessary for the payment of debts before specific legacies[5]; on the other hand, specific legacies are adeemed if the subject of the legacy cease to exist. Bond debts, at the beginning of the 18th century, when as already stated they offered the common form of investment, were often the subject of specific legacies, and the question arose whether payment of the debt to the testator would effect an ademption. It was agreed that this would be so if he had demanded the payment, but Lord Hardwicke[6], approving a distinction suggested before his time, held that, if the bond had been voluntarily discharged, there would be no ademption. This however was overruled by Lord Camden[7]; and in *Ashburner v. Macguire*[8] it was settled by Lord Thurlow that whenever the subject

Ademption of specific legacies.

---

[1] 5 M. and Cr. 29 (1840). Leighton v. Leighton, L. R. 18 Eq. 459.
[2] Prec. Chy. 300.
[3] 2 W. and T. 349.
[4] Wilson v. O'Leary, 7 Ch. 448.
[5] *Sayer v. Sayer*, Prec. Ch. 302, (1714).
[6] *Pettiward v. Pettiward*, Cas. temp., Finch, p. 152, see 2 W. and T. p. 248.
[7] *Atty.-Gen. v. Parkin*, Ambler, 566 (1769).
[8] 2 W. and T. 246 (1784).

of a specific legacy ceases to exist *in specie* the legacy is lost, without any reference to the presumed wishes of the testator[1].

A somewhat similar doctrine to that of the satisfaction of a debt by a legacy is that of the satisfaction of a covenant to settle property by the devolution upon the intended grantee, on the intended grantor's death intestate, of the property in question, or of property of the kind specified, if none in particular is indicated by the covenant. This doctrine was applied in *Wilcocks v. Wilcocks*[2] in 1706, and its principle was affirmed a few years later by Lord Cowper in a case[3] where personalty passed on the intestacy of a husband to his wife, to whom he had covenanted to leave a sum of money by will, and again in the leading case of *Lechmere v. Lechmere*[4] by Lord Talbot, where the covenant was to buy fee simple land, subject to certain consents, and to settle it to specified uses, and such land having been bought, but without the consents and without being so settled, on its coming by intestacy to the person who would, in the events that happened, have been entitled had the purchase and settlement been made in accordance with the deed, the Chancellor held that the covenant was thereby satisfied *pro tanto*.

Marshalling.

The opportunity which bond creditors had of obtaining payment out of the lands of their debtor on his decease, or out of the personalty at their discretion, while the simple contract creditors were restricted to the personalty only, led to the introduction of the doctrine of marshalling, which Equity applies wherever one who has two funds to have recourse to, would otherwise defeat the claims of another who has but one. The practice adopted in early days was to summarily forbid the creditor with two funds to touch that which was the sole resource of the other. Gilbert, C.B., in the middle of the last century, who, however, often represents as good equity what was already out of date, says that the course adopted in his

[1] **Harrison v. Jackson,** 7 C. D. 339.
[2] 2 Vern. 558.
[3] *Blandy v. Widmore,* 2 W. and T. 428 (1716).
[4] 2 W. and T. 412 (1735).

time was to hand over the bond to a trustee for the simple contract creditors, but long before they had been allowed to stand in the place of the bond creditors as against the real estate, to the extent to which these had exhausted the personalty, without the necessity for an action at law[1].

Lord Hardwicke held that, where a mortgagee of copyhold lands was paid out of the personalty, the simple contract creditors had no right to stand in his place against the lands, though he would have had they been freeholds. This decision was entirely forgotten till a note of it was unearthed in 1793, and it was shortly afterwards overruled by Lord Eldon[2], who laid down the general rule, stated above, in the broadest terms. The statutes subjecting real estate to simple contract debts, and placing such debts and specialty debts on an equal footing, have greatly diminished the importance of this doctrine, but in such a case as that of two mortgagees of whom one has a charge upon two estates and the other upon one of them only, it remains to give valuable assistance to the less favoured creditor. It is never applied, however, so as to prejudice the rights of the person marshalled against[3].

The same principle was applied between legatees, for instance, where one of two legacies was charged on the realty and the other not, the former was, if necessary, thrown upon the realty so as to leave the personalty for the latter. And so where creditors who might have proceeded against the realty exhausted the personalty, the legatees were permitted to stand in their place as against the realty, provided it were not specifically devised[4]. It was subsequently decided, in Lord Eldon's time[5], that all devises, even residuary devises, are specific, and so the legatees,—where there is no charge in question,—are now allowed to marshal against descended lands only.

Marshalling in favour of legatees was fully treated by Gilbert, C.B., and its main rules stated, but in his day the heir was

---

[1] Gilb. *Chancery*, p. 306. *Clifton v. Burt*, 1 P. W. 679 (1720). *Tipping v. Tipping*, 1 P. W. 729 (1721), Macclesfield.
[2] *Aldrich v. Cooper*, 2 W. and T. 82 (1802).
[3] **Webb v. Smith**, 30 C. D. 192.
[4] *Clifton v. Burt*, 1 P. W. 678 (1720).
[5] *Howe v. Lord Dartmouth*, 2 W. and T. 329, and see *Collins v. Lewis*, L. R. 8 Eq. 708.

treated with the same consideration almost as the devisee, and legatees were not allowed, by marshalling, to utterly exhaust his patrimony; indeed, unless they were near relations of the testator, or their legacies were given them for other meritorious consideration, this relief was not extended to them at all[1]. These modifications on the general rule have however been long abandoned.

Marshalling will not be allowed in aid of a bequest which is contrary to the Mortmain Act. This was decided by Lord Hardwicke soon after the passing of the Act[2].

Election.

"Where a man takes upon him to devise what he had no power over, upon a supposition that his will will be acquiesced in this Court compels the devisee, if he will take advantage of the will, to take entirely, not partially under it," so Lord Talbot ruled in *Streatfield v. Streatfield*[3]. The doctrine was well established by an earlier case, in which an heir, to whom the fee simple lands had been devised by his ancestor, was required to relinquish his claim either to them or to certain entailed lands to which he was by law entitled, but which had been devised by the ancestor to another[4]. It was finally decided, after some conflict of opinion, by the House of Lords[5], in 1816, that extrinsic evidence cannot be admitted to prove that the testator thought that certain specified property was his own, and therefore was intended by him to be included in a general devise, and thus to raise a case of election. The gift of what is not the testator's property must appear on the face of the will.

Modern decisions have placed this doctrine upon the ground of compensation, the devisee or legatee, who is compelled to elect, being required to compensate the devisee or legatee, who would otherwise be disappointed by his refusal to relinquish the property devised or bequeathed to the latter, out of the

[1] *Chancery*, p. 307.
[2] *Mogg v. Hodges*, 2 Ves. 83.
[3] 1 W. and T. 400 (1735).
[4] *Noys v. Mordaunt*, 1 W. and T.
p. 395 (1706).
[5] *Doe v. Chichester*, 4 Dow. 65. *Stratton v. Best*, 1 Ves. Jur. 285 (1791).

property devised or bequeathed to himself, so that if this be from the circumstances of the gift or devise impossible, there is no election[1].

Restraints upon Marriage.

Among the rules adopted from the civil law, as we have already seen, were rules avoiding conditions upon legacies in restraint of marriage, such conditions having been declared of no weight by the *Leges Julia et Papia Poppæa*. In early times these conditions without distinction were treated as void, but at the end of the 17th and the beginning of the 18th century distinctions began to be admitted, chiefly no doubt by reason of the slackening regard for the claims of the heir and of children, the usual legatees, the satisfaction of which had once been looked upon as a debt of nature. Hale, C. B., sitting with Clarendon, L. C., in 1663[2], held that, where a portion was given subject to a marriage with the consent of a specified person, and the condition was not observed, the portion must nevertheless be paid, for the condition was '*in terrorem*' only, but that had there been a limitation over, he said, it would have been otherwise. Six years later the same judge actually held that a devise on condition of marriage with consent, coupled with a gift over, was forfeited by breach of the condition, for, he said, devises were not governed by the civil law, and "there being a full breach of the condition as law will not, equity cannot help[3];" and the Lord Keeper Bridgman, who was nominally presiding in the Court, added the curious remark that "he was glad to see that a parent could settle his estate that it might be out of the power of a Court of Equity." By the middle of the following century it had become established, that conditions on devises of realty, unless in *general restraint* of marriage, were binding.

In the case of *Scott v. Tyler*[4], which was argued with great elaboration and consummate ability before Lord Thurlow[5], a

---

[1] *Bristowe v. Warde*, 2 Ves. Jur. 336, Loughborough. See **Vardon's Trusts**, 31 C. D. 275.

[2] *Belarsis v. Ermine*, 1 Ch. Ca. 22 (1663).

[3] *Fry v. Porter*, 1 Ch. Ca. 138.

[4] 2 W. and T. 120 (1787).

[5] By Mansfield, Scott (Lord Eldon), Graham, Alexander, Hardinge, Hargreave, Plumer and Stratford.

legacy had been given to the testator's daughter to be paid to her at the age of twenty-one if she were then unmarried, and if she married under that age with the consent of the specified persons to be settled upon her. She married under twenty-one without consent, and filed a bill against the residuary legatee to have the condition declared to be void. In his argument for the Defendant Mr Hargreave suggested that the whole doctrine of the invalidity of these conditions was based on a misapprehension of Roman Law, but it was, he admitted, too late to retract. He however argued that, though a condition subsequent upon a legacy in restraint of marriage would be void, yet a condition precedent would not be, for, in the absence of compliance, the legatee could never become entitled. He admitted that this distinction was directly opposed to the deliberately formed opinion of Lord Hardwicke, but it was, he said, approved by Lord Nottingham in *Popham v. Bamfield*[1] (not a case of marriage), where his Lordship said "precedent conditions must be literally performed, and this Court will never vest an estate where, by reason of a condition of precedent, it will not vest in him at law,...but with the conditions subsequent it is otherwise, and relief can be given against them if it is just and equitable." Lord Thurlow approved the distinction and dismissed the bill. The effect of these and later decisions may be summed up as follows: Conditions in restraint of marriage whether upon legacies or devises are good if they are conditions precedent. Conditions subsequent, if in general restraint, are binding in regard to devises (at any rate if they can be construed as intended to make a provision until marriage), but are not binding in regard to legacies; if in particular restraint, i.e. forbidding marriage with a particular person, they are binding in regard to devises, but not binding in regard to legacies unless the legacies be given over on non-compliance[2].

Marriage brocage contracts, that is contracts to procure marriages, have always been disfavoured in equity and were regularly set aside until Lord Somers' time[3]. He refused to

[1] 1 Vern. 83.
[2] Pollock on Contracts, 4th Ed., p. 309.
[3] *Hall v. Potter*, Show, P. C. 78.

follow the rule, but his judgment was reversed by the House of Lords, and the rule has obtained ever since.

3. *Married Women's Property.*

It has already been shown that, during the preceding period, Equity had refused to treat all the personal property in possession of a married woman as the Common Law did, as, during the continuance of the coverture, necessarily vested in her husband. During the last and the present centuries, it has gone further, and gradually, by extending its doctrine of separate estate, has placed married women in an even peculiarly favourable position as regards property given or settled to their sole use.

It was decided in 1725[1] that, if property were given for her separate use, even though conveyed directly to the married woman, it would be preserved for her, her husband being regarded as a trustee of it. This cannot, however, be said to have been settled till much later, for Lord Thurlow at the end of the century thought the interposition of trustees necessary to the creation of separate estate.

Separate estate.

In 1750, Lord Hardwicke[2] clearly stated as the rule of the Court that a married woman could as freely dispose of personalty held to her separate use by deed or will as if she were unmarried, but it was not till the great case of *Hulme v. Tennant*[3] came before Lord Thurlow, that it was decided that her general engagements, made without express reference to it, would nevertheless bind her separate estate in personalty. A married woman, the Chancellor said, is not legally incapable, as an infant is, and therefore such property as she can freely dispose of during the coverture ought to be liable to her debts. The method of securing real estate to a married woman adopted long before this time was to give the rents and profits for her separate use for life, and to give her a power of appointment by will or deed, or by will only, over the reversion in the land expectant upon her life estate. And in the case just mentioned, the Chancellor held that the rents and profits so given were

[1] *Bennet v. Davies*, 2 P. W. 316.   [2] *Peacock v. Monk*, 2 Ves. 190 (1750).
[3] 1 W. and T. 536 (1778).

liable for the debts, but, though the power of appointment was an unlimited one, he refused to direct its exercise so as to subject the reversion to the debts also.

Although Lord Thurlow's judgment was based entirely upon the admitted right of the wife to dispose of her property, yet in many subsequent cases the liability of the separate estate for engagements not referring expressly to it was placed on the ground that the engagements must be taken as appointments *pro tanto*, from which it followed that the wife's undertaking to pay must be in writing. This doctrine was, however, rejected by Lord Cottenham and Lord Brougham, who said that the liability of the separate estate is a corollary to the wife's power of disposition over it, and it was accordingly decided soon afterwards that, to the same extent as a man's contract made in the same form would bind his property, a married woman's would bind her separate estate[1], subject, however, to this, that the contract must be shown, by its express terms, the circumstances under which it was made, or other evidence, to have been made with reference to, and upon the faith or credit of that estate[2].

It had always been held, and without reference to the doctrine of separate estate, that, where a power of disposition was given to her, a wife could exercise it notwithstanding her coverture, but it was not finally settled, until a decision[3] of Lord Westbury in 1865, that where the fee simple of realty was held on trust for a married woman for her separate use, she could freely dispose of it by will or deed,—a power extended to her in the case of personalty more than a century before,—although, where lands were given in trust for her simply, on the analogy of the Common Law, and the restraining clause in the Statute of Wills, she could not have disposed of them without her husband's concurrence at all, and with it only by fine, recovery, or deed acknowledged, or by will.

The full liberty of disposition gradually acquired in this way was allowed to be limited by the imposition in the settlement on, or the conveyance to the married woman of

---

[1] See per Kindersley, V. C. *Vaughan v. Vanderstegen*, 2 Drew 165 (1853).

[2] *Johnson v. Gallager*, 3 D. F. J. 509 (1861).

[3] *Taylor v. Meads*, 34 L. J. Ch. 203.

a restraint on anticipation which was first introduced at Lord Thurlow's suggestion[1] into a settlement of which he was trustee, and, though it is repugnant to the principle that a power of disposing of it is incidental to the right to possess property, Lord Avanley, Lord Thurlow's successor, held the restraint to be valid.

An important extension of the doctrines of separate estate was made by a decision[2], that property held as separate estate during a prior coverture, is held again as such on the remarriage of a widow, although at the determination of her previous coverture all distinction due to the coverture between different parts of her property had lapsed, for separate estate, and, it may be added, the peculiar variety of separate estate with restraint on anticipation, exist only during the owner's coverture.

Recent statutes, beginning with the Divorce Act of 1856, have successively extended the right of married women to hold, at law, property to their separate use; and the last statute, the Married Women's Property Act of 1883, has practically put an end to the husband's interest in his wife's property other than his chance of curtesy or of acquisition on her death intestate[3].

Not only did Equity protect property settled to a married woman's separate use, but, from Lord Coventry's time, if a husband sought the assistance of the Court to recover property come to him through his wife, it required him to make some provision for her out of it. From *Jacobson v. Williams*[4], in 1717, it went further still, and the rule was established that, where either the husband,—or assignees in bankruptcy representing him,—was claiming in Equity, through his wife, property of considerable amount, she might come and insist on having a part settled to her separate

Equity to a settlement.

---

[1] See note to *Pybus v. Smith*, 3 Bro. C. C. 347.

[2] *Tullet v. Armstrong*, 1 Bea. 1 (1847). Langdale, M. R.

[3] Many of the old rules with regard to equitable separate estate have been held to apply to the separate estate created by this statute; thus a married woman's contract does not bind her separate estate unless she had, when contracting, some separate estate with regard to which she "might reasonably be deemed to have contracted." *Leak v. Driffield*, 29 Q. B. D. 98.

[4] P. W. 384.

use. In Lord Hardwicke's time this rule was carefully reconsidered and approved, and the amount which must be claimed to entitle the wife to apply to the Court was fixed at £200[1].

Although Lord Hardwicke had interfered to secure a provision for the wife where a legacy left to her was being recovered in the Spiritual Court, the right of the wife to come into Equity, when no application was pending there by the husband or his assignees, and to claim an 'equity to a settlement' out of property he, or they, were getting possession of, without the Court's interference, was not admitted till the leading case of *Elibank v. Montolieu*[2] was decided at the beginning of the century, but it was there established. And in a subsequent development of the same case it was determined that, the wife dying after making her claim and without releasing it, her children were entitled to insist upon it.

It was settled too, about the same time, that an assignment by the husband for valuable consideration before he actually received the property would not bar the wife's equity, though it would, if the property were got in during his life, bar her chance of survivorship[3].

The husband was at law, and, subject to the wife's equity to a settlement, in equity also, entitled to all the personalty of his wife not settled to her separate use, which he got possession of during the coverture, but her personalty, which at his death was still unreduced into his possession, reverted to her. Personalty therefore to which the wife was entitled in reversion unless it fell in during his life never came under the husband's control, and, even though the two concurred in assigning it, the assignment would be of no avail to bar the wife's title on her husband's death, for, by reason of her coverture, her assent would not bind her after her husband's death. And this was held in *Hornsby v. Lee*[4] in 1816. This case affords an excellent illustration of the protection given to married women. Even when the juristic capacity of married

The wife's reversion.

---

[1] *Jewson v. Moulson*, 2 Atk. 417 (1742). *March v. Head*, 3 Atk. 720.
[2] 1 W. and T. 486 (1801), Loughborough.
[3] *Macaulay v. Phillips*, 4 Ves. 19. *Johnson v. Johnson*, 1 J. and W. 472 (1820), Plumer, M. R.
[4] 2 W. and T. 906, Plumer, M. R.

women was treated by the Chancellors as far greater than it was at law, or subsequently in equity, this was for their advantage only. Thus, under Edward IV., where a conveyance of a wife's real estate had been made by her husband, without a fine but with her concurrence, and she, after her husband's death, sought to reclaim the lands by a '*cui in vita*,' the purchaser asked in vain for relief against what he naturally regarded as a fraudulent claim[1].

The Married Women's Property Acts, before referred to, are rapidly making all these doctrines obsolete.

The principle on which it is held, that, where one mortgages his estate as security for the debt of another, the mortgage shall have no further operation than its intended object requires, *Mortgage of* is a general one, and was recognised and applied *the wife's estate.* by Lord Nottingham in the case of attendant terms, but it received its most prominent applications with regard to mortgages of a wife's estate for her husband's debt.

So early as 15 Car. I., where a wife levied a fine to secure a lease to a mortgagee, the lease was not allowed to be used to bar her dower after the satisfaction of the mortgage[2]. And in 1702 the House of Lords, reversing Wright, L. K., decided that the widow's, not her late husband's heir, was entitled to an estate, which she and her husband, acting under a power, had mortgaged to secure his debt, and which had been reconveyed, on payment off, to him[3]. Following this, it was held soon after that, on the husband's death before redemption, the widow could file a bill to compel his executors to redeem her mortgaged estate[4]. And this was extended by Lord Hardwicke to enable the wife to stand in the mortgagee's place to recover the money, as any other surety might, if she paid the mortgage off[5].

A mere variation in the limitations of the proviso for redemption in the mortgage will not be taken as intended by the husband and wife to be an exercise of a power of resettlement, and indeed, before the case of *Jackson v. Innes*[6] was

[1] Ante, p. 83, and see pp. 93 and 142, and T. 1150.
[2] *Naylor v. Baldwin*, Rep. in Chy. 69.
[3] *Huntingdon v. Huntingdon*, 2 W.
[4] *Pocock v. Lee*, 2 Vern. 604 (1707).
[5] *Patersche v. Powlet*, 2 Atk. 384.
[6] 1 Bligh, 104.

discussed in the House of Lords, in 1819, it was thought that no form of limitation in the proviso for reconveyance in the mortgage, without an express recital, would suffice to effect a resettlement.

4. *Infants.*

After the abolition, on the Restoration, of the Court of Wards, and perhaps at an earlier period, the Court of Chancery undertook to appoint guardians for infants, upon petition, and claimed a general jurisdiction to interfere for the protection of infants in all cases. The leading case on the subject is *Eyre v. The Countess of Shaftesbury*[1], in which the Court interfered to support the authority of a testamentary guardian, Mr Justice Eyre, who was the survivor of three guardians appointed under the statute of 12 Car. II., which first allowed a father by his will to appoint guardians of his infant son. So firmly established did Lord Commissioner Gilbert consider the jurisdiction, that he traced the obligation of loyal obedience to the debt of gratitude due "for the protection which the infant receives at his first breathing vital air, since care is supposed to be taken of him by appointing proper guardians to manage him and his affairs." The jurisdiction, the Lords Commissioners said, was inherent in the King as *parens patriæ*, and was exercised by Chancery as representing him. The Defendant, the child's mother, in contempt of the order of the Court, carried him off and married him to the child of one of her friends, without the consent of the guardian, and for this the Court, following a practice already adopted, ordered her to be committed to prison. Most of the contempts alleged in the early cases are for marrying the ward to an improper person, or without obtaining the proper consents, and it is interesting to notice that the custom of child marriage, which was extremely prevalent among the wealthier classes during the 16th century, as the report of Henry VIII.'s divorce proceedings in the State Trials shows, survived into the 17th and 18th centuries also.

[1] 2 W. and T. 698 (1722).

The Court in Lord King's time[1], however, declined to treat the marriage of a ward by his guardian to the guardian's son, as a contempt where the ward was not a ward of Court; and Lord Eldon carried this further by refusing to interfere at all on behalf of an infant, except where there was property of the infant under the administration of the Court[2].

Lord Eldon claimed for his Court power to take away a child even from the father's custody[3], if the father were not in its opinion a fit person to be trusted with the care of the child, and by exercising this power in the case of a child of the poet Shelley he provoked the poet to address to him the well-known ode. Lord Macclesfield had, long before, claimed jurisdiction over the father of a ward of Court[4].

The custody of the father was, however, in ordinary cases regarded with such respect by the Court that it refused to decree the enforcement of an agreement by the father himself to surrender it[5]. "If the matter were *res integra*," said Lord Chelmsford[6] in reference to this, "I certainly should have a very strong opinion that this is opposed to a policy on which the best and dearest interests of society may depend." This view was shared by the Legislature, and Talfourd's Act enabled Chancery to give the custody of infants under seven years old to their mother; and the recent Infants' Custody Acts have extended this power and enabled the Court, for the infants' benefit, to enforce an agreement made by the father to surrender their custody[7].

The Court from the time of Lord Nottingham, made allowances for the maintenance of a child out of rents and profits to which he was absolutely entitled, and recent statutes[8]

---

[1] *Goodall v. Harris*, 2 P. W. 560 (1729).
[2] *Wellesley v. Duke of Beaufort*, 2 Russ. 21.
[3] *Shelley v. Westbrooke*, Jac. 266 n. The Common Law Courts only refused the father custody on the ground that he had shown his unfitness for it by grossly immoral conduct. See Seton, 4 Ed. p. 750.
[4] *Duke of Beaufort v. Bertie*, 1 P. W. 703.
[5] *St John v. St John*, 11 Ves. 530, Eldon.
[6] *Vansittart v. Vansittart*, 2 D. G. and Jo. 256 (1858).
[7] 2 and 3 Vic. c. 54. 36 and 37 V. c. 12.
[8] 23 and 24 V. c. 145, § 26. Conveyancing Act, 1881, § 43.

have greatly enlarged its power to make such allowances, extending it even to property to which the child is only contingently entitled.

The Legislature also intervened to extend the beneficial powers of the Court with regard to infants by Malins' Act, which enables the Court by its approval to give validity to a marriage settlement made by a female infant of 18, or a male infant of 20, where the infancy is the only objection to the settlement[1].

5. *Mortgages.*

We have seen that during the reign of Charles I. the right of the redemption of mortgages in equity was clearly established. This ruling, though it continued during the Commonwealth to be regarded as a somewhat oppressive and unwarrantable interference with deliberate contract, was never afterwards shaken, but, on the contrary, the mortgagor's interest was more and more fully protected by the Court, and this drew all questions connected with mortgages, whether concerning the conditions of redemption, the devolution of the right, or the rival claims of successive incumbrancers, into the forum where alone any other interest than that of the first mortgagee was recognised. The subject came before Lord Nottingham and his successors entirely unencumbered by rules of law, or traditions of earlier equity, and the elaborate chapter of the equitable code raised by their labours is a worthy monument to their care and ability. One doctrine only admitted by them is unworthy of the justice they professed to administer: the doctrine of 'tacking,' which allows a man, who intended to buy, and thought he had bought from a second, what the second had already sold to a third, by securing a perfectly adventitious addition to his shadowy right to cheat his rival of what he had in fact fairly bought and obtained.

From the first the maxim 'once a mortgage always a mortgage' was adopted: it is a rule, said Lord Nottingham,

[1] 20 and 21 Vict. c 57. See *Seaton v. Seaton,* 13 Ap. Ca. 61.

"that no mortgage by any artificial words can be altered, but only by subsequent agreement[1];" and in a case where the mortgage deed had provided that no one but the mortgagor or his direct heir should redeem, the same Chancellor allowed a jointress to do so, in spite of the deed[2]. This decision Lord North affirmed, and the rule has prevailed ever since, that no contemporaneous agreement shall put a restriction upon the right to redeem.

Redemption and foreclosure.

After a number of discussions as to who might sue for the redemption, it became settled by Lord Hardwicke's time that, practically, any one who, but for the mortgage (or in the case of a second or subsequent mortgagee, the mortgages antecedent to his own), would have been interested in the land, might do so.

The decree for redemption always involved alternatively, on non-compliance with its terms, foreclosure, and the mortgagee, as appeared at an earlier period, could sue for foreclosure in an original suit. The decree for foreclosure was not, however, absolutely final in every case, indeed, in 16 Car. II., it was described as 'in the nature of a mortgage' itself, and it was said that 'in cases of inevitable necessity' the Court would enlarge the time for payment even after the decree was signed and inrolled[3]. Later cases have put a limit to the indulgence once granted in this respect, and a foreclosure, after it has been made absolute, is not now reopened, unless the security is ample and good grounds are shown for the relief[4]. The time fixed for repayment of the mortgage money is more readily extended if application be made before it has expired, and if the interest and costs to date be paid, but even for this indulgence, since *Nanny v. Edwards*[5] was decided in 1827, some special ground must be shown. If, however, the mortgagee sues upon a collateral security to recover the mortgage money after foreclosure, his action will suffice to reopen the foreclosure at any time. This was decided in 1729[6], and a century later

[1] *Jason's Case*, 2 Ch. Ca. 33 (1680).
[2] *Howard v. Harris*, 2 W. and T. 1190.
[3] *Cocker v. Bevis*, 1 Ch. Ca. 61.
[4] See **Campbell v. Hoyland**, 7 C. D. 172.
[5] 4 Russ. 125. *Eyre v. Hanson*, 2 B. 479.
[6] *Dashwood v. Blightway*, 1 Eq. Ab. 317.

Lord Langdale, M. R., ruled that, conversely, if, having put it out of his power to reconvey the land, the mortgagee sues for the money, his suit will be stayed[1].

The usual terms of redemption are payment of principal, interest and costs. In *Howard v. Harris*[2], however, Lord North, in spite of the rule against giving interest upon interest, allowed the interest unpaid from time to time to be taken as added to the principal according to the terms of the mortgage. When a similar point came before Lord Hardwicke he said he would, if there were an agreement to that effect in writing, allow interest in arrear to be added to the principal[3], but only at the rate reserved by the mortgage. Apart from agreement, interest on interest is not allowed[4].

The mortgagor is not compelled to account for the profits. This was expressly decided by Lord Loughborough, in 1796, but the contrary rule has never existed, for if the mortgagee wants the profits he can take possession, though then he will be held strictly to account under a rule established from an early period[5], and he will even be charged an occupation rent if he occupy the premises himself. If he take possession unnecessarily, as if no interest is in arrear, he will suffer loss of interest by having the surplus profits, after allowing for the interest as it comes due, set off against the capital yearly. So Lord Hardwicke held[6]. But the rule does not apply if he is forced to take possession to preserve himself from loss[7]. In any case a mortgagee in possession is chargeable, not only with what he receives, in fact, but also with what he would have received, but for his wilful neglect[8].

The assignee of a mortgage debt was held to be entitled to all that was due, irrespective of what he had paid himself, as against the mortgagor, but not, according to Lord Jefferies, as against subsequent incumbrancers unless they had refused to

[1] *Lockhart v. Hardy*, 9 B. 349.
[2] 2 W. and T. 1178 (1683).
[3] *Thornhill v. Evans*, 2 Atk. 330 (1742).
[4] *Proctor v. Cooper*, Prec. Chy. 116 (1700).
[5] *Fulthorpe v. Foster*, 1 Vern. 476 (1687). *White v. City of London Brewery Co.* 42 C. D. 240.
[6] *Robinson v. Cumming*, 2 Atk. 410.
[7] *Davis v. May*, 19 Ves. 384 (1815). Grant, M. R.
[8] *Noyes v. Pollock*, 32 C. D. 53.

buy at the same rate[1], this distinction, however, was abandoned in Lord Hardwicke's time[2]. Of course, according to the rules already mentioned under the head of trusts, any purchaser of the mortgage who stands in a fiduciary relation to the mortgagor, or to a puisne mortgagee, cannot make a profit by charging his cestui que trust more than he paid himself.

A statute of 1734 allowed a mortgagor when sued at law by the mortgagee, in simple cases, to plead his mortgage and obtain a judgment for redemption, but the statute was of little importance, and Equity retained its practically exclusive hold over mortgages.

In the present century many additional powers for dealing with mortgages have been given to the Court by statutes, of which power to decree sale, in any case, instead of foreclosure, is one of the more important. Lord Hardwicke[3] had said that if the security were scanty, the mortgagee might demand a sale, but the Court never assumed a general jurisdiction to decree it.

In Equity the mortgagor was looked upon as owner in fee, save as against the mortgagee, and a husband was consequently, and according to Lord Hardwicke's decision in *Casborne* v. *Scarfe*[4], entitled to curtesy out of his wife's mortgaged lands. On the other hand, the mortgagee's interest was considered as personal assets, and Lord Nottingham decided that the mortgage money repaid after the mortgagee's death passed as personal estate to his executors, and not to his heir. It is interesting to notice that in the case where this question first arose, the Master of the Rolls modestly refused to give judgment because it was like to be a leading case[5].

Tacking.

The doctrine of tacking, to which reference has already been made, owes its establishment to Hale, C. B., who first

[1] *Phillips* v. *Vaughan*, 1 Vern. 336 (1686). *Williams* v. *Springfield*, 1 Vern. 476.
[2] *Morret* v. *Paske*, 2 Atk. 53.
[3] *Kinnoul* v. *Money*, 3 Swan, 202 n. 23 and 24 V. c. 145, § 71, Conveyancing Act, 1881, § 19.
[4] 2 W. and T. 1171 (1737).
[5] *Thornborough* v. *Baker*, 2 W. and T. 1165. *Tarbor* v. *Tarbor*, 3 Swan, p. 636.

admitted it in the Exchequer[1], and then, sitting with Bridgman L. K. in Chancery, in *Marsh* v. *Lee*[2], again based his judgment upon it, but it appears from this case that the doctrine had been suggested earlier. A mortgagor had mortgaged his estate successively to three persons, of whom the first held the legal estate, and the third had advanced his money without notice of the second mortgage, but had, upon advice of counsel, after a redemption suit by the second mortgagee against the mortgagor had been commenced, purchased the interest of the first mortgagee, and, as he had thus both law and equity, the Court decided he might shut out the second mortgagee until his own claims were satisfied. The Chief Baron described the legal estate bought from the first mortgagee as '*tabula in naufragio.*' Some of the early cases went an extreme length in admitting the protection of the legal estate, even where it was obtained by fraud, but this was restrained[3], and it is now settled that the puisne mortgagee cannot avail himself of the advantage of the legal estate unless he obtain it without anything to put a personal bar upon his user of it[4]. Lord Eldon went further, and said that notice to the first mortgagee of the second mortgage ought to make a conveyance of the legal estate from him useless for tacking, but this is now[5] decided the other way.

The whole doctrine was formulated in seven propositions in 1728 by Jekyll, M. R.[6], and, subject to the development just stated, these rules remain good. They provide, in addition to what has been said, that the puisne mortgagee who desires to tack must have a lien on the property for the debt for which he is seeking to obtain priority, created as such without notice of the mortgage to be tacked against. Even if the mortgagee have expressly agreed to make a further advance upon the security, if before making the advance he receive notice that a second mortgage has been made to some other person, he will not be

---

[1] *Hedworth* v. *Primate*, Hardress, 318, 14 Car. 2.
[2] 1 W. and T. 696.
[3] Per Hardwicke in *Garth* v. *Cotton*, 1 W. and T. 806.
[4] *Pilcher* v. *Rawlings*, 7 Ch. 259.

[5] *Peacock* v. *Burt.* 4 L. J., N. S. 33.
[6] *Brace* v. *The Duchess of Marlborough*, 2 P. W. 491. (A summary of the rules upon this subject is given in Coote on Mortgages, 5th Ed. p. 900.)

allowed to tack his further advance. This was decided by the House of Lords in 1861[1].

The doctrine was never extended so as to give special virtue to anything but the legal estate, for a conveyance of an equitable interest is an 'innocent conveyance.' And even as regards the legal estate the Court shrank from carrying it to its full extent, and where the legal estate and the subsequent lien were held in different rights it would not allow tacking[2].

The importance of the doctrine was much diminished when mere judgments were no longer allowed to create a charge on the lands of the debtor[3], and by the Vendor and Purchaser Act of 1870 the doctrine was temporally abolished, but it was revived in 1875 by the Land Transfer Act. It owes its origin, as Lord Hardwicke, who approved of it, said, to our divided system of judicature, for though "Courts of Equity break in upon the common law, where the necessity and conscience require it, still they allow superior force and strength to a legal title to estates[4]."

Consolidation.

Where a debtor owes to the same creditor two debts secured upon different properties of the debtor he is not allowed, against the wish of the creditor, to redeem one property without also redeeming the other, and this whether the creditor were the original lender in each case or an assignee of the debt and security in one or both of the cases only. This rule dates from the beginning of the present period, and it was founded upon the maxim that 'he who seeks equity must do equity'[5]. The right to consolidate availed against a purchaser of either of the equities of redemption from the mortgagor, and thus an additional risk was added to the many dangers which such a purchaser incurs. The extent of this risk has only quite recently, after some conflict of judicial opinion, been accurately and

[1] *Hopkinson v. Rolt*, 9 H. L. C. 514. *Bradford Banking Co. v. Briggs*, 12 Ap. Ca. 29.
[2] *Barnett v. Weston*, 12 Ves. 130 (Eldon).
[3] 27 and 28 Vic. c. 112.
[4] *Wortley v. Birkhead*, 2 Ves. Sen. 574.
[5] Francis, *Maxims of Equity*, p. 1.

definitely determined. The rule is that as against an assignee of the equity of redemption the right to consolidate must have existed as a present right *in esse* at the time of his purchase, and thus a subsequent mortgage by the mortgagor to the mortgagee cannot affect the right of the assignee to redeem[1].

The doctrine of consolidation, so far at least as it affects assignees, is now looked upon with disfavour, and the Conveyancing Act of 1881 enacts that, unless it is expressly provided in one of the mortgage deeds to the contrary, no consolidation of any mortgages made after the coming into operation of the Act shall be allowed.

Vendor's Lien.

A particular species of tacit mortgage constructed by Equity is worthy of notice. Where land is sold and the purchase-money remains unpaid there is, said the Court in 1684[2], "a natural equity that the land should stand charged with so much of the purchase-money as was not paid; and that without any special agreement for that purpose." On this was founded the vendor's lien. There was considerable conflict in subsequent cases as to what would serve to oust this implied lien, until the rule was settled by Lord Eldon in a judgment, which is an admirable example of its kind[3]. The lien, he said, is probably derived from the rule of the civil law, that on a sale the property does not pass without either payment or an agreement to give credit, and he expressed regret that it had ever been allowed without express contract. It is, according to this decision, a question of fact to be determined on all the circumstances, whether the lien was intended to be reserved or not, and the mere fact that a bill or other security is taken for the unpaid balance is not conclusive against the existence of the lien. I have stated on a previous page reasons for dissenting from the view that this lien is derived from the Roman Law. A reference to the originating case shows that though the 'natural equity' may have been consciously or unconsciously suggested by the civil rule, it was upon that, i.e. upon assumed

[1] **Jennings v. Jordan**, 6 Ap. Ca. 698.
[2] *Chapman v. Tanner*, 1 Vern. 267.
[3] *Mackreth v. Symmonds*, 1 W. and T. 355 (1808).

moral considerations arising out of the circumstances of the case, that the conception of the lien was founded.

Equitable Mortgages.

Mortgages by deposit of title-deeds were known at least from Lord Nottingham's time[1]. After the Statute of Frauds the question arose whether such a mortgage of realty was still permissible, and Lord Cowper held that it was[2], but the point was not finally settled until,—long after part performance had been decided to take contracts out of the statute,—a case came before the Court in 1783[3], in which Lord Loughborough said the delivery of the deeds was "a delivery of title to the plaintiff for valuable consideration." The Court he added " has nothing to do but supply legal formalities. In all these cases the contract is not *to be* performed but is executed," and so, according to Lord Eldon, the Chancellors repealed the statute so far as equitable mortgages are concerned. The facility of mortgaging established under this decision has proved to be a great convenience to land-owners, and by it some of the inconveniences arising from the difficulties of English law in regard to the conveyance of real estate have been made more tolerable. So common has the custom of borrowing money upon deposit become, that the unexplained absence of the documents of title is taken to be notice to a purchaser or mortgagee, upon a sale or mortgage of property, of the existence of an outstanding lien upon it.

Notice.

The doctrines of notice are of great importance in many departments of equity: purchase from a trustee with notice causes the buyer himself to be bound by the trust; a later incumbrancer advancing his money with notice cannot tack against an earlier; and many other instances might be given.

Cases occurred at an early period where actual notice to the party to be affected, that is to say, that the fact in question

---

[1] *Fitzjames v. Fitzjames*, Ca. temp, Finch, p. 10.
[2] *Hales v. Van Bereham*, 2 Vern. 617.
[3] *Russel v. Russel*, 1 W. and T. 780.

was brought to his knowledge, was not proved and yet he was held to have had 'notice.' Thus the Court under Lord Coventry, declared, in a passage[1] already quoted, that where lands were bought from a mortgagee it would take the purchaser to have notice of the mortgage, apparently because he would find it on the vendor's title-deeds if he made a proper examination, and notice by reference in deeds has been binding notice ever since Lord Nottingham's time, at least[2].

Another ground of constructive notice is the unexplained absence of deeds which the party bound ought to have expected to see, and, conversely, in *Peter v. Russel*[3], in 1716, Lord Harcourt refused to treat a loan to the mortgagor of the deeds, (a lease) borrowed on a plausible excuse, as notice of his intention to remortgage the property so as to postpone the first mortgagee, who had lent them, to a second mortgagee who was induced to advance his money upon seeing them.

So notice of occupation has been deemed to be notice of the terms of it since Lord Thurlow's time[4].

These rules have been said to rest upon "evidence of notice raising a presumption of notice so violent that the Court will not allow it to be rebutted," but it is obvious they really rest on negligence,—the Court has erected an 'average conveyancer,' and it penalises every one who takes less care than he. It is absurd to say the case rests on evidence of actual notice where the clearest evidence to disprove it would be ineffectual, and the effect is attained without reference to the opinion of the Court as to whether it existed or not.

Another kind of constructive notice, that of notice to the party's agent, rests on different grounds: it is a necessary precaution, and the identification of the principal and his deputy in this and many other cases is an incident of the extension of personalty which agency permits. *Notice to agent.*

This rule and the main exception to it can be traced to the beginning of the present period: "though notice to a man's counsel be notice to the party, yet where the counsel comes to

---

[1] *Bacon v. Bacon*, Toth. 133.
[2] *Bisco v. Banbury*, 1 Ch. Ca. 287.
[3] 1 Eq. Ca. Ab. 321.
[4] *Taylor v. Stibbert*, 2 Ves. Jur. 437.

have notice of the title in another affair, which it may be he has forgot when his client comes to advise with him a case with other circumstances; that shall not be such a notice as to bind the property," said Lord North in 1684[1]. Bridgman, L. K., in an earlier case had asked, with the feeling of one who had been a fashionable conveyancer, whether counsel could be expected to remember for ever? Lord Hardwicke approved the exception and it is well established[2]. It has even been suggested that it should be extended to personal notice also[3]. A distinction that there may be notice in a different transaction if it be near the other was adopted by Langdale, M. R., but this was exploded by the Court of Appeal[4].

Where the subject of notice is the fraud of the agent himself, of which he is of course aware, the principal is held not to be bound. This is a curious anomaly of recent date and hardly reconcileable with the reason given by Lord Hardwicke for the rule, that "he who trusts most should suffer most."[5]

Constructive notice has been recently put upon a statutory footing, but without any considerable alteration of the rules affecting it having been made[6].

Soon after the Registration Act of 7 Anne, it was held[7] that registration of a later conveyance should not secure priority over an earlier conveyance of the same land, if the later had been taken with notice of the earlier, for, said Lord Hardwicke, "taking the legal estate after notice of a prior right makes a person a *mala fide* purchaser," in accordance with Labeo's definition of *dolus malus*[8].

The legal estate has always been postponed when it has been taken with actual or constructive notice of an outstanding interest, save where, as in 'tacking', the purchaser has innocently obtained an equitable right of his own. But the legal estate will only be postponed to an equitable interest acquired

[1] *Preston v. Tubbin*, 1 Vern. 286 (1684).
[2] *Warwick v. Warwick*, 3 Atk. 294.
[3] *Hamilton v. Royse*, 2 S. and L. 327. Redesdale, C.
[4] *Hargreaves v. Rothwell*, 1 Kee. 159.
[5] *Kennedy v. Green*, 3 My. and K. 699.
[6] Conveyancing Act, 1882, § 3. See Hood and Challis, 3rd Ed. p. 166.
[7] *Blades v. Blades*, 1 Eq. Ab. 358, King C.
[8] *Le Neve v. Le Neve*, 2 W. and T. 26 (1747).

subsequently to the conveyance of the legal estate to the holder against whom relief is sought, on the ground of fraud. This rule was acted upon by Lord Harcourt in an early case[1]. At the end of the last century, however, Mr Justice Buller stated that it was "an established rule in a Court of Equity that a second mortgagee who has the title-deeds, without notice of any prior incumbrance, shall be preferred; because, if a mortgagee lends money upon mortgage without taking the title-deeds he enables the mortgagor to commit a fraud," and it appears that this was a correct statement of the practice of the Court at the time[2]. Lord Eldon repudiated this practice and returned to the view of Lord Harcourt, which had been adopted also by the judges who sat in the great case of *Ryall* v. *Rolles*[3], that the absence of the deeds when the money is lent is matter of evidence only, and this has been reaffirmed in a recent case[4]. Thus mere negligence in keeping the title-deeds or lending them to the mortgagor will not serve to postpone the legal owner. Of course, if his conduct amounted to an authority to some third person to sell or mortgage to the party claiming relief, the latter will have acquired a good title, but under, not against him.

6. *Fraud.*

The Court not only relieved against gross and palpable cases of fraud, where the party relieved had been intentionally deceived, but extended its interference to all cases of unfair dealing, even where there was an appearance of deliberate contract. The judges have always refused to define the boundaries of this interference, lest they should thereby suggest devices by which their jurisdiction might be evaded, but from the numerous decisions of the last two centuries some leading principles can be deduced.

From the year 1787 an action on the case for fraud, unconnected with any contract between the plaintiff and the defendant

---

[1] *Peter* v. *Russel*, 1 W. and T. 780.
[2] See *Evans* v. *Bicknell*, 6 Ves. p. 183. *Burnett* v. *Weston*, 12 Ves. 130.
[3] 2 W. and T. 799.
[4] **Northern Counties &c.** v. **Whipp**, 26 C. D. 487.

has been allowed at law[1], and after that time the Court of Equity was reluctant to give relief in cases where it could be fully obtained by an action for damages. Moreover, such an action was often more beneficial to the plaintiff than procedure in Equity, for a rule had long existed in that Court, a rule born of the essential viciousness of written evidence in disputed cases, by which the Chancellors refused to act upon the evidence of a single witness for the Plaintiff if it were directly contradicted by the Defendant, while at law the Defendant could give no evidence at all[2]. Where, however, rescission of a contract, or delivery up and cancellation of a deed was required, it still could be sought in Equity alone.

The equitable doctrine of estoppel by 'standing by' was laid down by Lord Macclesfield in these terms[3]: "when anything in order to a purchase is publicly transacted, and a person knowing thereof, and of his own right to the lands intended to be purchased, doth not give the purchaser notice of such right, he shall never afterwards be admitted to set up such right to avoid the purchase; for it is an apparent fraud in him not to give notice of his title to an intended purchaser, and in such case infancy or coverture shall be no excuse." And in a case, already cited, where a mortgagor of a lease, borrowed it from the mortgagee, who innocently lent it, and remortgaged it, Lord Harcourt gave as his reason for not postponing the first to the second mortgage that "he neither actively encouraged the Plaintiff to lend his money, nor passively, as by standing by and concealing the mortgage knowing the Plaintiff was about to advance money on the premises"[4]. The length to which this doctrine had been carried in the earlier cases[5] was curtailed to some extent by later decisions. Thus it was decided at the beginning of the 18th century that a party will not be prejudiced by his silence unless the circumstances, known to him, call upon him to speak. The rule is

Standing by.

[1] *Pasley v. Freeman*, 3 Term. Rep. 51, 2 Smith, L. C. 74.
[2] *Evans v. Bicknell*, 6 Ves. 183.
[3] *Savage v. Foster*, 2 W. and T. 680, (1722). There are a great number of these cases in the later 17th century reports. See *Hunsden v. Cheyney*, 2 Vern. 150 and note.
[4] *Peter v. Russel*, 1 Eq. Ca. Ab. 321 (1716), 1 W. and T. 780.
[5] *Edlin v. Battaly*, 2 Leo. 152 (27 Car. 2). *Hobbs v. Norton*, 1 Vern. 136.

"qui potest et debet vetare jubet[1]," and in modern cases this is taken to mean that the party to be prejudiced must have known of the other's mistake as to his, the former's, rights[2]. There is therefore no equity to recover the money expended if the spender lays it out over what he knows is another's land, as if a tenant, under no obligation to do so, and without agreement with his landlord, effects improvements on the land. This was so held early in the present century, and has since been approved in the House of Lords[3]. The recent Agricultural Holdings Acts, which have empowered a tenant under certain circumstances to charge the landlord with such improvements, rest on a different principle with which fraud has nothing to do.

In the cases just referred to the offending parties' right was postponed on the ground of his unduteous silence, but the principle was extended beyond this by a decision of Grant, M. R., that a trustee who represented to an intended mortgagee of the trust estate that there were no incumbrances upon it, whereas there was in fact already an incumbrance of which the trustee had had notice but which he had forgotten, must himself recoup the mortgagee the loss occasioned to him by the incumbrance, although the trustee had no interest in the estate[4]. This decision was founded upon a dictum of Lord Eldon in *Evans v. Bicknell*[5] that "it is a very old head of equity, that if a representation is made to another person going to deal in a matter of interest upon that representation, the former shall make that representation good, if he knows it to be false."

Since Lord Eldon's time the doctrine of 'making representations good' based upon this case has been the subject of much discussion, and the modern view is, that, putting aside estoppel, no claim for relief can be based upon any representation unless it either is a warranty or a term of contract or amounts to deceit at common law[6].

[1] *Osborne v. Lees*, 9 Mod. 96. *Hunning v. Ferrers*, Gilb. 85 (1711).
[2] **Willmot v. Barker**, 15 C. D. 96.
[3] *Pulling v. Armitage*, 12 Ves. p. 85. Grant, M. R. *Ramsden v. Dyson*, 1 L. R. H. L. 129.
[4] *Burrows v. Lock*, 10 Ves. 470, Grant M. R.
[5] 6 Ves. 182.
[6] Pollock on Contracts, Note N. **Peek v. Derry**, 14 Ap. Ca. 337. **Alderson v. Maddison**, 8 Ap. Ca. 467.

Catching Bargains.

In his celebrated judgment in *Chesterfield v. Janssen*[1] Lord Hardwicke in the classification of the frauds against which Equity would relieve, gave a special division to 'catching bargains with heirs, reversioners or expectants,' against which he said Equity had always relieved, even though no circumvention were charged, fraud being inferred from the transaction if "there were weakness on the one side (and) advantage taken of it on the other," and this partly on the ground of the deceit practised upon the father, ancestor or other relative of the heir, reversioner or expectant.

Cases where heirs who had pledged their future estates for present advances were released from their bargains, occurred in Equity from the time of Lord Ellesmere, but no definite rule was adopted, the relief being granted or rejected according as the individual Chancellor thought the case constituted an 'extremity' or not. Lord Nottingham expressed regret that the Civil Law rule of reopening bargains where less than half the value was given had not been applied, and he might well wish for some rule where the lack of it was so marked that again and again a Chancellor reversed the decree of his predecessor and left his own to be reversed by his successor, as happened in these cases at the end of the 17th century[2]. The favourite method of avoiding the usury laws of the period was to 'take up goods' at a high price for which credit was given, and immediately resell them for a much lower one in cash, a device so often illustrated in the Restoration drama, and against such bargains it was fairly settled the Court would generally relieve.

The whole doctrine was discussed in *Chesterfield v. Janssen*[3] with the care and ability its importance demanded. A man of full age, in possession of £7000 a year, but embarrassed by debt, borrowed £5000 in the open market from the Defendant on a bond to repay £10,000 at the death of the Duchess of

[1] 1 W. and T. 624.
[2] *Nott v. Johnson*, 2 Vern. 26.
(Nottingham, Jeffries, North). *Birney v. Pitt*, 2 Vern. 15.
[3] 1 W. and T. 624 (1750).

Marlborough, from whom he had expectations. After his death his representatives applied to have the bond set aside. The plaintiff's counsel relied on the precedents, and the analogy of the usury laws and of the Macedonian decree. The Defendant's counsel put their case on the broad ground that a "man's own act, without fraud, in full senses, and having absolute disposal," ought to bind him. Interest on money, they said, was then admitted to be legal and its allowance to be for the public benefit,—and on the latter point they cited the opinion of the philosopher Locke,—so long as the statutes against usury were not infringed; moreover the case, they urged, was analogous to a 'bottomry bond,' in which great profit had always been permitted on account of the risk of the principal; and finally they appealed to the Court to dismiss the suit, for "this Court," they said, "does not exercise or assume a legislative power, but disclaims it, and never will make a law to set aside contracts on public principles out of that cause, if good in law and conscience, let the convenience or inconvenience be what it will," for "*misera est servitus ubi jus vagum.*" The judges advised that there was no fraud proved, and the contract was not usurious, and with this the Chancellor agreed, but, on the ground of the position of the parties, he would nevertheless have set the contract aside, had not the expectant confirmed it after the death of the Duchess. The Court, he said, had undoubted jurisdiction to relieve against every species of fraud, and, though he 'utterly disclaimed' the power of legislation, the precedents had decided that in equity such a bargain as that in question must be ranked as fraudulent.

Subsequent Chancellors have often disapproved of the doctrine, but it was thoroughly established by the case just considered. It has not, however, been extended to contracts relating to interests in possession[1], for, if inequality be the sole ground of objection, to set aside these "there must be an inequality so strong, gross and manifest that it must be impossible to state it to a man of common sense without producing an exclamation at the inequality of it." On the other hand, in the case of reversions it was pressed so far that the question

---
[1] *Gwynne v. Heaton*, 1 Bro. C. C. 8 (Thurlow).

counsel asked in *Chesterfield v. Jannsen*, "shall the heir starve *ob heredis causam?*" was in danger of receiving an affirmative answer. The suggestion in Lord Hardwicke's judgment that the ground of the interference was the deceit practised on the ancestor was acted upon by Lord Brougham, who refused to set aside a contract approved by the ancestor[1], but this was considered contrary to precedent[2], and the validity of the suggestion has been recently denied[3].

The usury laws have been repealed, and a modern statute[4] has enacted that no *bona fide* purchase of a reversionary interest shall be set aside merely on the ground of undue value, but the principles laid down by Lord Hardwicke remain living doctrines of the Court[5]. They have indeed been extended to protect a borrower who had only 'general expectations' upon the credit of which the loan was made[6]. The terms upon which the bargain is set aside are generally the payment of the money actually advanced, with ordinary interest upon it, and the costs of the action.

Undue Influence.

Another characteristic doctrine of equity is that applied in cases of 'undue influence.' Obligations entered into under duress have always been unenforceable at law, but equity goes much further, and interferes wherever 'confidence is reposed and betrayed,' to set aside the obligation or conveyance obtained by unfair advantage.

Probably the earliest cases were, where purchases or other advantages were obtained by guardians from their wards by a misuse of the guardians' influence or authority, but early in the 18th century the Court went beyond these simple cases, and decreed that a bond given by a poor and ignorant man to one who had given him slight assistance in some litigation should be taken as security for the money advanced only[7], and Lord

[1] *King v. Hamlet*, 2 My. and K. 456.
[2] *Sugden*, Law of Property, p. 66.
[3] **Aylesford v. Morris**, 8 Ch. 492. (Selborne).
[4] 31 and 32 Vic. c. 4.
[5] *Benzon v. Cook*, 10 Ch. 392.
[6] *Neville v. Snelling*, 15 C. D. 679.
[7] *Proof v. Hines*, Ca. Talbot, 116 (1735).

Talbot said the Court would "not suffer any advantage to be taken of the extravagance and want of judgment, in the one case, and of the strong bias to obtain what (was) desired in the other," and he added that, had the Defendant been the Plaintiff's Solicitor, the decree would have been made without question. The principle on which relief would be given was not settled till *Hugenin v. Baseley*[1] came before Lord Eldon, in 1807. There a widow had made a voluntary settlement upon a clergyman who had obtained great influence over her, and she had deliberately refused to allow a power of revocation to be inserted[2]; Lord Eldon set the settlement aside, but, he said, adopting an opinion he had probably heard Lord Thurlow express, "it is not upon the feelings which a delicate and honourable man must experience, hearing these instruments taken altogether as I think myself bound to take them, nor upon any notion of discretion in this Court to prevent a voluntary gift by a man stripping himself entirely of his property, if undue influence is not imputed, that any judge sitting here has ever thought himself at liberty to interpose." Sir Samuel Romilly in his argument in the case had said "the relief stands upon a general principle, applying to all the variety of relations in which dominion may be exercised by one person over another," and this has been ever since approved. The Courts in recent times, however, under this head as under others, have been less ready than they formerly were to interfere, in the way Coke so bitterly resented, "to break men's contracts[3]."

Mistake[4].

No branch of Equity retained the indefiniteness characteristic of an extra legal and discretionary relief longer than that which dealt with mistake. This was chiefly because questions turning on mistake, unaccompanied by fraud or misrepresentation, came but rarely before the Court, except in suits for specific performance or for the rectification of settlements,

---

[1] 2 W. and T. 600.
[2] See *Ellison v. Ellison*, 1 W. and T. p. 291.
[3] See **Allcard v. Skinner**, 36 C. D. 145.
[4] On this head see *Specific Performance*, Fry, L. J., ch. xv., and Pollock on Contracts, ch. ix.

though in these suits such questions had often to be considered. Contracts, other than those of which Equity would decree specific performance, were usually proceeded upon in the courts of common law alone, and it was in these courts therefore that the effect upon the liability of the party in error of mistake, affecting the substance of a definite contract, was, for the most part, worked out, though some of the later decisions in Equity pushed the relief afforded,—by the plea of *non est factum* for instance[1],—somewhat further than the common law allowed.

Mistake (1) may affect the expression in an instrument intended to have a legal operation of the agreement actually made, or the record of an actual transaction, or (2) it may go to the substance of the agreement or other transaction itself.

(1) Under the first head come the cases in which the Court granted the rectification of writings and instruments in order to make their terms correspond with the real meaning and intentions of the parties. This was constantly

Mistake in the expression of agreement.

granted from the earliest time as against volunteers, but not, in accordance with the general practice of Equity, at least after Lord Hardwicke's time[2], so as to prejudice anyone who purchased upon the actual terms of the settlement without notice of the mistake affecting them. It must of course be shown that an agreement in the terms sought to be substituted for the written terms was actually arrived at, and the Chancellor just referred to refused relief where the evidence was not clear and definite[3], and, in later times, Lord St Leonards refused to act upon parol evidence only in the face of the defendant's denial[4]. The commonest cases were concerned with marriage settlements[5], and in these there was usually no dispute, and often the marriage articles, which, after marriage, the wife was incompetent to consent to vary, plainly demonstrated what the real agreement between the parties was.

[1] See Pollock on Contracts, p. 444, 5th Ed. *Vorley v. Cooke*, 1 Giff. 235 (1857).

[2] *Warwick v. Warwick*, 3 Atk. p. 293.

[3] *Henkle v. Royal Exchange Assurance Co.* 1 Ves. Snr. p. 318.

[4] *Mortimer v. Shortall*, 2 Dr. and W. 374 (1842).

[5] *Legg v. Goldwire*, 1 W. and T. 17 (1736).

At law the rule that parol testimony cannot be received to contradict, vary, add to, or subtract from the terms of a valid written instrument, had been adopted from remote antiquity[1], but where it was alleged that by mistake or surprise a term of the actual agreement was omitted from, or wrongly stated in the instrument, such testimony was always received in Equity on behalf of a defendant resisting a claim for specific performance based upon the instrument in its actual form. At the end of the last century several attempts were made to introduce the stricter rule of law into Equity, but even Lord Thurlow, though he expressed strong approval of the rule, and said that he thought that so much weight ought to be attached to the writing that it would in practice always prevail, recognised that error in the writing, though shown by parol evidence only, if due to mistake or surprise was a ground for equitable relief, and Lord Eldon, in *Townshend v. Stangroom*[2], stated that it was clearly settled that such matter could be relied on in defence, and he added, "I will not say that there are not cases in which it may be received to enable the Court to rectify a written agreement upon surprise and mistake, as well as fraud." Such cases had, as already shown, long before arisen and they still occur.

Parol evidence.

At the beginning of this period the Court still did not scruple to alter a will to make its wording conform to the testator's presumed intentions. If "there falleth out an unseen accident, which if the testator had foreseen, he would have altered his will, I shall consider it," Lord Nottingham declared[3], but this was not approved in the following century[4], and in 1798 the modern rule, that a will cannot be varied on the ground of mistake, unless the words alleged to be mistaken are clearly inconsistent with the intention shown by the will itself, was definitely laid down by Sir Pepper Arden, M.R.[5] To this may be added, though it

Rectification of wills.

---

[1] Taylor on Evidence, 8th Ed. p. 963.
[2] 6 Ves. 330. See *Specific Performance* post, p. 253.
[3] *Winkfield v. Combe*, 2 Ch. Cas. 16 (1679).
[4] See *Mostyn v. Mostyn*, 5 H. L. Ca. 155.
[5] *Mellish v. Mellish*, 4 Ves. 44.

properly falls under the second division of 'mistake,' that, where a disposition purports to have been made entirely on the assumption that a state of circumstances exists which in fact does not exist, it will be treated as not made. Thus, where, by a codicil, a testator revoked legacies on the ground that the legatees were dead, while in fact they survived him, Lord Eldon ordered the legacies to be paid[1].

The peculiar construction of releases in Equity, which restricts their operation to matters within the contemplation of the parties, rests also partly on mistake of expression, and partly on mistake going to the substance of the transaction. This construction accorded with principles settled before the present period, and was, in fact, a development of the rule that words are to be understood *secundum subjectam materiam*, for "the chief and governing rule of construction is drawn from the end or cause," and it was so put by Francis in 1737[2]. He states the rule thus: "general words in a release of all demands, or the like, shall be restrained by the particular occasion, and shall be intended only of all demands concerning the thing released." Equity will go even further and set aside a release made on the footing of accounts which turn out to be seriously inaccurate[3].

Releases.

(2) The jurisdiction to set aside a release just mentioned is a small survival of extensive powers once wielded by the Court. "Another impediment of assent," says the author of the 'Treatise of Equity[4],' "is ignorance and error whether in fact or in law; if it be the cause and motive of the agreement. And if the mistake is discovered before any step is taken towards performance, it is just that he should have liberty to retract; at least upon satisfying the other of the damage that he has sustained on losing his bargain. But if the contract is either wholly or in part performed, and no compensation can be given him,...then it is absolutely binding notwithstanding the error. Yet this

Mistake in matter of substance.

---

[1] *Campbell v. French*, 3 Ves. 321. Pollock on Contracts, p. 707, 5th Ed. cf. the 'dependent relative revocation' of wills.

[2] *Treatise of Equity*, p. 50.

[3] *Gandy v. Macaulay*, 31 C. D. 1.

[4] p. 10.

is not to be understood when there proves to be an error in the thing or subject, for which he bargained. For then the business is null itself, by the general laws of contracting, inasmuch as in all bargains, the matter, about which they are concerned, and all the qualities of it, good or bad, ought to be clearly understood; and without such a distinct knowledge the parties cannot be supposed to yield a full consent." The Court, moreover, as the same writer shows in his *Maxims*[1], would interfere to set aside a bargain if, by subsequent 'accident,' it turned out to be unexpectedly onerous, or if it was 'unreasonable[2],' "as forty years' purchase for lands, or an extravagant price for stock, as was given in the *South Sea* year." Gradually, however, relief, in many of these cases ceased to be obtainable.

If there is a mutual mistake going to the essence of the agreement[3] then equity would set the agreement aside, and still will do so[4]. Thus in *Bingham v. Bingham*[5] where the Defendant had agreed to sell to the Plaintiff an estate which turned out to be, in fact, the Plaintiff's own, the purchase-money was ordered to be refunded; "for though no fraud appeared, and the Defendant apprehended he had a right, yet there was a plain mistake such as the Court was warranted to relieve against, and not to suffer the Defendant to run away with the money in consideration of the sale of an estate, to which he had no right." This decision has been followed in recent times by the House of Lords[6].

The mistake may be that of one party only. If there is no agreement, "if the Court is satisfied that the true intent of one of the parties was to do one thing, and he by mistake has signed an agreement to do another, that agreement will not be enforced against him, but the parties will be restored to their original position, and the agreement will be treated as if it had never been entered into[7]," a modern

Unilateral mistake.

[1] VII.
[2] *Treatise*, p. 11.
[3] ("the cause and motive of the agreement.")
[4] *Earl Beauchamp v. Winn*, L. R. 6, H. L. p. 233.
[5] 1 Ves. Snr. 126 (1748 M. R. sitting for Lord Hardwicke).
[6] *Cooper v. Phibbs*, L. R. 2 H. L. 149.
[7] *Paget v. Marshall*, 28 C. D. 263.

judge has said, and on this point there has been no difference between the earlier and the later equity. In such a case Lord Romilly offered the Defendant the alternatives of taking what the Plaintiff had, in fact, agreed to give, or having the whole rescinded. In these cases, as elsewhere, if an instrument purporting to contain the true agreement were executed, it could not be varied or cancelled to the prejudice of a purchaser without notice[1].

Where a real agreement has been entered into, but one of the parties would not have agreed but for a mistake, the rule is less clear. If the error related to matter of importance, down to recent times Equity would certainly have set the agreement aside, or, at least, would have refused to enforce it. Nearly all the cases where the question was discussed were cases in which 'mistake' was raised as a defence to a suit for specific performance. "No doubt, if one party thought he had purchased *bona fide*, and the other thought he had not sold, that is a ground to set aside the contract," Lord Thurlow declared[2], but in many cases, where this defence was raised, the Chancellors, and especially Lord Eldon[3], merely stayed their hands, and "left the Plaintiff to pursue his remedy at law." "Perhaps some of the cases on this subject go too far," said James, L. J., in a recent case[4], "but, for the most part, the cases where a Defendant has escaped on the ground of a mistake, not contributed to by the Plaintiff, have been cases where a hardship amounting to injustice would have been inflicted upon him by holding him to his bargain, and it was unreasonable to hold him to it." And so the current has now set against allowing a mistake, affecting only the party's motive for agreeing, of which the other party had no suspicion, and to which he did not contribute, in cases where there is no fiduciary relation between the parties to raise an independent equity, to diminish the liabilities of the party mistaken, or the rights of the other. It is difficult to see why the latter should not be treated as a purchaser without notice, for such he is,

---

[1] *Garrard v. Frankel,* 30 B. 445 (1862).

[2] *Calverley v. Williams,* 1 Ves. 210.

[3] See *Stapylton v. Scott,* 13 Ves. p. 427.

[4] **Tamplin v. Jones,** 15 C. D. 215.

and so be unaffected by the possible 'equity' affecting the contract.

In the passage quoted above from the 'Treatise of Equity' mistakes of fact and law are classed together as if no regard were paid to the common principle 'ignorantia juris haud excusat,' but Lord Hardwicke refused to admit an error as to the legal consequences of known facts,—in the particular case the construction of a will,—as a ground for relief[1]; and in the Exchequer in Equity, it was said in 1835, that, though "it is a maxim of equity that parties making a mistake of fact shall not be held bound", (yet) "when they make a mistake in law they cannot afterwards be heard to say that the contract shall on that account be set aside[2]." In *Cooper v. Phibbs*[3], already referred to, Lord Westbury narrowed down the exception which he admitted to exist, so as to make it apply to public general law only, not to matters of private right, while in other modern cases[4] there has been considerable discussion as to whether the exception exists at all, and in 1876 Mellish, L. J., declared that Equity "has power to relieve against mistakes in law as well as against mistakes of fact; that is to say, if there is any equitable ground which makes it under the particular facts of the case inequitable that the party who received the money should retain it[5]."

Mistake of law.

Compromise.

Where doubtful rights are compromised, though it afterwards prove that the rights lay, in fact, wholly on one side, Equity has refused to allow the compromise to be disturbed, and a case of this is found so early as 19 Car. II.[6]

Family arrangements too were specially protected by the 18th century Chancellors[7]: the Court, said Lord Hardwicke[8], "will be glad to lay hold of any just ground to carry (them) into

---

[1] *Pullen v. Ready*, 2 Atk. 591.
[2] *Marshall v. Collett*, 1 Y. and C. Ex. p. 238.
[3] 2 L. R. H. L. 149.
[4] 3 C. D. 350.
[5] *Rogers v. Ingham*, 3 C. D. p. 357.
[6] *Frank v. Frank*, 1 Cas. in Chy. 34.

The reporter remarks that there was no consideration, but see *Miles v. New Zealand &c.*, Co. 32. C. D. 266.
[7] *Cann v. Cann*, 1 P. W. 727. Macclesfield.
[8] *Stapilton v. Stapilton*, 2 W. and T. p. 931.

execution and to establish the peace of a family." But, on the other hand, no concealment of anything known to the parties to the arrangement, and relevant to its subject can be allowed, and, if any such exist, it will be fatal, as Lord Talbot held, and Lord Eldon agreed, to the whole settlement[1].

8. *Penalties.*

Relief against penalties was given by the earlier Chancellors, without any definite rule, where the cases brought before them seemed unduly hard, but when, during the present period, Equity settled down to more judicial fashions, this relief was confined between stricter limits, but within those limits it was freely given. The refusal to allow a bond creditor to exact the penalty was of earlier date than the relief given to the mortgagor, and in Lord Somers' Act[2] it was recognised by fulfilment of the condition, though after the day fixed, being made pleadable at law. It was the regular practice of the Court whenever a penalty to secure payment of money came before it, to retain the cause until an issue '*quantum damnificatus*' had been tried at law, and then to allow relief on payment of the amount so found.

On the other hand, when application was made to Lord Macclesfield[3], in 1721, to relieve against a forfeiture of copyholds, for waste and leasing against the custom of the manor, he refused, for, he said, "it is recompense that gives this Court a handle to grant relief. The true ground of relief against penalties is from the original intent of the case, where the penalty is designed, only to secure money, and the Court gives him all that he expected or designed," and he went on to distinguish penalties imposed by law from those founded on the agreement of parties, and against the former, Equity, he said, would never relieve. There is no doubt the rule was here too strictly put, and the Chancellor subsequently often relieved against penalties even where they were not intended merely to secure the payment of money,—for example penal-

[1] *Pusey v. Desbouverie*, 3 P. W. 315. *Gordon v. Gordon*, 3 Swan, 400.
[2] 16 Anne, c. 16, § 20.
[3] *Peachy v. Duke of Somerset*, 2 W. and T. 1245.

ties in leases sanctioning covenants therein contained. This particular kind of relief was regulated by a statute of 4 George II.[1]

Lord Thurlow[2] placed the rule on its modern basis, when, in continuing an injunction against the enforcement of a bond entered into to secure the use of a room to the Defendant, according to an agreement, he said, "the only question was whether this was to be considered as a penalty, or as assessed damages." And he added, "The rule that, where a penalty was inserted merely to secure the performance of a collateral object, the enjoyment of the object is considered the principal intent of the deed, and the penalty only as accessional, and therefore only to secure the damages really incurred, is too strongly established in equity to be shaken."

The common law courts themselves ultimately refused to enforce agreements for penalties, and adopted the principle enunciated by Lord Thurlow[3]. The chief question, in modern cases, has always been whether a sum fixed in an agreement as payable in default of compliance with its primary terms is to be taken as a penalty, or as liquidated damages, and, after much discussion, the principles of the distinction have now been fairly settled by an elaborate judgment of Jessel, M. R.[4]

9. *Sureties.*

It has already been shown that sureties were regarded with peculiar favour in Equity, and during the present period further doctrines for their protection were introduced, and the old ones were extended and established so as to greatly improve their position.

Lord Cowper refused to allow a master to sue a surety for the good conduct of his apprentice, partly on the ground that the master's ordinary diligence would have prevented the loss[5], but Lord King decided in 1725 that a principal creditor would

---

[1] c. 28, § 3. See now Conveyancing Act, 1881, § 14.
[2] *Sloman v. Walter*, 2 W. and T. 1257.
[3] *Kemble v. Farren*, 6 Bing. 141.

Astley v. Weldon, 2 B. and P. 346.
[4] *Wallis v. Smith*, 21 C. D. 245.
[5] *Montague v. Tidcome*, 2 Vern. 518. The master had given a counterbond.

not be barred against a surety by mere negligence unaccompanied by fraud[1]. At the end of the century, in *Rees v. Berrington*[2], Lord Loughborough laid down the rule as to the discharge of the surety by the creditor's acts in these words, " there shall be no transaction with the principal debtor, without acquainting the person who has a great interest in it...It is the clearest and most evident equity not to carry on any transaction without the privity of him (the surety) who must necessarily have a concern in every transaction with the principal debtor. You shall not keep him bound, and transact his affairs without consulting him."

Under Lord Eldon there was a reaction from the previous anxiety to assist the surety, and a little more regard has since been paid to the rights of the creditor. Mere passiveness, Lord Eldon[3] held, extending Lord King's ruling, would not prejudice the creditor, for if the surety desired to be quit of his contract he could pay the debt and sue the debtor for repayment, or, ever since Lord Guilford's time[4], he could sue the debtor without first paying the debt himself. And he also held that an agreement to give the debtor time would not release the surety unless it were a positive contract between the debtor and the creditor, for that only would prevent the surety from suing the former himself[5]. And ever since, a contract to give the debtor time, but saving the creditor's rights against the surety, has left the latter's position unchanged.

The right of a surety to contribution from his co-sureties after paying more than his share of the debt was, in 1787, extended to cases where the co-sureties became such by separate instruments[6], and soon afterwards the action of assumpsit was moulded by the liberal-minded lawyers who then presided in the common law courts to enable them to give this, as several other species of equitable relief, at law.

[1] *Shepherd v. Beecher*, 2 P. W. 288.
[2] 2 W. and T. 1106.
[3] *Eyre v. Everett*, 2 Russ. 381.
[4] *Ranelaugh v. Haynes*, 1 Vern. 189 (1683).
[5] *Samuel v. Howarth*, 3 Mer. 272. In this case Lord Eldon said the principles governing the liability of sureties had then been adopted at common law.
[6] *Dering v. Winchelsea*, 1 W. and T. 114. Eyre, L. C. B. **Steel v. Dixon**, 17 C. D. 325.

At law, however, one who was principal debtor on the face of the bond was not allowed to show that he was intended to be surety only, whereas in equity,—where the principles of technical estoppel, which Lord Ellesmere had characterised as 'lying fictions,' never prevailed,—he could always do this.

On paying the debt the surety is entitled to stand in the creditor's shoes, and to sue on all his securities, and this without any agreement, though, until the case next cited, at least, it was the custom for him to take counter bonds from the debtor for indemnity. The early case of *Parsons v. Briddock*[1] goes very far in this respect, for in it the surety was allowed to recover against the debtor's bail, who had become bound in an action which the creditor had commenced against the debtor.

Lord Eldon[2] refused to enforce for the surety securities actually discharged at law by the payment, but a section was inserted in the Mercantile Law Amendment Act of 1856 to remove the difficulty this refusal created. It enacts that bonds paid by a surety shall be enforceable by him against the other obligors, notwithstanding the technical discharge of the obligation.

10. *Specific Performance.*

The performance in specie of obligations, particularly those arising out of contract, was during the 18th century, but especially under Lord Eldon at the close of that period, developed into the most important branch of equitable jurisdiction after trusts and administration.

It would not be enforced, Lord Macclesfield decided, where the agreement was for the delivery of unspecified chattels or choses-in-action (in the case before him £1000 stock)[3], not even though the parties had expressly agreed to reject the alternative of payment of the difference in the market price on the day. This is ac- *What agreements are specifically enforced.*

---

[1] 2 Vern. 608 (1708).
[2] *Copis v. Middleton*, 1 T. and R. 229.
[3] *Cuddee v. Rutter*, 1 W. and T. 906 (1720).

cording to Lord Hardwicke[1], because the value of goods varies according to time and circumstances, and, by compelling specific performance, Equity might ruin a defendant, although the plaintiff's damages might not exceed a shilling. Lord Redesdale, half a century later, returned to the older reason, the original basis of equitable interference, and placed the refusal of specific performance in the cases referred to above on the ground that damages were adequate; but the logical ground, and that upon which in recent times the test of the grant or refusal of specific performance rests, is that when specific property is sold, it becomes in equity forthwith the purchaser's property[2], but where the property is not specified its ownership cannot pass.

Lord Hardwicke displayed some inclination to depart from the rule laid down in *Cuddee v. Rutter*, but by Lord Eldon's time it had become well established. The converse rule was acted upon in *Somerset v. Cookson*[3], where the claim was for delivery of a Greek patera, the property of the Plaintiff, and Lord Talbot overruled a demurrer objecting to the suit on the ground that a bill would not lie "for anything merely personal any more than it would for a horse or a cow." Lord Guilford in the case of the "Pusey horn[4]," fifty years before, had stated his view, that the delivery of a chattel of special value might be enforced in equity.

By the Statute of Frauds, an agreement for the sale of an interest in lands is unenforceable, unless there be a written memorandum of the contract, but in 1701 the House of Lords decided[5] that, where a verbal contract, though otherwise within the statute, had been partially performed, specific performance of the whole contract might be granted, and so the rule has ever since remained. The same conclusion, that part performance takes the agreement out of the statute, was, as has been shown above, adopted many years

Part performance.

---

[1] *Buxton v. Lyster*, 3 Atk. 382 (1746).
[2] *Holroyd v. Marshall*, 10 Ho. Lo. Ca. 209 (Westbury), and see *Official Receiver v. Tailby*, 13 Ap. Ca. 523.
[3] *Somerset v. Cookson*, 1 W. and T.
962 (1735).
[4] *Pusey v. Pusey*, 1 W. and T. 961 (1684).
[5] *Lester v. Foxcroft*, 1 W. and T. 881. **Maddison v. Alderson**, 8 Ap. Ca. 467.

later in regard to equitable mortgages also. The statute prevents a plaintiff who is suing for specific performance of an agreement within its terms, from proving a parol variation of the written contract, or showing that, by fraud, mistake or surprise, the writing does not contain the true agreement, and asking for relief according to the variation or true agreement. So the Master of the Rolls held in 1802[1]. But a defendant may give evidence of fraud or mistake in the agreement as written, or of a subsequent variation of its terms, by way of defence, for the statute operates only to prevent the enforcement of the agreements it affects, it does not enable agreements, otherwise invalid, to be insisted upon. In *Joynes v. Statham*[2] Lord Hardwicke had said that such evidence was frequently given, and, he had added, that it would be equally available if the Defendant were Plaintiff, but this, as has just been shown, was subsequently overruled. Following the main rule, however, it was decided that a plaintiff might obtain specific performance of a parol variation if the variation be evidenced by part performance[3] of its terms.

In the case of penalties the Court had at an early period refused to look upon failure to keep to an agreed day as of vital importance; for 'time is not of the essence of a contract' was its ordinary rule. And, in accordance with this principle, a plaintiff was allowed to sue for performance though he had himself failed to be ready by the day fixed, even though the agreement provided that it should be void in such a case. Sir S. Romilly in his argument in *Seton v. Slade*[4], admitting that the old latitude as regards time was by his day restrained in equity, yet urged that the Plaintiff's failure to keep the day was no defence, and, he said, Lord Thurlow had scouted the suggestion that it was. Lord Eldon agreed to this, but he suggested that a clause might be inserted in contracts to make time essential, and, although Lord Thurlow would not have allowed such a clause to have effect, he thought it would be good. Ever since, the

<small>Time not of the essence of the agreement.</small>

---

[1] *Wollam v. Hearn*, 2 W. and T. 508. (Grant, M. R.)
[2] 3 Atk. 388.
[3] *Legal v. Muller*, 2 Ves. 279.
[4] 2 W. and T. 542.

agreement of the parties making time of the essence of the contract, has been respected[1]. Before this dictum time had sometimes been held to be essential on account of the nature of the property sold, if, for instance, it were a reversionary interest[2].

In *Seton v. Slade* Lord Eldon said that many hard cases had occurred through specific performance with compensation being directed, where the vendor had not got what he had agreed to convey, so that the purchaser missed the object of his purchase. The rule was, however, settled during his own chancellorship that either vendor or purchaser could insist on specific performance, where the vendor could convey substantially, but not exactly, the interest he had agreed to sell[3].

In the earlier part of this period the Court repeatedly refused specific performance of agreements of which it did not approve. Guilford, L. K., said that "he would not carry (the agreement) into execution for the benefit of a stranger": and he added that articles, out of which an equity could be raised for a decree *in specie*, ought to be obtained with all imaginable fairness, and without any mixture tending to surprise or circumvention[4], and Lord Macclesfield was "clear of opinion, that this Court was not bound to decree a specific execution of articles where they appeared to be unreasonable, or founded on

A discretion- a fraud, or where it would be unjust, or unconscion-
ary relief. able to assist them; that, though there was no direct fraud proved, yet from the great undervalue of the land, and that without any expense on the Plaintiff's part, (the agreement before him) appeared to him to be an unreasonable and shameful contract[5]." And the relief was sometimes refused on the ground of the excess or inadequacy of the sale price alone[6]. Unfairness, hardship, want of mutuality, and inadequacy of consideration still appear as defences to claims for specific performance, but they are now bound down within narrow

---

[1] *Hudson v. Bartram*, 3 Madd. 440. Leach, V. C.

[2] *Newman v. Rodgers*, 4 Bro. C. C. 393, Loughborough.

[3] *Guest v. Homfray*, 5 Ves. 818. Grant, M. R. *Mortlock v. Homfray*, 10 Ves. 315. Eldon.

[4] *Phillips v. Duke of Bucks*, 1 Vern. 228 (1683).

[5] *Young v. Clerk*, Prec. Ch. 538.

[6] Francis, *Maxims*, 11.

limits, and would not be allowed to prevent the Court enforcing an agreement fully understood and deliberately entered into by the Defendant and unaffected by fraud. Inadequacy of consideration, it has been expressly decided, amounts to nothing more than evidence of fraud[1].

Lord Eldon did much to mark out the lines on which the grant of this relief would be allowed, and from his time the discretion always claimed in allowing it has been 'judicial,' and, in fact, the epithet has long been entirely unwarranted.

He also introduced[2] the practice of sending references as to the title to the property to be conveyed straight to the Master, wherever the title alone was in question between the parties.

It has been pointed out in the preceding pages that Equity, following the civil law, and indeed the common law also, looked upon restraints on marriage with much disfavour, and in the exercise of their discretion with regard to specific performance, on similar grounds, the Chancellors refused to enforce agreements for the separation of husband and wife[3]. At the beginning of this century, however, giving way to the necessities of social life, Equity began to enforce "the minor and auxiliary parts of the agreement to separate, while (it still professed) to repudiate the principal and essential part and motive of it[4]." Ultimately, in 1847, the House of Lords decided that agreements to separate were no longer against 'the policy of the law[5].'

Agreement between husband and wife.

Agreements between husband and wife could not be entered into directly, and it was necessary that trustees for the wife should contract on her behalf[6], but this formality has been dispensed with in recent years, first, where the one consort was actually suing for a divorce[7], and then in all cases[8]. Now the difficulty has been entirely removed by statute[9].

[1] *Stilwell v. Wilkins*, Jac. 282.
[2] 3 Twiss, *Life of Eldon*, p. 443. *Fullager v. Clarke*, 18 Ves. 482.
[3] *Wilkes v. Wilkes*, 2 Dick. 791 (1757, Clarke, M. R.).
[4] *Frampton v. Frampton*, 4 B. 293 (Langdale, M. R.).
[5] *Wilson v. Wilson*, 1 H. L. C. 538.
[6] *Hope v. Hope*, 22 B. 351 (Romilly, M. R.).
[7] *Vansittart v. Vansittart*, 4 K. and J. 62 (Hatherley, C.).
[8] **Besant v. Wood**, 12 C. D. 622. (Jessel, M. R. In this case the whole law with regard to such agreements is carefully considered.)
[9] Married Women's Property Act, 1883.

11. *Injunction.*

The weapon of injunction was wielded by the Court until the present century with little of its later effect. Wherever a *prima facie* case for the exercise of equitable interference to stay actions at law was established, the 'common injunction' might be obtained, on motion or at the hearing, but special injunctions for the preservation of property and the like, though well known, were little used.

"Prevention of mischief by injunction is a head of Equity upon which instances few and far between are to be found before (Lord Eldon's) time. Lord Thurlow would hardly grant an injunction where the parties had a remedy at law. Before his time there are not more than half-a-dozen instances of each species of injunction, and in these relief was as often denied as granted. Now injunction is, it is well known, the right arm of the Court, pervading the workshop of the artizan, the studio of the artist, entering alike into the miner's shaft and the merchant's counting-house. Almost all the principles upon which this relief is granted or refused, the terms and conditions upon which it is dissolved, revived, continued, extended and made perpetual are to be found in Lord Eldon's judgments alone[1]." Lord Eldon's panegyrist in the passage just quoted rather underrates the work of earlier Chancellors on this head, and he had no conception, of course, of the advance made since Lord Eldon's time, which has so extended the jurisdiction that the grant of injunctions, especially in 'light and air' cases, has come to be a great part of the most important work of the equity courts on 'motion days,' but the passage is still substantially accurate.

The Copyright Act of Anne and the discovery, (for it is considered it was a discovery not a creation,) of copyright under it, was the occasion of many applications for injunctions to the Court; for the protection of copyright, it is plain, depends on the summary suppression of piracies by offenders who are probably impecunious, and whom it would be therefore useless to sue for damages.

Copyright.

[1] Eldon as a Law Reformer, *Law Review*, vol. 2, p. 282.

In assenting to such applications the Court strictly preserved the discretionary power it always claimed over the remedies exclusively administered by it, as specific performance and injunction[1]. Thus Lord Eldon exercised practically a censorship of the press, which Lord Macclesfield had previously claimed, by refusing to protect from piracy books of which he disapproved, among others Southey's *Wat Tyler* and Byron's *Cain*[2].

Lord Hardwicke on the occasion of applications for injunctions to protect copyright, decided the important points, that an abridgement of a book, provided it be made with the exercise of care and labour, is not an infringement of the copyright[3], and that the writer of a letter may restrain the publication of it by the person to whom he has addressed it, although it is made by his own act, the property of the latter[4]: a rule of which Lord Eldon disapproved, but which would surely have been made by Parliament if the Chancellor had not anticipated it.

Equitable Waste.

The subject of equitable waste, to prevent which injunctions were granted by Equity from Lord Nottingham's time, and, as already shown, in some instances, at least, so early as the reign of Elizabeth, is worthy of separate consideration, and chiefly on account of Lord Hardwicke's celebrated judgment in *Garth v. Cotton*[5], which not only fully confirmed the doctrine, that waste permitted at law might be restrained in equity, but established and secured the strict settlement of lands in the form it till recently retained. It was settled before that case occurred that a tenant in tail after possibility of issue extinct, or a tenant for life without impeachment of waste,

---

[1] Sec. 25 (8) of the Judicature Act of 1873, has not altered the principles upon which injunctions are granted. N. L. Ry. Co. v. G. N. Ry. Co. 11 Q. B. D. 30.

[2] Camp. Vol. 7. p. 663. *Lord Byron v. Dugdale*, 1 L. J. Ch. 239. There can be no copyright in a publication of an immoral, indecent, seditious, libellous or irreligious nature.

[3] *Gyles v. Wilcock*, 2 Atk. 142 (cited in Campbell).

[4] See *Gee v. Pritchard*, 2 Swan, 414 (cited in Campbell).

[5] 1 W. and T. 820.

would not be allowed to destroy the mansion house or to cut ornamental timber[1].

In *Garth v. Cotton* a settlement had been made on the tenant for life, for 99 years, if he should so long live, with remainder to trustees to preserve contingent remainders, with remainder to the eldest son in tail and other remainders, and with remainder over to the Defendant's testator. The tenant for life was impeachable for voluntary waste, but, before any son was born, he made an arrangement with the Defendant's testator to cut the timber and divide the proceeds. The Plaintiff, the eldest son of the tenant for life, now sued to recover the money paid under this arrangement.

Lord Hardwicke said the case turned entirely on the existence of the trustees to preserve contingent remainders, the addition of whom to the settlement had been devised about 100 years before in consequence of the decision,—in *Chudleigh's case*[2],—that if there were no estate interpolated between that of the tenant for life and that of the remainderman, they two, before the contingent remainders vested, could combine to destroy them.

Lord Harcourt had decided, in 1710, that an assignee with notice from these trustees would himself be bound by the trust[3], and Lord King, in 1732, that, "in common sense, reason and justice," and therefore in equity, if the trustees assisted to destroy the contingent remainders they were guilty of a breach of trust[4].

The question in the present case was whether the trustees might have applied to the Court to stay the committal of the waste, because, if they might, they ought to have done so, and their neglect of duty could not be allowed to prejudice their cestui-que trust, although he was then unborn. Lord Hardwicke decided that they might have done so, and consequently gave judgment for the Plaintiff. The fact that the life tenant and the remainderman had a legal right he paid no heed to, for he said, "in all cases where a legal right is acquired or

---

[1] 1 W. and T. p. 841. *Lord Barnard's Case*, 2 Vern. 738. (Cowper.)
[2] 1 Co. 120.
[3] *Pye v. Gorges*, 1 P. W. 128.
[4] *Mansell v. Mansell*, 2 P. W. 676.

exercised by fraud or collusion, contrary to conscience, it is the office of this Court to enjoin it, or to decree a compensation."— And, as to a further objection on account of the death of the Defendant's testator, he said, "Equity disclaims the maxim that a personal remedy dies with the person wherever the remedy is proper for that jurisdiction," and he adduced precedents from Lord Nottingham's time in support of this proposition.

The restraint of equitable waste where the life tenancy is given 'without impeachment of waste' and the settlement creating the tenancy does not expressly show an intention to confer a right to commit it, has received statutory sanction in the Judicature Act[1].

12. *Discovery.*

The grant of discovery in aid of actions at law became a regular branch of the practice of the Court, for at law, though the method of examining the witnesses whom the parties were allowed to call, was far superior to that adopted in Chancery, the rules of evidence, which Bentham described as devised to exclude the testimony of every one who was likely to know anything about the matter, were strictly adhered to until the second quarter of the present century. Therefore, when the evidence of the Defendant was required by the Plaintiff, or that of the Plaintiff by the Defendant, a bill had to be filed in equity, and the same course was necessary if evidence had to be taken abroad, or, before the hearing, at home. The practice was to file a bill in the ordinary way, but never to bring it to a hearing, unless the whole dispute was retained in Chancery, and in later days this would only be done where an 'adequate, complete and beneficial remedy' was not to be had at law.

All through the present period the evidence on behalf of each party was taken without any information being allowed to reach him with regard to the evidence which was concurrently taken on behalf of the other. The necessary consequence of

[1] Sec. 25 (3). **Baker v. Sebright**, 13 C. D. 179.

a departure from this principle, the Chancellors believed, would be perjury,..."if after publication (of the evidence) passed, and people seeing where a cause pinched, they should then be at liberty to look out witnesses to bolster up a faulty part of the cause[1]." Following out this principle what is now the fundamental rule of discovery was arrived at: that the right of a party to the benefit of the other party's oath is limited to a discovery of such facts as relate to his own case, and does not extend to a discovery of the manner in which the other party's case is to be established, or to the evidence which relates exclusively to it[2]. This rule was not however fully settled, and regularly applied in every case, till the end of the period or even later.

The practice of attaching interrogatories to the bill, which, unless the Defendant could establish a good plea or demurrer, he was bound to answer, enabled the "plaintiff in Equity to obtain from the Defendant a discovery upon oath as to all matters of fact which, being well pleaded in the bill, were material to the plaintiff's case about to come on for trial, and which the Defendant (did) not by his form of pleading admit[3]."

One of the most important rules in regard to discovery was laid down by Lord Nottingham in *Basset v. Nosworthy*[4], namely, that discovery would not be decreed against a purchaser for value without notice of the claim which the discovery was sought to support. The rule arose out of a doctrine which had from the earliest time been adopted in equity, and was always afterwards accepted down to the Judicature Act, that no relief should be given against a purchaser for value without notice, but in later times the protection afforded by the rule was considerably attenuated.

Purchase for valuable consideration without notice.

Lord Thurlow would not allow the plea against a legal right, as dower, pursued under the concurrent jurisdiction in equity[5], and Lord Loughborough described the plea as only a shield

---

[1] *Jones v. Purefoy*, 1 Vern. 46 (1682).
[2] Wigram on Discovery, Prop. III.
[3] Wigram, Prop. III. *Duncalf v. Blake*, 1 Atk. 52. (Hardwicke.)
[4] 2 W. and T. p. 1 (1673).
[5] *Williams v. Lambe*, 3 Bro. C. C. 264, and Belt's note.

to the possession of land, but this Lord Eldon overruled, allowing a mortgagee to plead it against a tenant in tail who was seeking to recover the deeds from him[1]. Lord Romilly made a further inroad upon the doctrine by refusing to admit it as a defence by a second mortgagee against a foreclosure suit by a first mortgagee, and the House of Lords supported his decision on the extraordinary ground that foreclosure was not relief[2].

Since the Judicature Act it has been held that the plea is no longer good even as a bar to discovery in aid of an ejectment action[3], for it only availed, since Lord Thurlow's time, where recourse was had to the auxiliary jurisdiction of the Court of Chancery, and the jurisdiction of the Supreme Court is in every branch independent and complete.

One plea allowed to excuse an answer has just been referred to; another that the answer would subject the Defendant to a penalty or a forfeiture, which like the first dated from long before the present period, has always been maintained as a general principle[4] though in particular cases it has been declared by statute to be no longer a reason for refusing discovery[5].

Since the amalgamation of the Courts of Chancery and Common Law, subsidiary suits for discovery only are no longer required or permitted, but orders for discovery are made on interlocutory application in the substantive action[6].

[1] *Walwyn v. Lee*, 9 Ves. 24.
[2] *Collyer v. Finch*, 5 H. L. C. 905. Lord Cranworth said, "it (foreclosure) is calling on the party to exercise his right now or never." Its result, however, is to deprive the mortgagee of his property, if he cannot redeem.
[3] **Ind Coope and Co. v. Emmersen**, 12 Ap. Ca. 300.
[4] *Bird v. Hardwicke*, 1 Vern. 109, (1682).
[5] e.g. 6 and 7 W. IV. c. 24.
[6] Rules of the Supreme Court, O. 31.

CHAPTER XIII.

REFORM IN CHANCERY.

THE last years of Lord Eldon's Chancellorship were marked by the commencement of a persistent and determined attack upon the abuses which had grown up in the Chancery, or, inherent in its practice from the first, had developed until they could no longer be tolerated. Complaints, as we have seen, had been made almost continuously from the reign of Elizabeth of the manner in which equity was administered, but they had, except in the time of the Commonwealth, and on the occasion of Lord Macclesfield's disgrace, neither been very wide-spread, nor been pressed with any great vigour. The case now was entirely different. On the one hand, the evils complained of had greatly increased, on the other, far more searching enquiry now began to be made into public abuses, and far less patience was shown in enduring them. Within Parliament a number of public spirited reformers had arisen, who were neither bound to silence by attachment to the Government of the day, nor exclusively occupied by endeavours to secure the defeat of all its undertakings, and their own succession to its place. Some of them were members of the common law Bar,—for during Lord Eldon's time a sharp division had arisen between the counsel who practised in equity, and no longer went circuit, and those who practised in the common law courts,—and these were peculiarly alive to the absurdities of the Chancery procedure; some of them were men, like Sir Samuel Romilly, who had been bred in the Court of Chancery, but who had escaped the blindness that familiarity with abuses is apt to generate; and some were laymen, who were shocked

The demand for reform.

at the ruin in which they saw litigants involved, and the inconveniences which the lack of efficient legal institutions entailed. Outside Parliament too a keen interest in legal reform had arisen. The great success of the Code Napoléon, and the writings of Bentham and his followers had much to do with this[1], and the growing wealth of the country and its increasing trade brought forcibly home to every man of business the need for Courts where rights could be plainly declared and speedily secured. During the last century the great estates of the country had at irregular intervals struggled slowly through Chancery, and their proprietors had come to regard the delays and expenses of the process as inevitable, if unpleasant incidents of ownership, but the merchant and middle classes were less patient, and, moreover, the Court was even less fitted for the decision of the disputes in which they were likely to be interested than for the administration of estates. "The number of suitors in Chancery is nothing compared to the community, or this Court would long ago have been abolished as a nuisance," Sir Samuel Romilly asserted[2], and the number of persons interested was now rapidly increasing.

It was not indeed the Chancery only that needed reforming; the procedure and practice of the common law courts had become buried under a mass of technicalities and fictions such that the steps which were really necessary for the discovery of the parties' rights were generally but a small proportion of those which had actually to be taken in an action, while the remaining steps, not only increased the cost and duration of the litigation, but formed so many traps for an unwary pleader or advocate, and caused the time of the judges to be constantly occupied in the discussion of the merest legal conundrums, which bore no "relation to the merits of any controversies except those of pedants," or "in the direction of a machinery which wholly belonged to the past[3]."

[1] Parkes' *History of the Court of Chancery*, to which frequent reference has been made in these pages, was published in 1828. It is a vigorous indictment of the Court and its administrators, in which the author, a Birmingham solicitor, did his best to collect all that was known, or had been said, against the one or the other.

[2] Camp. Vol. II. p. 379 n.

[3] *The Reign of Queen Victoria* 'Ad-

Uncertainty as to the result of his suit, inevitable expense, which often made judgment in his favour more disadvantageous than abandonment of the right declared to be his, and almost incredible delays before the end of the suit was reached awaited any one who was unfortunate enough to be involved in litigation in Equity.

The uncertainty was not the consequence of any arbitrariness of the decisions of the Equity judges, for, as we have seen, it was now thoroughly settled that the rules of Equity, as they were found in the Reports, were to be observed. The difficulty arose in part from the mass of these reports, and the contradictions of the dicta they contained. The mass of reports at the present time is far greater, but contradictions, in cases of recognised authority, have become few, and, thanks to the simplification of the law and the excellence of the modern digests and text-books, the number of the reported cases does not now often occasion any very grave difficulty in ascertaining beforehand the probable decisions of the Courts. But the case was very different at the beginning of the century. Sir Samuel Romilly, who was the greatest equity lawyer of his day, described the responsibility of advising his clients as unbearably great, and Mr Park, who was also a lawyer in considerable practice, wrote, in 1828, the following plaintive passages[1]. "It is scarcely possible to conceive of the anxiety, the oppressiveness, the burdensomeness of the life of an English jurisconsult in active practice. His mind is never free, it is always groaning under a load of mental labour in which he can never find a resting-place." "The interminable accumulation of the materials of law prospectively, an accumulation beyond the natural strength of man to keep pace with,—added to the unavoidable defection of the memory, retrospectively, places the chamber lawyer always in the condition of a horse who is carrying beyond his weight." But an even greater source of uncertainty was the state of the law of real property, with which the questions debated in Chancery were so much involved. "No person can have had much experience in Courts of

ministration of the Law.' Bowen, L. J.

[1] Contre-Projet to the Humphreysian Code, p. xxii.

Equity," says the Report of Lord Eldon's Commission, "without feeling that many suits owe their origin to, and many others are greatly protracted by questions arising from the niceties and subtleties of the law and practice of conveyancing[1]."

The costliness of proceedings in Equity was due partly to the number of unnecessary officials who had been foisted upon the Court, or had remained there long after their original usefulness had ceased; partly to the manner in which the evidence in contested cases was taken; and partly to the prolixity of the pleadings.

<small>Costliness of proceeding in Equity.</small>

The 'Six Clerks' furnish a striking example of the 'harpies of office' who not only taxed the hapless suitors, but, from fear for their privileges, offered a most strenuous opposition to improvement of every kind. They had once, as we have seen, been the attornies of the Court, but, as business increased, and the original simplicity of procedure vanished, parties found it necessary to employ special agents to take charge of suits on their behalf. These agents, Solicitors as they were called, were formally recognised by the Legislature in 1729[2], but before that they had practically superseded the Six Clerks as the litigants' representatives. At the beginning of the century the latter had become utterly useless: what work remained in their offices was done by deputy, and it was quite possible for a solicitor engaged in extensive practice to pass his life without ever seeing any of them. Their spokesman, who attended before the Commission of 1825, said that their duties consisted in filing and preserving records, entering them, certifying to the Court respecting them, and signing copies, that for the discharge of these each Clerk attended two months in the year, and that they might occasionally all have to consult over matters so important as the form of an engrossment, but he could not say that an occasion for consultation had ever occurred[3].

<small>The Six Clerks.</small>

[1] Report of 1826, p. 34. The Commissioners were careful to add that any alteration in the system "must be made with the greatest caution."
[2] 2 Geo. II. c. 23.
[3] Parkes, p. 576. Even Lord Eldon's Commission thought that suitors did not derive adequate benefit from the fees paid to the Six Clerks, and suggested that these officials should be used to tax bills of costs. Report of 1826, p. 33.

The Six Clerks had, however, or rather their underclerks had, opportunities for facilitating or hindering the weary progress of a cause, and it was therefore deemed advisable by solicitors to take a certain number of office copies of documents, which were otherwise unnecessary, that the profit on the copying might serve the purpose of the 'expedition money' which the orders of the 18th century Chancellors had suppressed. Thus the intention of a salutary order of Lord Hardwicke, that no unnecessary copies need be taken, was defeated.

The manner in which the evidence in Chancery was taken had always been a serious discredit to the Court; it remained at the beginning of the 19th practically the same as it was at the end of the 17th century, although all the fire of the criticism of the Commonwealth Reformers had been directed upon it.

If the witnesses were examined in London they were taken before one of the Examiners of the Court, and, in the absence of anybody representing either party to the suit, a set of interrogatories previously prepared[1], and often couched in technical and precise language which the witnesses could not understand, was put to them. Inasmuch as one witness might refuse to answer, or fail to give the evidence expected, as a matter of precaution, several were usually called to prove each point, though had the evidence been taken by the agent of the parties orally, one would generally have sufficed. After the examination in chief the witness might be cross-examined, by the same examiner[2], upon interrogatories prepared without any knowledge of, or reference to, his previous answers, but, as the Commissioners of 1850 reported many years after[3], such cross-examination was "so

Evidence in Chancery.

---

[1] Blackstone, III. p. 449. Parkes, p. 456. Lord Eldon's Commission could think of no alteration "which would, upon the whole, operate as an improvement." They were satisfied that "the instances are very rare, in which there is even any suspicion of ultimate injustice, in consequence of the existing mode of taking evidence." Report of 1826, p. 14.

[2] This was an innovation in Lord Eldon's time, the old rule required a different examiner. It was expressly allowed by Order 26 of Ap. 1828.

[3] Report of 1852, p. 8.

ineffective and dangerous that it (was) seldom resorted to, except where the witness (was) known to be friendly to the cross-examining party, and (had) previously communicated facts to be the subject of a friendly cross-examination." When the examination took place in the country its cost and ineffectiveness were even greater, for then the examination was by a commission[1] of untrained persons, who had to be paid and supported by the parties at the town or towns to which the commission was directed, often for weeks together. This evil was to some extent modified by the appointment of solicitors only upon these commissions after the Report of the Commission of 1825.

The inadequacy of such examinations, in really contested cases, to procure satisfactory evidence for a judge to act on, who saw, and had power to call before him, none of the witnesses, is obvious. The suppression of the depositions taken for formal defects or because the interrogatories were leading, and the grant of further commissions, frequently occurred, and when to the depositions were added the affidavits, which were admitted to prove subordinate points, and the bill and answer, the cause, it was truly said, was buried beneath a sea of paper.

Often the discovery of truth by these means was so hopeless that parties were sent to try an issue[2] at law, and sometimes again and again in the same cause.

The bill and answer were portentous documents. The first "stated the Plaintiff's case at full length and three times over. There was the first part, in which the story was circumstantially set forth. Then came the part which charged its truth against the Defendant,—or, in other words, which set it forth all over again in an aggrieved tone. Lastly, came the interrogating part which converted the original allegations into a chain of subtly framed inquiries addressed to the Defendant, minutely dovetailed and circuit- *The Pleadings.*

---

[1] Two commissioners were appointed by each party. They and their clerks were sworn to secrecy until after publication. The procedure in the Ecclesiastical Courts was the same. There is a good description of it in *Ten Thousand a Year*.

[2] It was at this time a fictitious issue on a wager.

ously arranged so as to surround a slippery conscience and to stop up every earth. No layman, however intelligent, could compose the 'answer' without professional aid[1]."

"I remember," said Lord Campbell in 1859[2], "when bills in Equity told the same story over and over again, and each time more obscurely than on the previous occasion. When the answer came, the great object in drawing it up was, that, however long it might be, it should form only one sentence, in order that, if part of it had to be read, it should be necessary to read the whole."

An almost continuous complaint of the delays of Chancery had existed from the reign of Elizabeth. Now and then an energetic Chancellor had, by great exertions, swept away the accumulation of causes waiting to be reached, and, according to their biographers, at least two Chancellors of the 18th century had fallen victims to their efforts to do this[3]. But the postponements of Lord Hardwicke's judgments made it finally impossible for any of his successors to ever get level with their cause-lists, and Lord Eldon had been even more dilatory than his predecessors. It is unnecessary to dwell upon the complaints made in the House of Commons and in the press of the day of the number of causes waiting after hearing for Lord Eldon's judgment, on the tales of cargoes rotting while he considered to whom they belonged, and of frantic appeals from ruined families that some end might be put to the fatal continuance of their suits, or to consider the defence made by Mr Twiss[4] to these charges. The facts are indisputable[5], that a common administration suit, where the parties were not hostile, took from three to five years; that eminent counsel stated that no man could begin a contested suit and hope to see its end; that clients were advised to compromise good claims, and to yield to bad ones, rather than risk a suit; and that, on the average, causes took

Marginal note: Delays in Chancery.

[1] Bowen, L. J. *The Reign of Queen Victoria.* 'Administration of the Law.'
[2] Ho. Lo. 1 July, 1859, quoted by Warren. *Law Studies.*
[3] Guilford, L. K., and Talbot, C. See Parkes, pp. 223 and 319.
[4] *Life of Eldon,* 2nd Ed. Vol. III. p. 359.
[5] See the Report of 1826, pp. 9 and 13, and C. P. Cooper's *Proceedings in Parliament,* p. 86.

at least three years to reach the top of the list after they were ready for hearing. The delays after the cause was ready for hearing, which, as it was said, were the worst delays of all, for the litigants were then making a direct demand for the Court's assistance, were due to the insufficiency of the judicial strength of the Court for its work. To these had to be added the delays due to the cumbersome procedure necessary to get ready for hearing, of which some idea may be gathered from what has already been said[1], and the greater delays, after hearing, in the Master's offices, if, as happened at some stage in almost every cause, enquiries were directed[2].

The work of the Court had long far outrun its capacity for discharging it. The average number of bills filed in Lord Hardwicke's time was about 2150, in 1801 it had sunk to 1225, but by 1824, after the appointment, in 1813 of a Vice-Chancellor, it had risen again to about the old number, and it was now increasing[3]. But whereas the money in Court in 1745 was under 1¾ million pounds, it was in 1825 over 39 millions. From these figures,—from the absolute decrease in the number of suits during the latter half of the 18th century and its slow increase after an additional judge was added to the Court, while the wealth and population of the country were steadily and rapidly growing and the amounts at stake in the suits actually litigated became so much greater,—the reformers argued that the inefficiency of the Court, its delays and expense, had driven suitors from its doors; that they, in fact, amounted to a denial of justice, and this inference was undoubtedly just. Lord Eldon's time was greatly taken up by his political avocations, by his duties as president of the House of Lords, the necessity of his attendance there to hear appeals, the important business in Bankruptcy cast upon him as Chancellor, and by other multifarious occupations, so that he had but little time left at his

[1] See ante, p. 155. As an instance of the delays permitted a defendant could not, in general, dismiss a vexatious suit for want of prosecution till after 1¾ years from the Plaintiff's last real step in it. Report of 1826, p. 13, and see pp. 68....

[2] Report of 1826, p. 18.

[3] C. P. Cooper, *Proceedings in Parliament*, &c., p. 103, (1828).

disposal to attend to his work as an equity judge[1]. The Master of the Rolls, carrying out the theory that he was only the Chancellor's deputy, never sat when the Chancellor was sitting, and therefore did not sit in the morning, except for a few days in the year, but sat, for three or four days a week, from 6 to 10 in the evening. So that, at the best, he and his chief did the work of a single judge between them.

It may be stated at once how this particular defect was met. First came the appointment of a Vice-Chancellor in 1813, then, soon after Lord Eldon's retirement, it was arranged that the Master of the Rolls should sit in the morning, and by an Act of 1833[2] he was empowered to hear motions and conduct all Court work, instead of hearing causes only, and about the same time the Bankruptcy business, other than appeals, was removed from the Chancellor's shoulders[3]. In 1841[4] two new Vice-Chancellors were created, and lastly, ten years later[5], two Lords Justices were appointed to hear appeals from the Master of the Rolls and the Vice-Chancellors, and to them the remainder of the Bankruptcy business, the hearing of appeals, was committed also. By these changes the judicial force of the Court was ultimately, that is, by 1851, increased more than five-fold.

Appointment of additional judges in Equity.

Very few cases, said the Commissioners in 1826[6], could be brought to a final decision without inquiries before a Master. A large portion of the business of the Court was administrative, and the inquiries for creditors and next of kin, the ascertaining of classes of legatees, the sales of estates and distributions of the proceeds, and the taking of accounts, which the administration involved, were conducted in the Masters' offices, and there too discussions on the sufficiency of answers, objections to

---

[1] He attended from two to five mornings a week in the House of Lords. Even when he was in Court but little of his time was devoted to hearing equity causes. It was taken up by bankruptcy and lunacy matters, and "the incessant intervention of other business specially brought before him on the plea of immediate urgency and importance." Report of 1826, p. 16.
[2] 3 and 4 W. IV. c. 94.
[3] 1 and 2 W. IV. c. 56. Lord Eldon's Commission reported against this reform, p. 35.
[4] 4 and 5 V. c. 52.
[5] 14 and 15 V. c. 83.
[6] Report, p. 18.

pleadings for scandal, and many other interlocutory matters were heard. The offices were under no direct control by the judges, and their business was conducted privately without the salutary influence which an open court always exerts on the administration of justice, but their chief defect was the frequent misconduct and incapacity of the Masters themselves, who had, and whose clerks had, a direct interest in the protraction of the proceedings before them[1], and who, when they had the desire, lacked the necessary dignity and authority to check the delays and irregularities of shuffling or dishonest litigants. They, as the Chancellor and his deputies, could not take the direct evidence of witnesses, but were obliged in every case to search through masses of affidavits for the facts on which they founded their reports to the Court. The method of appeal from their decision, by motion to the Court, leading, if successful, to fresh enquiries, added to the expenses and delays the system entailed.

<small>The Masters' offices.</small>

Repeated motions were made in Parliament for returns of the causes awaiting judgment in Chancery, and for commissions to enquire into the state of the Chancery procedure, and into the condition of law and legal procedure generally. Mr Michael Angelo Taylor, for instance, session after session called the attention of Parliament to the delays in Chancery[2]; and, in 1828, Lord Brougham, then Mr Brougham, the most ardent and celebrated of the pioneers of legal reform, moved for a Commission "to enquire into the defects occasioned by time or otherwise in the laws of this Realm, and into the measures necessary for reforming the same," and made a speech[3] in support of his motion which, though dealing mainly with the Courts of Common Law, forcibly attracted public attention to the abuses and absurdities prevailing in the administration of every branch of our law. Before this, in 1825, the Commission,

---

[1] Lord Eldon's Commission said that payment for office copies was the principal source from which the Masters' remuneration was drawn, but this they were convinced, though the contrary was loudly asserted, led to no abuse. It would be more beneficial, they advised, for suitors to pay the Masters a fixed salary, but that would be unjust to the public. Report of 1826, p. 23.

[2] See Hansard, 2nd ser. XVIII. p. 315.

[3] *ibid.* p. 127.

whose report has been already referred to, had been appointed to enquire into the Chancery practice and procedure. It was composed of Chancery lawyers and Masters, and presided over by Lord Eldon.

This Commission made its Report in 1826, after taking an enormous mass of evidence, from which many of the facts stated in the preceding pages of this chapter have been taken[1]. The Report dealt in a very timid and partial manner with the abuses the evidence disclosed, and the 188 propositions which were attached to it were described at the time as framed merely to prune the luxuriance of these evils, and in no way to touch their roots. And the *Times*, not unfairly, spoke of it as an apology for all the abuses of the Chancery[2]. No alteration had been made, said the Commissioners, in the general system of the practice of the Court since Whitelock's orders of 1656, and they had none to suggest[3]. For the amendment of the method of taking evidence, the Report suggested only that skilled Commissioners be chosen for country commissions, and, to meet the delays of causes ready for hearing, it suggested no reform at all. A few miserable shillings might have been saved and causes advanced a week or two in the lists if all the propositions had been carried out, but no measure would have been taken to get judgments through in a time more conformable to the expedition indispensable in a good administration[4]. But even such improvements as the Commission thought necessary were not then obtainable, for whatever chance of being immediately carried into effect their recommendations had, was lost by an attack which Lord Redesdale, next to Lord Eldon the most influential member of the Commission, made upon them. He attributed most of the failures of the Court to the ignorance and misdeeds of the solicitors, and he expressed regret that they had ever been admitted to practice in it at all, and many of the inconveniences which were not attributable to them, he considered irremediable.

The Report of 1826.

[1] The *Times* newspaper published a series of articles upon the Report, and a summary of the evidence. These are printed in the appendix to Parkes.
[2] Parkes, p. 530.
[3] Report, p. 10.
[4] C. P. Cooper, *Lettres sur la Chancellerie*.

No Act was passed until 1833 for the improvement of the Court, but the publication of the evidence and report, and the discussion to which this gave rise, prepared the way for reform.

In 1827 Lord Lyndhurst, who as Copely, M. R., had introduced into Parliament a bill for the amendment of Chancery procedure, became Chancellor, and in the next year he published a set of orders, which, without making any fundamental changes, in some degree improved the practice in the Masters' Chambers, and expedited the progress of causes before the hearing[1]. And in 1831 Lord Brougham, who had succeeded Lord Lyndhurst, published additional orders, still further curtailing the times allowed for some of the interlocutory steps of the suit[2]. Orders of 1828 and 1831.

In 1833 the first important procedure amendment Act[3] was passed. It abolished some of the unnecessary offices, and provided that, for the future, the fees (which were diminished and regulated) should be paid to the Suitors' Fund, the emoluments of the officials being henceforth to be by way of salary[4], and the officials were forbidden under pain of prosecution to take gratuities. The old deputy Registrars, it was provided, should do duty nominally as well as actually as Registrars, and should attend the judges and draw up decrees, which were no longer to contain the long recitals that had made them as lengthy and expensive as the rest of the paper proceedings. Suits in Equity were to be commenced by an open writ prepared by the Plaintiff and issued under an office seal, analogous to the Writ of Summons simultaneously introduced at law, instead of the old subpœna under the Great Seal. No one was to be compelled to take office copies, and thus further necessary expense was avoided. To save the time of the Court, applications for time to answer and for The Chancery Regulation Act 1833.

---

[1] *Code of Chancery Practice.* Kennedy, p. 185. (O. 4. Plaintiff to deliver his exceptions to the answer within two months. 48. Decree to be taken into the Master's office within two months. 51. Master may fix time for proceeding on it; 56. and may give conduct of enquiry to another party if Plaintiff do not proceed diligently; 58. and may proceed *de die in diem;* and may examine witnesses, on the inquiry, *viva voce.*)

[2] Kennedy, p. 209.

[3] 3 and 4 Will. IV. c. 94.

[4] This reform was not fully carried out till 1852.

leave to amend bills, &c., were to be made to the Masters, and to reach the judges only when the Masters' decisions were objected to; and, to control the dilatoriness of the Masters' offices, they were directed to report annually to the Chancellor on the work pending before them. It was by this statute also that the Master of the Rolls, as already stated, was made an efficient judge.

The Act provided too that the number of the Six Clerks should be gradually reduced to two, but they were soon after swept entirely away, along with a host of other useless officials by an Act[1] of 1842.

During the twenty years following these reforms, numerous orders were, from time to time, issued, the more important of them with the sanction of Parliament[2], for the improvement of Chancery practice and procedure, and, without making any alteration in the general plan described above, they effected considerable amendments in detail, especially by reducing the pleadings to more reasonable limits, restricting the times allowed for taking the different steps, minimising the delay and expense which the necessity for a bill of revivor upon the death of any of the numerous parties to a suit entailed, and facilitating the process of getting a suit taken *pro confesso* where the defendant absconded. No substantial further improvement, however, was made until 1850.

In the meantime great changes had taken place in the common law courts, and in the law itself. The old fictitious forms had been, for the most part, swept away, the practice of the three courts assimilated, and, by the Acts passed on the reports of the great Real Property Commission,— the Fines and Recoveries Act, the Inheritance Act, the Wills Act, and the Real Property Amendment Act of 1845,—the law of Real Property had been greatly

<small>Reforms in law and in the common law courts.</small>

---

[1] 5 and 6 V. c. 103.
[2] 3 and 4 V. c. 94. Brougham's Orders 1833, Cottenham's 1841, Lyndhurst's 1842 and 1845. For list see Daniell's *Ch. Practice*, 2nd ed. p. xxv.
[3] Orders of 1841 and 1845. A partial power to take bills *pro confesso*

where defendants absconded, or, being in custody, refused to appear was given by 5 Geo. II. c. 25. 45 Geo. III. c. 124, extended it to cases of privileged defendants who refused to appear, and 11 Geo. IV. c. 36, extended it still further. Daniell's *Ch. Practice*, 2nd ed. p. 473.

rationalised and simplified, its main principles being preserved.

The judicial staff of the Court of Chancery had, as we have seen, been greatly increased, but its business had grown greater also. The ancient equity jurisdiction of the Exchequer, which in the present century had become very ineffective, had, in 1841, been transferred to the Chancery[1]. And the early Joint-Stock and Winding-up Acts[2], and the enormous multiplication of Joint-Stock Companies, had introduced into Equity a mass of new business which bade fair to equal all the other work of the Court put together.

Increase of business in Equity.

Notwithstanding the important improvements effected, the procedure of both equity and common law courts was still quite unsuited for the expeditious and satisfactory disposal of the questions that came before them, and the Commissioners were appointed upon whose labours the Common Law Procedure Acts of 1852 and 1854 and the Chancery Amendment Acts of 1852 were founded.

Some immediate steps however were taken in 1850, pending the appointment and return of the Chancery Commission; Lord Cottenham's orders were issued, and Sir George Turner's Act "to diminish the delay and expense of proceedings in the High Court of Chancery[3]" was passed.

In introducing his bill, Sir George Turner stated that it had originally comprised a scheme for rearranging the preliminary proceedings of suits, and the Masters' Offices, but that, on the issue of the orders referred to, with the same object, that part of the bill had been dropped. In explaining the purpose of the clauses that remained he said[4], "hitherto it has been the rule of the Court to administer complete justice in all cases in which it interferes; for instance, the Court would not deal with a portion of the property, it would have the whole property before it, as well as all the parties in any way interested in it, although they might not be in any manner interested in the particular question which had

Sir George Turner's Act.

[1] 5 V. c. 5.
[2] 7 and 8 V. c. 110, 11 and 12 V. c. 45, 12 and 13 V. c. 108.
[3] 13 and 14 V. c. 35.
[4] Headlam's Supplement to Daniell's Practice, p. 174. Hansard, cxi. p. 1128.

brought the case under the notice of the Court. The consequences of this endeavour on the part of the Court to do complete justice, was that in many instances it incurred the opprobrium of doing injustice. The heavy expenses of Chancery proceedings chiefly resulted from this attempt to work out a perfect system of justice[1]." "Take, for example," he continued, "a simple case, that of a question arising as to the right to a share in a residuary estate: the claimant files a bill, and all persons interested in the estate, though having no interest whatever in the particular question, are made parties to the suit, and served with an order of the Court. The suit comes on for hearing, and is referred to the Master's Office, where all accounts are required to be taken, and a great expenditure of time and money takes place before a very simple point can be settled." These were the evils that the Act[2] was intended to remove, and, in spite of the apologetic language in which they are explained, it is plain they were gross and oppressive evils, the more intolerable because of their utter gratuitousness. The plan adopted was to allow any one who desired a decision of the Court upon a question of construction arising out of a will, a question of title on a purchase, or other similar matter, to obtain it by stating a 'special case' without pleadings. Another source of unnecessary litigation, the impossibility of executors and administrators distributing the estate so as to be safe against unexpected claims of creditors, without the cumbersome and expensive process of an administration suit, was, to some extent, met by allowing them to obtain a decree for administration, by a 'motion of course' without any preliminary proceedings, but this was rendered obsolete a few years later by the passing of an Act which made the administration itself unnecessary.

Summary relief.

Lord Cottenham's orders, which were issued in the same

[1] "It is one principal advantage of our system of Equitable jurisdiction that, by embracing the interests of all parties who can possibly be affected by its decision in any suit, it not only does complete justice in every suit instituted, but prevents all future litigation respecting the same rights of property." Report of 1826, p. 26. The rule was relaxed if the parties were very numerous; e.g. in the early unincorporated company cases.

[2] 13 and 14 V. c. 35.

year 1850, effected other important improvements, especially by the introduction, or rather the very great extension, of means for obtaining relief upon summary application.

The old rule had been very strict, that no final relief could be given till, after all the preliminary stages had been duly gone through, the hearing was reached. An Act of 1734[1] had enabled the Court, before the hearing, to make a binding decree in foreclosure suits on the Defendant's motion; during Lord Eldon's time all sorts of devices by way of motion were adopted to draw a decree from him[2]; in 1812, as already mentioned, Sir Samuel Romilly's Charity Act had allowed summary applications to be made by petition in Charity cases, and just before this time the Trustee Act had extended this boon to simple applications connected with the appointment of new trustees, but this was all. The Orders of 1850 therefore made a great innovation when they allowed numerous applications by 'claims,' to be made direct to the Court[3]. A creditor or legatee seeking payment of a debt or legacy out of the assets of a deceased person; a next of kin seeking an account; an executor seeking administration; a mortgagee or mortgagor seeking foreclosure or redemption; and any claimant who was entitled to specific performance of an agreement, dissolution of a partnership, the appointment of a trustee, or liberty to use his trustee's name, without leave, and any other claimant, with leave, could file a 'claim' for the relief he desired, and serve on the respondent a summons to show cause why such relief should not be granted, without bill and without answer being necessary, unless the claimant desired, or the Court directed it. The claim was then considered by the Court on motion, the evidence being given upon affidavit. Claims were at once so largely employed that, as the Commissioners of 1850 reported, between the end of May 1850 and the beginning of January 1852, 1969 were filed; upon these 863 decrees and orders had been made, and 245 of them only

Claims.

[1] 7 Geo. II. c. 20.
[2] See p. 272, ante, note.
[3] "The effect of these orders is, as respects a very large number of cases cognizable in equity, almost entirely to supersede the use of written pleadings." Headlam's Supp. p. 199.

remained in the list for decision at the end of January 1852, the remainder having been withdrawn or compromised[1].

The claims however, useful as they were, were but a step towards a further improvement, and were little used after the Chancery Reform Acts of 1852, and were finally abolished in 1860.

The orders just referred to also extended the powers of the Masters upon references, and further orders of the same year abolished appointments before them, limited to one hour[2], which it had been the custom to make, but which had entailed the greatest inconvenience in conducting complicated enquiries, and directed them to proceed with their enquiries continuously. And the same orders gave the Masters valuable additional powers of proceeding in the absence of parties who neglected to attend before them, and effected a very considerable saving by directing parties to references to be classified according to their interests. This was the last attempt to make Masters' Offices work satisfactorily, for, two years later, the Masters themselves were entirely abolished so far as regarded the future working of the Court. That was the commencement of effective reform. Delay and expense were the necessary concomitants of the administration of 'parlour justice,' in which the Master and the opposing solicitors were all anxious to accommodate each other, and there was neither publicity nor any definite rule as to time to urge them to activity. And while the practice in the Masters' Offices remained in such a state as to destroy all hopes of speedy justice, and they were unable to dispose of ordinary contested matters in less than three or four years, it might well be said of the introduction of claims, and the other reforms, that "it is a mere mockery to entice parties into a slough of despond by making the entrance easy of access, if the months and years of struggle to which suitors are doomed serve only to prove the *facilis descensus Averni*[3]."

The Commission appointed in 1850 to enquire into the procedure of the Chancery, and the fees paid by the suitors, to

[1] Report, 1852, p. 13.
[2] Headlam's Supp. p. 235.
[3] Miller's 'Orders of the Court of Chancery.' Supp. p. iv.

which subjects of enquiry, in the following year, the jurisdiction itself was added, was an exceedingly strong one. It consisted of Lord Romilly, the Master of the Rolls, Turner and James, afterwards Lords Justices, Bethell and Page Wood, who as Lord Westbury and Lord Hatherley respectively were afterwards Chancellors, and several others. They were, as the earlier Commission had been, distinctly representative of the Court whose jurisdiction and procedure they undertook to investigate, but the spirit of the two Commissions was very different. The work of the early reformers, the addresses of Brougham and his friends, and the evidence taken before the first Commission had forced the existence of the grave inconveniences and abuses in Chancery upon every one's notice, and the increasing study of foreign systems, as well as the success of the great but partial improvements already effected in our own, had removed the hopeless acquiescence with which many who recognised these inconveniences and abuses had once regarded them. Several of the Commissioners, and particularly Sir Richard Bethell and Mr Turner, were indeed pronounced reformers, and had already submitted measures for the improvement of our legal institutions to Parliament. The name of the former will ever stand along with the names of Romilly and Brougham at an earlier, and of Cairns and Selborne at a later day, identified with much that marks the difference between the organised failure of our judicial institutions in the first quarter of this century and their comparative success in the fourth.

The Chancery Commission of 1850.

"From the commencement of our investigation," says their first report[1], "we have felt that considerable alterations in the jurisdiction of the Court of Chancery must form part of any complete scheme for improving the administration of justice. The mischiefs which arise from the system of several distinct Courts proceeding on distinct and in some cases antagonistic principles are extensive and deep rooted. It happens that in many cases parties in the course of the same litigation are driven backwards and forwards from Courts of Law to Courts of Equity, and from Courts of Equity

Jurisdiction.

[1] 1852, p. 1.

to Courts of Law." The Commissioners refused to discuss the question of fusing the rival jurisdictions, postponing it for a future report, but meanwhile they declared, as Lord Brougham, who despaired of the attainment of the greater undertaking, had declared years before, that "a practical and effectual remedy for many of the evils in question may be found in such a transfer or blending of jurisdiction, coupled with such other practical amendments, as will render each Court competent to administer complete justice in the cases which fall under its cognizance[1]." In accordance with this suggestion, for the next twenty years, reforms took the direction of steadily extending the common ground of the jurisdictions of the Common Law and the Chancery Courts, seeking to make each completely capable of dealing with suits properly begun in it, and, where the suit might be commenced in either, leaving the greater convenience of the procedure of the one or the other to settle in which it should in fact be commenced.

The Commissioners then turn to the manner of taking evidence in Chancery, which still remained as it is described at the beginning of this chapter. They advised that the system of examining witnesses upon written interrogatories should be abolished, that affidavit evidence should be generally admissible, but that any party should have a right to have the witness produced for *viva voce* examination, and that either party, and also the Court, should have power to compel witnesses to give evidence in any proceeding. Where a witness was examined *viva voce* it should be, they advised, in the presence of both parties, or their agents, who should be at liberty to examine and cross-examine, and before a competent person, who should take a note of the answers given[2].

Evidence.

The Commissioners referred in forcible and indignant language to the cumbersome and expensive character of the proceedings before the hearing. There was, they said, no difference between friendly and hostile suits in this respect, although after the preliminary proceedings were concluded, the former could, by consent, be expeditiously heard as 'short causes[3].' The 'claims' and 'special cases,' to which reference has

[1] p. 3.   [2] p. 40.   [3] p. 10.

been made, had effected considerable improvement, but their usefulness was marred by the lack of any compulsory process for obtaining evidence upon them. "We are of opinion," they said, "that the proper progress of Chancery Reform is in the same direction, that is to say, to substitute in every case which admits of it, the shortest and most summary process, with the least amount of preliminary written pleadings, and to bring the parties by themselves or their counsel to state their cases with as little delay as possible to the tribunal which has to decide. It is a matter of frequent occurrence in the Court to see cases encumbered with statements and counter-statements, evidence and counter-evidence, with which the parties have been for years harassing each other, although there has been throughout no substantial dispute as to the facts; and the real question lies within a very narrow compass, and would have been probably evolved in the first instance, if the Court had had the power summarily to ascertain and deal with the facts[1]." Summary procedure.

The Report from which these passages have been taken is a careful and elaborate document, dealing with many defects in Chancery procedure besides those here referred to. Its suggestions were carried into effect without delay by three statutes of 1852, and by a series of general orders published in the same year[2].

By these the office of Master in Chancery was wholly swept away, and it was provided that, for the future, the Chancery judges should sit in chambers for a portion of their time for the dispatch of business, as the Common Law judges had long done. The Chamber business was to be conducted, for the most part, as it had been under the Masters, by Chief Clerks, but every litigant was to have the right to adjourn any question, with the decision of which he was not satisfied, directly to the judge, and the judges, that is, the Master of the Rolls and the Vice-Chancellors, were to have respectively complete control of the Chambers attached to their Courts. So vanished one of the oldest, and certainly the best Abolition of the Masters.

[1] p. 14.
[2] 15 and 16 V. cc. 80, 86, 87. General Orders, 1852. *Law Review*, vol. 17, p. 165.

abused and the least efficient of all the institutions of the Court.

The old rules as to parties, requiring in many cases hosts of unnecessary suitors to be involved in litigation which could not affect their rights, were altered. Executors and administrators had always been allowed to represent the personal estate legally vested in them, and in like manner, by an Order of 1841, trustees with a power of sale over realty had been admitted to represent such realty, and now the principle of representation was extended, a single legatee or cestui que trust being permitted to sue for administration without joining his fellow beneficiaries, the Court having power to add any party it thought fit, and it was provided that no suit should be dismissed for misjoinder. In place of bills of revivor on passage of interest, orders 'as of course' were substituted.

Parties.

The forms of bill and answer had been somewhat improved since the descriptions given above fully applied to them, but now the bill was directed to consist of a concise narrative arranged in numbered paragraphs, without interrogatories, and power to interrogate opposite parties separately, not only where the procedure was by bill, but where it was by motion or petition, and to summon witnesses and examine and cross-examine them orally before examiners, was conferred. The answers, pleas and demurrers were to be sworn, whether in town or in the country, before Commissioners to take oaths, who some years before had replaced the Masters Extraordinary.

Pleadings.

Methods of summary application were largely introduced, as the Commissioners had recommended. Applications by summons at Chambers, of which in recent years we have seen so large an extension, were now first allowed, common administration decrees being made thus obtainable without any pleadings at all, and it was provided that the Plaintiff, at any time after the answer but before reply, might move, upon affidavit evidence, for any decree or order which he was entitled to, and the Court might thereupon grant or refuse the motion, or give directions as to the future conduct of the suit.

Summons at chambers.

The inappropriateness of the Chancery procedure and modes

of taking evidence for the discovery of the facts of a contested case had, as we have seen, often led to parties being sent to try an issue at law, but there was no such excuse for what was an equally frequent practice, the sending of pure questions of law, which arose in equity, for argument before the common law judges. The Chancellors were generally experts in the Common Law themselves, and had often presided in the Courts where it was administered; and the counsel who practised before them, after the distinction became marked, were more accustomed to deal with dry legal questions than those who confined themselves to the other side were; moreover the equity judges did not profess to be bound by the result of the common law judges' deliberations and decisions, but disregarded them if they conflicted with their own views. Lord Eldon was accustomed to reflect with pride that he had sent issues first to the King's Bench, and then to the Common Pleas, for a decision on a point of law, and had finally demonstrated to himself in Chancery that both the decisions so obtained were wrong[1]. This scandal also was put an end to by the Acts of 1852, and it was provided that a Chancery judge should decide questions of law arising before him for himself, and should decide also any questions of title relevant to the grant of equitable relief. *Issues of law abolished.*

The part of these reforms that gave least satisfaction at the time was that relating to the taking of evidence. A section[2] of the principal Act had said emphatically that the existing practice as to the examination of witnesses should be abolished, and this was acknowledged to be so far good, but the substituted method, which allowed either party to insist that the evidence be taken orally before an examiner, was not a success. In 1854 the Commissioners drew up a memorandum on the subject[3], and recommended that either party should be permitted in all cases to adduce evidence in chief in support of his case either by affidavit or by the oral examination of witnesses, who refused to make affidavits, before an examiner, and that the opposite parties *Further changes in the mode of taking evidence.*

---

[1] See note to *White v. Lisle*, 3 Swan, 342. *Law Review*, vol. 17, p. 188.
[2] 15 and 16 Vict. c. 86, § 28.
[3] Report of 1856, p. 23.

should have the right to cross-examine the deponents upon their affidavits or oral depositions either orally before an Examiner, or by written interrogatories, and this recommendation was carried into effect by an order of January 1855[1].

A further Commission was appointed in 1859 specially to enquire into this subject, and it reported that the procedure before an examiner led to delay and expense. Suitors repeatedly neglected to keep their appointments, and the examiner exercised no efficient control over the proceedings. "With respect to material facts which are disputed," the Commissioners reported, "we have come to the conclusion that the only reasonable course is to take the evidence *ore tenus* before the Court which is to decide on the whole case, the evil arising from the evidence being taken before one functionary and its weight and effect decided on by another is an evil of principle and not of detail," and therefore they advised that all evidence should be taken *viva voce* at the hearing, or by Affidavit simply. Thus at last official approval was stamped upon a view which had been repeatedly urged upon the Court from the time of Henry VIII.[2] onward. No doubt the explanation of the long-maintained refusal to admit *viva voce* evidence at the hearing is, that in many of the cases debated in Chancery the facts were either not seriously disputed or could be established by documentary evidence, and in these affidavits or depositions had been an inexpensive and convenient method of laying the facts before the Court, and a procedure which was suitable for these cases, was, as in other instances, applied also to others to which it was utterly unsuited. Even now the veteran Lord St Leonards, who was a member of the Commission, refused to join in the report; "the constant demand on a judge in Equity," he said, "to decide points of law, and to consider the bearings of the evidence requires quiet and calm in the Court itself....The course of the Court should not be interrupted by addresses to a jury, the introduction of Common Law Counsel, and all the wrangling of trials at Nisi Prius," and he advised

---

[1] See O. 19 of the Consolidated Orders of 1860.

[2] *Treatise on the Masters*, ante, p. 60. Blackstone, 3, p. 374.

that a further trial should be given to the system of taking evidence before an examiner[1].

In spite of this protest, however, the rule was introduced[2] that, though evidence was in general to be taken by affidavit, or by an *ex parte* examination of (unfriendly) witnesses before an examiner, the depositions being treated as an affidavit, a party might apply for an order that disputed facts be determined by oral evidence at the hearing, whether of the cause itself or of any motion or petition And it was provided that either party should be at liberty to compel the other to produce any witnesses, who had made affidavits or depositions on his behalf, for cross-examination before the Court or before an examiner, the Court retaining in all cases the power conferred in 1852, to summon witnesses before itself, at its discretion.

These great reforms in the procedure and practice of the Chancery Courts were appropriately concluded by the issue in 1860, under Lord Campbell's authority, of a table of Consolidated Orders which had been drawn up by Lord Chelmsford's direction in the previous year. *The consolidated orders.* The publication of these orders and the abrogation, with some unimportant exceptions, of all the earlier general orders of the Court,— "bringing order out of confusion, and harmony out of discord,...by separating those orders which (were) subsisting from a mass of others which (had) become defunct,"—was well described by the consolidators[3] as likely to effect "a great and unmixed good." It comprised about six hundred rules, dating, in some instances, from as far back as the sixteenth century, and it, for the first time in the history of Chancery, presented a consistent, complete and authoritative statement of the practice as settled by express orders[4]. A great part of the existing code of rules and orders, which since the Judicature Acts has been drawn up for use in all the Courts, was taken from this source.

---

[1] Report of 1860.
[2] Order of February, 1861, 23 and 24 Vict. c. 128.
[3] See their report prefixed to the Orders.

[4] Some subsequent general orders were issued, but none of importance except those of 1861, as to evidence, already mentioned to.

The improvement of the Court of Chancery about this time was simultaneous with an even wider reaching improvement of the Courts of Common Law. A Commission had been appointed to enquire into their working also, and a great procedure reform was effected by the Common Law Procedure Acts of 1852 and 1854 as the result of their labours. The main object of the Acts was to secure that the actual merits of every case should be brought before the judges unobscured by accidental and artificial questions arising upon the pleadings[1], but they also did something to secure that complete adaptability of the common law courts for finally determining every action brought within them, which the Chancery Commissioners of 1850 had indicated as one of the aims of the reformers. Power was given to the common law courts to allow parties to be interrogated by their opponents, to order discovery of documents, to direct specific delivery of goods, to grant injunctions, and to hear interpleader actions, and equitable pleas were allowed to be urged in defence to common law actions[2].

The Common Law Procedure Acts.

Before this, jurisdiction had been conferred on the common law courts to order evidence to be taken abroad, first in India only, by an Act of 13 Geo. III., and then generally, by 1 Will. IV. c. 22, which also enabled them to examine on commission *de bene esse*, before the trial, witnesses likely to be unable, from sickness or absence from the country, to attend at it, and, by the Evidence Amendment Acts[3] the restrictions upon the admission of the testimony of interested witnesses, of the parties to the litigation, and of the husband or wife of a party had been successively removed. By these improvements the Auxiliary Jurisdiction of Equity was practically swept away, bills for discovery being no longer rendered necessary by the nominal refusal to admit the evidence obtainable by means of them, and appli-

The Auxiliary Jurisdiction in Equity superseded.

---

[1] See Introduction to Day's *Common Law Procedure Acts.*
[2] C. L. P. Act 1854, §§ 78 to 86.
[3] 3 and 4 W. 4, c. 42. 6 and 7 Vict. c. 85. 14 and 15 Vict. c. 99. 16 and 17 Vict. c. 83. See Day's *C L. P. Acts*, 4th ed. p. 261, where the history of the improvement of the law of evidence is sketched.

cations to stay actions at law were to some extent curtailed. The equity powers conferred upon the common law Courts were, however, but partially exercised, for the Courts held that they could act upon them only where the right asserted was plain, undeniable and conclusive.

On the other hand, the distinctive common law power of granting damages was conferred upon the Chancery Courts wherever they had jurisdiction to grant specific performance or injunction[1], the amount to be assessed by the judge or by a jury, but this power also was little used.

In 1860, Lord Campbell introduced into Parliament the bill upon which the third Common Law Procedure Act was founded. The bill proposed, in accordance with the final recommendations of the Common Law Commission, to confer extended equitable jurisdiction upon the common law courts in matters coming before them, and to enable them to prohibit the equity courts from interfering in common law actions. These proposals were strongly opposed by Lord St Leonards and the other law lords, and the Vice-Chancellors addressed a memorial[2] to Parliament in which they urged that the common law procedure and machinery were unfitted for determining equitable questions, though they were sufficient to secure justice where a case was brought down to a single issue of law or fact, whether it depended upon a legal or equitable title, and this the existing statutes permitted, and they plainly hinted that the common law judges did not possess the necessary knowledge of equity to administer the proposed powers. The common law judges, on the other hand, who almost unanimously approved of the bill, in their reply, pointed out that the clauses objected to only amplified powers which for six years had been found to work well, and that they were necessary to prevent parties being driven, in many cases, to sue both at Law and in Equity, and to prevent them running the risk, if they sued on the one side, of being themselves sued on the other.

The proposals of 1860.

In the end the clauses were dropped, and but small additions were made by the Act to the equitable powers of the

[1] Cairns' Act, 21 and 22 Vict. c. 27. [2] Warren, L. S., Ed. 1863, p. 545.

Common Law Courts; they were enabled to give relief against forfeiture of leases for non-payment of rent or non-insurance, and the jurisdiction to try interpleader actions conferred by the Act of 1854 was extended to cases where the rival claims had not a common origin[1].

No further advance was made towards the complete equipment of all the Courts with all the powers necessary to enable them to do complete justice in every case brought before them. Several years passed without any organic reform, and then the Judicature Commission of 1867 was appointed, and, as the result of its labours, the fusion of all the Courts and of the rival systems of Equity and Common Law into a single Supreme Court and a single system of civil judicature was determined upon.

Meanwhile, considerable alterations were made in the substance of the law. The Trustee Relief Act, 1847[2], extending an earlier Act of George III., enabled trustees and executors to bring into Court the funds subject to their care, and enabled the Court to make orders as to the application of the trust money, and the administration of the trust upon petition, as already mentioned; the Trustee Acts of 1850 and 1852[3], which replaced and extended some earlier Acts, enabled it to convey, by a vesting order, properly vested in lunatic, absent or infant trustees or mortgagees, and to appoint and vest the trust property in new trustees wherever it was inexpedient, difficult or impracticable for this to be done without its assistance; the Leases and Sales of Settled Estates Acts[4] cast new administrative work upon the Court, and, to some extent, anticipated the extensive control which more recent statutes[5] have given tenants for life and other limited owners over the settled property; and the earlier Joint Stock Acts, consolidated and replaced by the Companies Acts of 1862 and 1867, organised and regulated the important

Substantive reforms in equity.

[1] 23 and 24 V. c. 126, §§ 1—18. Day's C. L. P. Acts, 4th Ed. Introduction, p. 10.
[2] 10 and 11 V. c. 96; 36 Geo. III. c. 52.
[3] 13 and 14 V. c. 60, 15 and 16 V. c. 55; 11 Geo. IV. c. 60; 4 and 5 V. c. 23; 1 and 2 V. c. 69.
[4] 19 and 20 V. c. 120; 21 and 22 V. c. 77.
[5] The Settled Land Acts of 1882 and 1884.

business which had grown up with the introduction of the new trading corporations. To the Acts just enumerated must be added the Trustee and Mortgage Act of 1860[1], which embodied in a statute many of the common-form provisions of settlements and mortgages relating to sales, purchases and investments by trustees, and to powers of sale, of appointing a receiver, and of insuring by mortgagees,—a device to shorten documents which later statutes[2] have extensively adopted,— and the Law of Property Amendment Acts[3] of the previous and the same year respectively. By these latter Acts it was provided that a license to commit a particular breach of a covenant in a lease should no longer avoid the whole covenant; that relief might be given once, against a forfeiture for failure to insure, if it were not due to fraud or gross negligence, equity having previously refused to relieve in any case, because of the risk the neglect had occasioned; that where lands were charged by a will with debts, the devisee, or, if there were no sufficient devise, the executor might sell them, though no power of sale were given by the will; that an executor who had paid everything due under a lease and set aside sufficient money to meet any sum agreed to be expended under it, might distribute the estate without personal risk; and that, in any case, if an executor gave such notice for creditors to come in and prove their debts, as the Court was accustomed to give in an administration suit, he might safely distribute without providing for claims on the estate of which he had no notice. Trustees and executors were enabled to apply to the Court for advice, and were protected from liability on account of the trust moneys, except for what they actually received, and for losses which occurred by reason of their default, and they were permitted, subject to the terms of their trusts, to invest the trust property in any investments authorised by the Court[4].

The division of the systems of Equity and Common Law

[1] 23 and 24 V. c. 145.
[2] Particularly the Conveyancing Act of 1881.
[3] Lord St Leonards' Act, 22 and 23 V. c. 35, and Lord Cranworth's Act, 23 and 24 V. c. 38.
[4] See now the Conveyancing Act, 1881, and the Trustee Act, 1888.

which it was now decided to abandon, was peculiar to England and the colonies and states descended from her. The inconveniences it created, and the additional cost and risk, and the unnecessary delays it occasioned had steadily increased with the elaboration and development of the law, and the great improvements effected in procedure, which had attracted and admitted into the Courts an enormously increased mass of judicial business, had only made the evils incidental to the separation less easy to be borne. Lord Bacon and Lord Hardwicke had agreed in magnifying the danger that the certainty of the Common Law, which they described as the bulwark of liberty, would be lost if the judges administered Equity: "All the arguments drawn from the ease and convenience of the suitors, the preventing vexation and delay, and saving of expense, seem to conclude to uniting (law and equity) in the same Court," Lord Hardwicke admitted[1], but, he added, "the arguments drawn from the necessity or utility of preserving the rules of law entire, and not leaving it in the power of judges to new mould and vary those rules at discretion, by insensibly blending law and equity together, hold for keeping them divided."

Fusion of Equity and Common Law.

The discretionary powers of the equity judges, as we have seen, had long since vanished, and the question now, therefore, was whether one-half of the rules affecting a class of subjects should be administered by one judge and the rest by another, or whether each should administer the whole. Since the practical abolition of the auxiliary jurisdiction by the grant of full powers of discovery to the common law courts, and the admission of interested witnesses, the business of Equity had, no doubt, become more than ever distinct in character from that of Common Law, administrative and protective rather than remedial or punitive, and in a great degree each Court had been enabled to bring to an end matters properly commenced before it, but there was still the danger of beginning wrongly, and all the advantages of a division of labour could be, and in fact have been, preserved without maintaining the separation of the Courts. It was felt that the time was fully

[1] Letter to Lord Kames. Appendix to Parkes.

ripe for an attempt to fuse the two jurisdictions together, and all parties were anxious that the attempt should be made.

The first Judicature Act was passed in 1873 under the auspices of Lord Selborne and Lord Cairns. It provided for the consolidation of all the existing superior Courts into one Supreme Court, consisting of two primary divisions, a High Court of Justice and a Court of Appeal. The former was subdivided into several divisions of which one was to be the Chancery Division. To the High Court of Justice were transferred the jurisdictions of all the amalgamated Courts, and all pending business. *The Judicature Acts.* Law and Equity, it was provided, were to be administered concurrently by every division of the Court, in all civil matters, the same relief being granted upon equitable claims or defences, or equities incidentally occurring, as would have previously been granted in the Court of Chancery; no proceeding in the Court was to be stayed by injunction analogous to the old common injunction but the power for any branch of the Court to stay proceedings before itself was of course to be retained; and the Court was to determine the entire controversy in every matter that came before it.

By the 25th section of the Act rules upon certain of the points where differences between Law and Equity had existed, deciding in favour of the latter, were laid down, and it was enacted generally that in the case of conflict, the rules of Equity should prevail. Actions upon matters of the nature previously within the exclusive jurisdiction of the Court of Chancery, were assigned to the Chancery Division, but power to transfer from one Division to another was reserved. A general system of procedure for all the Divisions was drawn up, and has since been elaborated in detail by rules of Court issued under a subsequent Act. And an appeal from the judges of each of the Divisions was allowed to the Court of Appeal.

The fusion of Equity and Common Law effected by this Act and the amending Act of 1875, which preserved its plan, was followed a few years later by a rehousing of all the Courts. The common law courts had remained at Westminster in and about the Hall assigned to them by Edward III., and there also the Chancellor had sat in term time. The other equity judges had been bestowed in various makeshift courts scattered about Lincoln's Inn, except the Master of the Rolls, who, after he ceased to sit in the Rolls Chapel, as he did in early times, found a court in the adjoining Rolls Yard. Each judge had had his chambers where he pleased, and the different offices attached to the Courts were scattered about in several places in and around Chancery Lane. The distances between the different courts, the chambers and the offices had occasioned great inconvenience, and it was therefore an important change for the better when on the appropriate occasion[1] of the fusion of their jurisdictions, the courts, the judges' chambers and the judicial offices were all combined in a single block of buildings.

Nothing but good has resulted from the reunion of the two jurisdictions; the administration of justice has been facilitated and made both cheaper and more certain. The rules of law have certainly not been injuriously affected because their effect has been studied, together with the qualifying effect of the corresponding rules of equity, and the spirit in which the reforms of procedure and jurisdiction were devised continues to animate the judges; and, at length, it can be truly said that the judges are occupied in an endeavour to discover the real merits of the cases that come before them, and to carry out the substantial intention of the rules of the system they have to administer, without allowing mere technicalities or formal difficulties to stand in the way.

No one can rest satisfied with the form in which the law of our country has been allowed to lie obscured. The piles of reports and the numerous statutes, from which it has to be quarried out, make it far oftener difficult to determine what its deliverance is on a particular question, even for a lawyer, than it need or ought to be, and make it generally impossible for any one else, in spite of the excellence of the text-books written to expound it. Still its substance is generally felt to be reasonable and just, and to be adequate to the needs of the community whose concerns it regulates. A great part of its

[1] The Judicature Acts came into operation in 1875, the new Law Courts were opened in 1882.

excellence is due to the efforts of the judges who created and developed the rules and principles of Equity in the Court of Chancery, and when the manifold abuses of practice and procedure which they tolerated, and the needless complexities which, in some instances, they introduced into the law are remembered, their work in improving, extending and rationalising the crudity and narrowness of a mediæval code must be remembered also.

The further history of Equity, and of its administration, after the abolition of the Court of Chancery, does not fall within the scope of this essay.

INDEX.

A.

Accident, 145.
Account, 148.
Accountant-General appointed, 174.
Administration, 89, 139, 210.
Answer, the
  in the Calendars, 66.
  in the 16th century, 120.
Appeals to the House of Lords, 167, (and see *Rehearing*).
Arrears in Chancery,
  in the 17th century, 155.
  in Lord Eldon's time, 270.
Atkyns, Sir R., on equity, 115.
Attendant terms, 137.
Austin on equity, 11.
  on judicial legislation, 188.
Auxiliary jurisdiction in equity superseded, 288.

B.

Bacon, Sir N., 97.
Bacon, Lord, 102.
  speech on taking his seat, 103.
  orders, 104.
Becket, 23.
Bill in equity, 119.
  in the Calendars, 61.
  in modern equity, 269.
Bills of peace, 149.
Bills of Sale Acts, 207.
Blackstone on equity, 1, 177.
Boddenho's case, 14.
Bridgman, Sir O.,
  inventor of trustees to preserve contingent remainders, 165.
  on equitable assignments, 206.
  on notice, 236.

Brougham, Lord,
  on law reform, 273.
  orders, 275.

C.

Calendars, their contents, 48.
Campbell, Lord,
  on bills in equity, 270.
  proposal to give further equity powers to the common law courts, 289.
Cantelow's case, 80.
Carbeston, petition of the tenants of, 18.
Case, the action on the,
  and equity, 11.
  and the improvement of the land, 180.
  for fraud, 171, 181.
Catching bargains, 240.
Censorship of the press in equity, 259.
Chambers, summons in, in equity, 284.
Chancellor, the
  head of the Chancery, 9.
  his position before the reign of Richard II., 23.
  references of petitions to him under Edward I., 27; Edward II., 28; Edward III., 31.
  petition to him, 34.
  power to grant a special assize, 41.
  not to question judgments, 43.
  acting committee of the Council, 57.
  sole judge in Chancery, 58.
Chancellor, the Lord,
  the Lord Keeper to have the same jurisdiction as the Chancellor, 97.
  plan to abolish the office, 172.
  his multifarious duties, 271.

298   INDEX.

Chancellors (and Lord Keepers):
  lay Chancellors, 44.
  the ecclesiastical Chancellors, 94.
  lawyers appointed, 96.
  from Wolsey to the Commonwealth, 94.
  Wolsey, 95.
  Sir T. More, 96.
  Sir N. Bacon, 97.
  Sir C. Hatton, 98.
  Ellesmere, 98.
  Bacon, 102.
  Dr Williams, 105.
  Coventry, 105.
  Whitelock (Lord Commissioner), 156.
  Clarendon, 164.
  Sir O. Bridgman, 169.
  Nottingham, 169.
  Guilford, 171.
  Jefferies, 171.
  Somers, 172.
  Cowper, 174.
  Macclesfield, 174.
  Talbot, 175.
  Hardwicke, 175.
  Northington, 179.
  Thurlow, 179.
  Eldon, 181.
  (and see the several titles.)
Chancery, the,
  writs issued out of it, 9, 25.
  horses to carry the rolls, 31.
  fixed at Westminster, 31.
  directions to apply in, 35.
  common law in, 26, 49.
  officials, 61, 156.
  increase of business under Henry VIII., 97; under Elizabeth, 155.
  abuses at the time of the Commonwealth, 155.
  resolution to abolish, 159.
  attacks on it in 1699, 172.
  state of the Chancery under Lord Eldon, 264.
  damages in Chancery, 289.
  (and see *Chancellor, Commission* and *Equity*.)
Charities, 142.

Choses-in-action,
  assignments in equity, 138, 206.
Claims, 279.
Commission,
  Lord Eldon's, 267, 274.
  of 1850 on the Chancery, 281.
  of 1859 on evidence, 286.
  of 1867, the judicature commission, 290.
Common Law,
  in Chancery, 26, 49.
  defects in the early common law, 42, 71.
  procedure in, under Ed. I., 50.
  improvement under Henry VIII. and Elizabeth, 108.
  development after the Restoration, 165.
  development under Lord Mansfield, 180.
  reforms of real property law, 276.
  issues sent to, 285.
Common Law Procedure Acts, 288.
Commons, the House of,
  complaints against the Chancery, 37.
  protest against appeals to the House of Lords, 168.
Commonwealth, attempted reforms of the Chancery, 154.
Compromise, 249.
Consideration, 196.
Contingent remainders, 165, 260.
Contract,
  cases in the Calendars, 86.
  assumpsit for breach, 87.
  rectification and rescission for mistake, 244, 245.
  penalties in, 250.
  time not of the essence, 255.
Conversion, 202.
Copyright, 258.
Costliness of equity, 267.
Costs,
  power to give, 39.
  security for, 46, 66, 118.
  on insufficient answer, 120.
  none on demurrers, 120.

INDEX.

Costs,
 in Cromwell's ordinances, 161.
 deposit for, on petition for rehearing, 171, 178.
 full costs where bill heard on answer only, 178.
 Hardwicke's orders as to fees, 178.
Council, the,
 judicial powers, 16, 37.
 ordinance for its governance, 17.
 of a lord, 7, 40.
 its relation to the Chancellor, 57.
Court,
 of Chancery, *see Chancery*.
 of Requests, 18.
 of Wards, 137, 225.
Courts in mediæval England, 8.
Coventry, Lord, 105.
 his orders, 106, 123.
Cowper, Lord, 174.
Cromwell's ordinances, 160.
Cross-examination,
 none in early equity, 69, 121.
 by cross interrogatories, 268.
 oral, 286.
Curia Regis reorganised by Henry II., 7.

D.

Damages in equity, 289.
Death, remedy in equity does not abate on, 261.
Deceit, action for, 181, 238.
Decrees,
 in early equity, 57, 69.
 in the 16th century, 123.
 not to contain recitals, 275.
 only bound the person, 89.
De Donis, the statute of, Lord Ellesmere on, 137.
Delays in Chancery, 122, 270, 271.
Discovery, 77, 151, 261, 263.
Discretion in equity,
 under the early chancellors, 100.
 Lord Hardwicke upon it, 175.
 Sir Joseph Jekyll upon it, 176.
 Lord Eldon upon it, 182.
 in regard to specific performance, 256.

E.

Ecclesiastical Chancellors, 94.
Ecclesiastical Courts, 79.
Ejectment action, 108, 111, 149.
Eldon, Lord, 181.
 refused to abandon the concurrent jurisdiction, 180.
 on discretion in equity, 182.
 work in regard to specific performance, 256.
 work in regard to injunction, 258.
 delays in Chancery in his time, 270.
 small time at his disposal for sitting in equity, 271.
 his commission on the Chancery, 274.
Election, 217.
Ellesmere, Lord, 98.
 contest with Coke over injunctions, 109.
 judgment in the Earl of Oxford's case, 111.
 on equity, 112.
 letter to his client, 123.
 on *De Donis*, 137.
 on estoppels, 253.
Equity,
 meanings of equity, 1.
 origin of English equity, 3, 20, 35.
 and the action on the case, 11.
 nature of early equity, 38.
 procedure in early equity, 51.
 in the Calendars, 71, 76, 93.
 under Henry VIII., 92.
 under the Ecclesiastical Chancellors, 95.
 Lord Ellesmere on equity, 100.
 precedents and Roman Law in early equity, 100.
 Lord Bacon on equity, 102.
 development after the establishment of the right to issue injunctions, 116.
 from Wolsey to the Commonwealth, 129.
 development after the Restoration, 166.

300 INDEX.

Equity,
  Lord Nottingham's part in this development, 170.
  Lord Hardwicke on equity, 176.
  Lord Eldon on equity, 182.
  growth of modern equity, 184.
  scarcity of equity reports in the 18th century, 187.
  arguments in the leading cases, 188.
  influence of Roman Law on modern equity, 189.
  new judges appointed, 272.
  report on the jurisdiction of equity, 281.
  auxiliary jurisdiction superseded, 288.
  in common law courts, 289.
  substantive reforms in equity, 290.
  fusion of equity and common law jurisdictions, 292.
  (see also *Chancery, Chancellor, Discretion*.)
Equity to a settlement, 222.
Estoppel in early equity, 92.
  ,, Lord Ellesmere on, 253.
Estrepment, writ of, 150.
Evidence,
  in early equity, 67.
  suits to perpetuate testimony, 77, 152.
  in the 15th and 16th centuries, 121, 123.
  publication, 122, 262.
  ad informandum conscientiam judicis, 123.
  written evidence required in some cases, 171.
  de bene esse, proposal to allow common law courts to order this to be taken, 173.
  extrinsic evidence, 217.
  parol evidence, 245.
  in Chancery in Lord Eldon's time, 268.
  vivâ voce evidence introduced, 282, 285.
  Commission of 1859 on evidence, 286.
  new rules, 287.
  improvement of the rules of evidence, 288.

Examination of defendants in equity, 44, 66.
Examiner in equity, 268.
Exchequer, equity jurisdiction abolished, 277.
Executors, 86, 89, 139.

F.

Fictions in law and equity, 265.
Fines and Recoveries Act, 276.
Fleta, 9, 10, 24.
Forfeitures relieved against, 109, 250.
Forgery and duress, 73.
Forma pauperis, suits in, 126.
Fraud, 144, 237.
Fraud on a power, 210.
Freehold, where to be answered for, 7, 110.

H.

Huls v. Hyncley, 52.
Hardwicke, Lord, 175.
  letter to Lord Kames, 105, 166, 175, 292.
  delay in giving his judgments, 177.
  orders, 178.
Hatton, Sir C., on equity, 98.
Holmes, Mr Justice, on the origin of uses, 78.

I.

Infant marriages, 225.
Infants,
  discovery from, 152.
  custody and guardianship, 225.
  settlements, 227.
Injunctions,
  to stay proceedings at law, 89, 116, 293.
  the contest over them, 109.
  in the 16th and 17th centuries, 150.
  at common law, 150.
  in modern equity, 258.
Issues,
  of facts not tried in Chancery, 28.
  ,, sent to be tried at law, 269.
  of law abolished, 285.

INDEX. 301

Interest,
 compound, allowed, 229.
 allowed at law, 241.

J.

Jefferies, Lord, 171.
 order for full costs to be paid, 173.
Jenkins on equity, 115.
Joint ownership in equity, 205.
Judges, additional, appointed in equity, 272.
Judgments, the Statute against their reversal, 42, 114.
Judicature Acts, 293.
Jury, trial by, 72.
Justician, the chief, 8, 24.

K.

King,
 judicial powers of the, 13.
 claim to power to grant *privilegia*, 22.
Kirkeham, M. R., directions of Ed. IV. on his appointment, 60.

L.

Læsio fidei, 79, 87.
Leading cases, 186.
Legacies, 140, 213.
Locke King's Acts, 211.
Lyndhurst's orders, 275.

M.

Macclesfield, Lord, 174.
 impeached for bribery, 174.
Mansfield, Lord,
 and the improvement of the law, 180.
 on consideration, 196.
Marriage, restraints upon, 218.
Married women,
 allowed to sue in equity in early times, 142.
 discovery from, 152.
 separate estate, 142, 220.
 restraint on anticipation, 222.
 equity to a settlement, 222.
 the wife's reversion, 223.

Married women,
 mortgage of the wife's estate, 224.
 agreements between husband and wife, 257.
Marshalling, 215.
Master of the Rolls, 27, 60, 127, 272.
Masters in Chancery, 59, 127.
 references to them, 125.
 enquiries before them, 273.
 last reforms of their offices, 280.
 abolished, 283.
Masters extraordinary, 128.
Mistake, 146, 243.
 of law, 249.
More, Sir T., 96.
Mortgages, 88, 143, 227.
 right of redemption established, 143.
 conditions of redemption in the Commonwealth bill, 160
 rules adopted by Lord Nottingham, 227.
 redemption and foreclosure, 228.
 sale, 230.
 tacking, 227, 230.
 consolidation, 232.
 vendor's lien, 233.
 equitable mortgages, 234.
Motions, 124.
 in Lord Eldon's time, 272, 279.

N.

Ne exeat, 151.
Northington, Henley, Lord, 179.
 judgment in *Burgess v. Wheate*, 194.
Notice, 234.
 to agent, 235.
 purchase for value without notice, 262.
Nottingham, Lord, the 'father of equity,' 169.
 his work in regard to trusts, 192.
 ,,   ,,   ,, mortgages, 227.

O.

Orders,
 Bacon's, 104, 119.
 Coventry's, 106.

Orders,
Whitelock's, 157.
Cromwell's ordinances, 161.
Clarendon's, 164.
Hardwicke's, 178.
Orders of 1828 and 1831, 275.
Cottenham's, 277, 279.
consolidated orders of 1860, 287.
Outrage, suppressed by the Chancellor, 62, 71, 152.
Oxford, case of the Earl of, 111.

P.

Park on English law, 266,
Parkes' *History of the Court of Chancery*, 265.
Parliament,
judicial powers of, 19.
petitions of the Commons against the Chancery, 37.
proceedings in, concerning the Chancery, 157, 172, 273.
Barebone's, 157.
Parnyng, an early lay chancellor, 44.
Part performance, 254.
Parties, new rules as to, 277, 284.
Partition, 149.
Penalties, 89, 145, 250.
Personalty, primarily liable for debts, 211.
Petitions in Chancery, 126.
Petitions to Parliament,
referred to the Chancellor, 26, 28, 33, 40, 46.
triers appointed, 19.
Pike on common law in Chancery, 50.
Pleading,
in equity, 51, 61, 128, 269, 284.
in the early common law, 50.
Poor plaintiffs in equity, 42, 65, 126.
Powers, 207.
illusory appointments, 209.
fraud on a power, 210.
Precedent, influence of, in equity, 100, 177, 188.
Publication, 122.
no evidence after, 262.

R.

Real property reforms, 276.
Rectification, of mistakes, 146.
in settlements, 244.
in wills, 245.
Redesdale, Lord,
on the report of Lord Eldon's Commission, 274.
Registrars, the old, abolished, 275.
Rehearing, petition for, 124, 155, 171, 178.
Releases, 246.
Reply, 67, 121.
Reports, scarcity of, until the present century, 187.
Reversions, sales of, 242.
Roman Law, influence on equity, 100, 189, 206.
Romilly, Sir S.
on Chancery, 265.
on the uncertainty of our law, 266.

S.

Salman and trustee, 78.
Scire facias, 54.
Separate estate, 142, 220.
Separation deeds, 257.
Set off, 149.
Six clerks, 128, 267, 276.
Solicitors, 128, 267, 274.
Somers, Lord, 173.
law reform bill, 173.
Special case, relief on, 278.
Specific performance, 88, 147, 253.
Standing by, 238.
Statute of Frauds, 170, 192, 254.
Statute of Uses, 133.
Statute of Wills, 134.
Stauneford on the common law jurisdiction, 55.
Story on equity, 2.
Subpoena,
petition against, 43.
origin of, 45.
replaced by an open writ of summons, 159, 275.
Summary procedure in equity, 277, 283.
Sureties, 146, 251.

T.

Tenures, abolition of, 165.
Thorpe, an early lay chancellor, 44.
Thurlow, Lord, 179.
   author of the restraint on anticipation, 222.
Trade disputes in the Calendars, 73.
Trustee,
   liability, 137, 199.
   receipt, 197.
   remuneration, 202.
Trustee relief Acts, 290.
Trustee Acts, 290.
Trusts and uses,
   origin, 78.
   in the Year Books, 82.
   in the Calendars, 84.
   in the 16th century, 130.
   after the Statute of Uses, 135.
   foundation of the modern rules, 192.
   resulting, 195.
   voluntary, 196.
   executory, 197.
   precatory, 198.
   investment of trust money, 200.
Turner, L. J., Chancery Amendment Act, 277.

U.

Uncertainty of the law, 266.
Undue influence, 242.
Uses (*see* Trusts and Uses).

V.

Vendor's lien, 232.
Vice-chancellors appointed, 272.

W.

Waste, injunctions to stay, 150, 259.
Whitelocke, 156.
Wills,
   of land reintroduced by the aid of uses, 81, 84.
   Statute of Wills, 134.
   after the statute, 134.
   inofficious wills, 141.
   nuncupative, abolished, 212.
   revocation, 212.
   rectification, 245.
Wolsey, the last of the Ecclesiastical Chancellors, 95.
Writs,
   procedure by writ, 9.
   consimili casu, 10.
   writ to the Sheriff of London, 22 Ed. III., 31.
   asked for in the bills in the calendars, 61.

Y.

York, claim of the Duke to the Crown tried in Parliament, 21.

www.ingramcontent.com/pod-product-compliance
Lightning Source LLC
Chambersburg PA
CBHW030808230426
43667CB00008B/1111